Lives of the Master

The Rest of
the Jesus Story

by Glenn Sanderfur

Based upon the
Psychic Readings of Edgar Cayce

A.R.E.® PRESS • VIRGINIA BEACH • VIRGINIA

May 1989, 2nd Printing

TABLE OF CONTENTS

But there are also many other things which Jesus did; were every one of them to be written, I suppose that the world itself could not contain the books that would be written.   **John 21:25**

DEDICATION

This book is dedicated in humble gratitude to the Master of Masters—Jesus the Christ—whose love for us became in the beginning a redemptive journey, the magnitude of which we can never fathom and the scope of which we never before dared dream. It is a journey which will continue until the last lost sheep is in the fold.

This book is the story of the Good Shepherd who has, from the foundations of time, again and again through sacrifice and martyrdom shown the way to the wandering flock.

ACKNOWLEDGMENTS

Acknowledgment is hereby given to my friend, Gary D. Rose, whose encouragement, inspiration, research, and advice were invaluable, especially in the early days when the writing of this story seemed so overwhelming and improbable.

Appreciation is also expressed to Nell Clairmonte, who began the chronicle years ago but joyously yielded the task and shared in this endeavor.

To these and all others whose love of the Christ and whose many contributions have been so motivating and valuable, I can only convey my heartfelt and genuine thanks.

INTRODUCTION

I first ran into the premise that Jesus had lived prior lives while reading *Edgar Cayce's Story of Jesus*, by Jeffrey Furst, several years ago. It was based upon psychic information given by Edgar Cayce in the first half of the twentieth century.

The idea was revolutionary. My Southern Baptist religious background was too limited in scope to allow the "Son of God" multiple lives on earth. And yet as I thought of the concept more, I began to "know" that it was correct. After all, my religious upbringing didn't accommodate reincarnation either, but I was convinced I had lived prior lives.

It occurred to me that a study should be made of the prior lives of Jesus which Cayce had mentioned to see what support there might be for them outside of the readings and what lessons could be learned from the lives. In time, the idea grew stronger and began to approach compulsion. Would we witness an orderly progression in spirituality of this soul? Had he erred and experienced the kind of problems the rest of us have? I was convinced there would be value in such a study.

In time, after no one else had made this study, I began to consider the possibility of doing it myself. I had no illusions, however, about the ease of the task nor of the desired qualifications. Some Biblical scholar should, I felt, make the study. Ultimately, I decided to research the subject and possibly write an article on my findings; there probably would not be enough material, I thought then, for a book. The project encompassed an eight-year period, and at times completion seemed virtually impossible. I experienced some intuitive and near-psychic experiences, however, which helped me in the research and encouraged me in the writing. Information concerning prior lives of Jesus—from often unrelated and divergent sources—soon became voluminous.

Edgar Cayce's longtime secretary, Gladys Davis (Turner), told me shortly before her death in 1986 that the information on prior lives of Jesus had excited and interested Mr. Cayce more than any other topic discussed in his psychic revelations. She was pleased that the subject was finally being studied in some depth.

The study has been one of love punctuated by an undeniable

sense of duty. I have, in the process, learned much and developed a genuine feeling of closeness and love for the Master. Another result has been a decided conviction about the validity of the Cayce readings—at least on the subject of Jesus' previous lives. The fact that Cayce gave this information before some of the sources of support discussed in this book had actually been "discovered" in archaeological finds adds further credibility to his achievement.

I believe there are a number of benefits to be derived from the story of the Master's lives. The Master becomes a more meaningful and relevant pattern for us to follow. It is a pattern with threads reaching into many of the world's major religions. The accomplishments of the man Jesus become all the more significant when viewed from the perspective of his earlier less-perfect lives. There emerges with this broader picture a sense of divine, cosmic orchestration which is awesome, inspiring, and comforting to us mortals. There is logic and meaning to things which heretofore had to be taken solely on faith.

I want others to experience some of the benefits which have been mine as a result of the study of Jesus' prior lives. That is the purpose of this book.

*   *   *   *   *

Unless otherwise noted in the text, references to or quotes from the Bible will be that of the Revised Standard Version.

For the sake of simplicity in these chapters, unless the wording or context clearly indicates otherwise, references to Edgar Cayce will actually be to him in psychic trance and to the information which came through him while in such a state. The Edgar Cayce psychic readings will be identified by a reading number. The original readings are housed at the A.R.E. Library and the Edgar Cayce Foundation in Virginia Beach, Virginia.

CHAPTER ONE

Edgar Cayce

The place and timing of his birth were surely no accident. A southern, mid-American, small-town environment helped him avoid the intensive, choking public scrutiny which he might have found in a large metropolitan area. The age was one of good communication but luckily did not possess today's mass media techniques which often result in overnight, instant fame and publicity. Edgar Cayce's psychic ability was thus allowed to bloom, develop, and adjust gradually to public exposure and skepticism. Yet his special talent was documented well enough to avoid obscurity and loss to subsequent generations.

The psychic material recorded and received from Edgar Cayce constitutes the greatest mass of such information ever accumulated. It covers practically every subject imaginable and from the early years on was tested and proven to be accurate in the health and medical fields.

Edgar Cayce was born near Hopkinsville, in western Kentucky, on March 18, 1877. The Cayce family had been area natives for a couple of generations and were respected, thrifty, hard-working rural people.

Edgar's schooling stopped at the eighth-grade level, but a thirst for knowledge fueled his learning experiences throughout life. One day, in preparing for his classroom lessons, he discovered that by sleeping on a book he could learn

3

its contents word for word. This experience and one in which an angelic-type person appeared to him marked the beginning of his psychic orientation. The young Edgar asked the "angel" for power to help heal others. It was a request which was certainly fulfilled in later years.

Edgar's first full-time job was as a merchant, but talent at photography soon moved him into this profession where he was quite successful in businesses in Kentucky and Alabama. During these early years he married Gertrude Evans, an attractive young Hopkinsville native. They were to remain happily married for the rest of their lives and raise two boys, Hugh Lynn and Edgar Evans. Gertrude became a valuable assistant and support to Edgar in his psychic life and work.

It was while still in Hopkinsville that Edgar, at the age of 24, developed a throat problem and became unable to speak. A traveling showman and hypnotist put him to sleep, and Edgar— under hypnosis—diagnosed his own problem and gave directions on how to cure it. The treatment worked, and he could speak again. Soon it was discovered that Edgar, through hypnosis, could also diagnose other peoples' ills and give advice for their healing. Often the treatments were unconventional and scoffed at by the traditional medical profession, but they worked—even on cases viewed by others as incurable.

Cayce received his first national publicity when Dr. Wesley H. Ketchum, a local doctor who had been working with him, presented a medical convention report on Edgar's strange ability. On October 9, 1910, an article in the *New York Times* on Ketchum's presentation also brought Cayce a rash of publicity and requests for healing.

His working arrangement with Dr. Ketchum eventually ended, and Edgar, now living in Selma, Alabama, hired a local stenographer, Gladys Davis, to record his psychic readings. Thus she began her remarkable accomplishment of recording over 14,000 of these.

A routine for giving readings was established almost from the beginning. Cayce would lie down on a couch or bed with his face up. As soon as he felt relaxed, an assistant would give him some suggestions, and he would go into a deep sleep. The assistant would read a prepared directive asking for spiritual guidance before asking the questions to which people desired answers.

Cayce would then give answers from his deep sleep in a voice slightly different from that of his normal conscious state.

Unexpectedly Cayce's psychic career took a new turn. At Dayton, Ohio, in 1923, he began speaking about subjects other than physical ailments. He started giving information on philosophical issues such as the meaning of life, the origin of humanity, and humanity's relationship to God. Humanity was portrayed as a creation and expression of God present in this material world as a result of choice and a forgetfulness of its divine source. The return to God might be accomplished through a series of lives and learning experiences. Cayce had surfaced a subject—reincarnation—which seemed to be outside his traditional Protestant Christian background.

From the very beginning, Edgar Cayce had been wary about the psychic information that came through him when he entered the hypnotic, trance-like, sleep state, and he promised to quit the practice altogether if any harm ever came to anyone on account of it. This never happened, and eventually he fully accepted the validity of the information, including that about past lives. He even followed the psychic advice to relocate his family and work to Virginia Beach, Virginia, a small fishing village when he arrived there in 1925. Here he spent the rest of his life and established a permanent organization to carry on his work.

Today at Virginia Beach, the Association for Research and Enlightenment, Inc., with over 50,000 members worldwide, continues the work begun by Edgar Cayce. This membership organization is assisted by the Edgar Cayce Foundation and Atlantic University. Cayce's psychic readings are housed in a unique metaphysical library, which also includes over 50,000 volumes on subjects related to the readings. Between 75 and 100 books have now been written specifically about Edgar Cayce or his work, and research into concepts from the readings continues at an expanding rate.

In 1942, the first biography of Edgar Cayce, *There Is a River*, was written by Thomas Sugrue. Jess Stearn's *The Sleeping Prophet* followed in 1967 and became a national best seller.

The material in the Cayce readings covers a wide array of subjects and interests. In addition to health and medical material, the readings include information on topics such as ancient civilizations, prehistory, archaeology, religion, philosophy, psychology, parapsychology, meditation, dreams, earth changes, and prophecies about the future. Jess Stearn in his biography called Edgar Cayce "one of the most remarkable psychics of all time." Author/theologian Richard Drummond ranks Cayce with such Christian spiritual giants as St. Francis of Assisi, Martin Luther, St. John of the Cross, Teresa of Avila, Ignatius Loyola, Francis Xavier, Jakob Boehme, George Fox, John Wesley, and Rudolph Steiner.[1]

Edgar Cayce gave us material that has healed thousands of persons from illnesses and health problems. But perhaps even more important, this psychic material can potentially help men and women find new directions for thinking about and dealing with their lives. The philosophy of the readings stresses the unity and oneness of God and humanity—in fact, of all God's creation. Service to all people is given as the ideal for humanity and the passport for traveling the road back to godhood—that state of perfection and oneness of our purpose and our will with God's. Two themes of unparalleled promise stand out in bold relief: We are children of God, and the life of each soul is continuous and eternal.

Cayce in his trance state was asked the reason for his unusual psychic talent. The answer which came back offers promise to the rest of us:

Only as a gift of Him who has given, "If ye keep my ways, I will love thee, will abide with thee, and bring to thy remembrance *all* things from the foundation of the world."   2072-8

Psychic talent whose accuracy can be tested and verified in some of its subject areas should logically carry a degree of accuracy into those areas that cannot be proven or disproven. Thus, Edgar Cayce, whose psychic medical record was excellent, should be able to provide us with a fairly accurate psychic window on past events and prehistory. When, for example, his psychic source tells us that Jesus did or said certain things, such comments are deserving of some respect. When the details are not inconsistent with the Bible and history, they are worthy of even more attention. And when we find ancient documents and historical facts which agree with his psychic revelations, then we may be justified in according them a significant degree of respect and authority.

Some persons may be disturbed at the idea of using information from a psychic, especially one who, while in a trance, gives us material from an unknown source. There are Biblical injunctions against certain occult or psychic practices, and yet both the Old and New Testaments would be empty and meaningless without the psychic experiences of its characters. Its spiritual message is written in the words of prophets and the paranormal deeds of its saints. The careful questioning and evaluation of psychic practices and material, therefore, is appropriate and to be encouraged.

After sifting through the almost conflicting advice of the Bible regarding the use of psychic phenomena and prophetic utterances, a meaningful rule or guide does seem to emerge. First, the psychic information must be accurate and stand the test of veracity through time. Secondly, it must be of a nature which points one unerringly to God and, from a Christian viewpoint, the Christ.[2] If these criteria can be met, then, in the words of Paul, the talents of prophecy, speaking in tongues, and the like are in fact gifts of the Spirit. Jesus' directions on distinguishing the true prophet from the evil beguiler is to look at his fruits—the results which flow from his works.

For this author, the psychic information of Edgar Cayce clearly meets the above tests of validation. Each person, however, is invited to examine the coming chapters and make his or her own judgment on the veracity and value of Cayce's psychic story concerning the lives of the Master.

* * * * *

An analysis of some of the non-conventional philosophical and religious information from Edgar Cayce—especially as it relates to this book—can be better done today than just a few years ago. Recent archaeological discoveries and the availability of documents from these finds allow us to look at material contemporaneous with the times of early Christianity and other historical periods and to examine texts which have been immune from editing and change through the intervening years. The material in many of these ancient documents is quite relevant and germane to information given by the Edgar Cayce source which is the subject matter of this book.

Edgar Cayce died in January, 1945, and all of his psychic information predates that year. In the late 1940s and into the

1950s, a number of significant documents, most of which had been lost for centuries, were discovered at Qumran near the Dead Sea in Palestine (now Israel) and at Nag Hammadi in Egypt.

The scrolls and documents found at Qumran are generally believed to have been written between 250 B.C. and 68 A.D., preserved, and then hidden by a sect of the Essenes, a monastic religious group. This sect is mentioned frequently in the Cayce readings, and its historical existence and general beliefs are documented by Jewish historians Philo, Josephus, and Pliny. Cayce said the meaning of the term "Essene" is expectancy. (254-109) Certainly the Essene history and documents indicate they were expecting and preparing for a messianic figure.

Some of the works discovered at Qumran were heretofore unknown by modern scholars or were known only by reference in other material. Interpretation and analysis of the documents have been slow, and some critics have even charged deliberate delay and cover-up by Christian scholars who feared that the original authorship of Jesus' teachings and sayings might be jeopardized. Most of the documents, however, are now publicly available, and they do not impugn the message of Jesus. The impact of the documents on our understanding of early Christian messianic concepts, however, has been profound.

> They [the messianic concepts] were being shaped by writings and teachings emanating largely from the Essenes, and widely regarded as inspired. Until it became possible in recent times to be fully aware of this, and to have access to much of the literature, the true story of Christian beginnings could not be ascertained. Our perspectives were incorrect and almost inevitably so were our conclusions. The circumstances have not yet been apprehended by the vast majority of Christians.[3]

The first books of the Egyptian Nag Hammadi library were discovered in December, 1945, but their publication too has been greatly delayed because of a number of political and scholarly obstacles. Their full interpretation—and impact—is just beginning.

The Nag Hammadi library is primarily a collection of early Christian Gnostic works. Gnosticism was a powerful force among early Christians who claimed to "know" the hidden and true meaning of Jesus' teachings. For two or three centuries it existed side by side with more conservative and traditional Christian groups. With the conversion of the Roman Empire to conventional Christianity, however, the chance of Gnostic Christianity surviving became remote, especially with the subsequent efforts to standardize Christianity and declare variants to be heretical. Yet some scholars today surmise that in the Gnostic material may be found the doctrine and teachings which most nearly conform to those of Jesus and the apostles.[4]

The Essenes may have been forerunners of the Gnostics, although there is a substantial difference in many of their teachings and beliefs. The Qumran documents certainly reveal tendencies which became Gnosticism.[5] The history of Gnosticism as derived from the Nag Hammadi library begins about where the Dead Sea Scrolls Essenic history ends. Generally, the Dead Sea or Qumran documents refer to Old Testament events, whereas the Nag Hammadi texts relate to early Christianity and the New Testament.

As we have seen, the two major and most important discoveries of ancient documents have been at the Dead Sea and Nag Hammadi, but other texts which were thought to be lost or non-existent have also surfaced in the last century or so and will be used as sources of reference.

The fact that a document is old and unavailable for centuries does not make it authentic. On the other hand, there are common threads of philosophy which run through many of them and which bear on the subject of this book. They deserve serious scrutiny and consideration and will be referred to frequently in the chapters ahead.

CHAPTER TWO

Story of the Master

(as suggested by the Edgar Cayce readings)

> *Then Jesus said: "Behold, Father, she
> wanders the earth pursued by evil. Far from thy
> Breath she is going astray. She is trying to flee
> bitter Chaos, and does not know how she is to
> escape. Send me forth, O Father, therefore, and I,
> bearing the seal shall descend and wander all
> Aeons through, all mysteries reveal. I shall
> manifest the forms of the gods and teach the
> secrets of the holy way . . . "*
> *(Early Christian Naassene Psalm)*

**An overview of the lives of the Master told in story
form:**

*Many aeons ago before the foundations of time, God existed. In
an act of love, God created beings to be companions and co-
creators with Him. Thus the souls of each of us came into being.*
    *The first soul created, the one we now call our Elder Brother,
was very special to God and helped in the rest of creation.*
    It was a perfect time as the newly formed souls enjoyed

everything God had created. There were also angels and archangels and all kinds of animal, plant, and mineral life existing in many planets and worlds. A part of God was given to each soul, and all life thus became a reflection of God.

To the souls, however, God gave a unique ability—that of free will. They could do whatever they wanted, even things that God did not desire and which distorted the creative plan. This gift, which God would not take back nor control, shows the immense love which our Creator had for each of us. After all, God is love. It is a love which we cannot comprehend—just as we cannot comprehend God.

Although the angels did not have as much freedom of will as the souls, some of them defied God, and there was a war in heaven. The leader of the revolting angels was Lucifer or Satan, who was eventually cast out of heaven. This war affected all of creation, including earth and the souls who now live here. The conflict will be long and difficult; however, God and the loyal angels will ultimately prevail.

As ages passed, many souls began to experiment with God's creation and to do things which were not part of the plan. As they did so, they gradually lost their closeness to God and forgot their divinity—the spark of God within each of them. Only vaguely could these souls recall their Creator and remember the purpose for which they were created. It was a sad situation which continued to get worse, and there seemed to be no solution. God could destroy the lost souls but could not control them nor stop the errors they were making.

When the souls had first entered the earth and matter, they could do so by just willing it. They could leave their bodies and return to the spiritual realms in the same manner. But as time went on, it became more and more difficult to leave the material world in this way. Eventually there came a time when these souls could not voluntarily leave the bodies they had entered no matter how hard they tried. They had to wait until death. Even then, their souls could not return to the spiritual heavens, and they could only come back into the material world by being born into new bodies. It was an endless and hopeless circle. There was no way of escape or return to the heavenly Father.

Finally, God confessed to our Elder Brother deep sorrow over having created the souls and given them their free will. Now those who had misused their willpower would have to be destroyed.

But Elder Brother could not accept the destruction of his lost brethren. He gathered other souls around him who were not yet entrapped in matter, and they discussed and planned ways to help the lost ones. Elder Brother agreed to talk to God about the situation.

As he approached God, he fell down at His feet and pleaded: "Almighty Father, You have created the souls in Your wisdom and love. They were meant to be companions to You and to help in the creation of worlds to come. But they have gone astray. Do not destroy them, I beseech you. Send me to show them the way back to Your favor and their true home. Send me and these other souls who have not forgotten You. I will be their leader, and together we will save the lost souls and show them the way home."

God was moved by this unselfish display of love. These souls had not lost their heavenly estate, and yet they were willing to risk it in order to help those who were lost. They wanted their erring brothers also to share in their heritage.

God could not say "no" to them. He blessed Elder Brother and the faithful souls and urged them to begin their mission of mercy. God warned them, however, that the job would be difficult and the outcome uncertain.

At this time in the earth's development, the largest land mass and the islands surrounding it were called Atlantis. It was a beautiful land, but souls had become involved in the evolution and creation of the plants and animals of the area and had not faithfully continued God's desire for creation. They had developed pests, undesirable weeds, and ferocious beasts that preyed on everything, including the soul bodies. Even worse, the souls had created body forms that were mixtures of various types of life. Some bodies contained animal parts, such as hooves, fur, scales, and horns. Others even had plant characteristics like leaves and tree trunks. Our soul memory has preserved these monstrosities in the legends of mermaids, satyrs, unicorns, and other strange body forms.

Elder Brother and the other unfallen sons of God came to Atlantis and to the souls lost in these strange body forms. They did not enter any of the earth bodies, however, because these were now polluted forms of creation. They came in spirit form only yet were able to communicate with the lost souls. Elder Brother was their leader, and he was called Amilius on this occasion.

They talked to the lost souls and reminded them of their divine origin. Amilius and his friends tried to rekindle the memories of the beginning and the heavenly estate of all souls but to no avail. The souls trapped in the body forms and matter only laughed at the sons of God and continued in their selfish lusts and misuse of materiality. Their sensual world was as far as they could see or remember.

Even Amilius and the sons of God almost got lost in this world of matter. Reluctantly they decided to give up on their mission and return to God while they still could. They sadly left their lost and trapped brothers and returned to the heavens. As they met the Father, they asked His forgiveness for their failure but begged God for patience and forbearance with the lost souls.

Elder Brother came again to God in his role as spokesman for the unfallen souls. He asked God for another chance to help the lost brothers. Although still loving all the souls that had been created, God was more discouraged than ever about the lost ones and the chances of their ever returning to Him.

God said to Elder Brother, "I cannot help the lost souls until they realize the awfulness of their plight and ask for My help. I speak to them, but they cannot hear Me. Until someone lives a perfect life of love and shows the way, there is no hope. Then will the barriers between us be removed. But for now they have forgotten who they are and are incapable of unselfish love and a return to godhood."

Elder Brother replied: "All that You say, O Father, is true. They know not the way and will not listen. If they cannot hear You, then let me go again and speak to them. Let me live the perfect life and be an example of love. Then will they remember who they are and come back to You."

But God said, "You have spoken well, firstborn son, and I love you all the more for your courage and mercy, but it is not enough. The lost souls can no longer understand one who is a spiritual being. They can only recognize an example in one like themselves; they will not listen to any except their own. Unfortunately the body forms are now so corrupted that a soul will not be able to return to spirituality after entering a material body. I will not let you do this thing and risk losing you."

Elder Brother and the loyal souls pondered the truth of God's words. The loss of their erring brothers seemed inevitable.

And then Elder Brother made a suggestion. "Let us ask God to create a new body form for souls to inhabit on earth. Let us take on these new bodies and in them show our brothers the way back to God. I will serve as a model for the new earth body. I will enter the first body, and you may follow me in similar bodies. We will live lives of love and show our brothers the way to God."

When Elder Brother presented this plan to God, there was no immediate response. Finally after much deliberation, God spoke and said, "I do not wish for any soul to perish." Therefore a plan was agreed to, which would unfold in this way:

1. Each soul must meet its errors or sins over and over again

until it has learned to meet them correctly in love instead of in selfishness. No soul, however, will be given more than it can handle at any one time.

2. Each soul would be allowed many opportunities through earthly lives to overcome this world of materiality and soul selfishness. Only if a soul repeatedly continues in selfishness and shuns the light of love will it lose any further opportunity of salvation and be cast into outer darkness.

3. To help the souls realize their separation from God, Lucifer or the devil would be allowed to tempt the souls and lead them into extreme depths of depravity. Only then might each soul be in a position to recognize its totally hopeless condition and begin to seek a return to the Father. In disillusion and suffering through time, space, and patience might the soul come to the realization that its real will is the will of God and that in the practice of this will is happiness and heaven.

4. Realizing the difficulty of the situation, God proposed that each sin of the soul should be forgiven and its consequences avoided whenever the soul forgives that sin in others.

5. The confused lines of communication might be restored between God and the lost souls if some soul were to live a perfect life of love in materiality.

6. While there are other planes and places for soul development, the task of overcoming selfishness or disobedience to God's will must be completed on earth if it was begun there.

7. When a soul has replaced selfishness with a genuine love for others in both its thought and conduct, it may then finally leave the earth plane and move on to other realms on its return journey to the Father.

God reflected upon this plan and saw that it was good. When souls reached the extremes of degradation and separation from God, they might then be willing to search for something better. At that point there was a possibility that the memory of their lost heritage could then be rekindled. If that happened, the plan allowed the lost souls a way of escape and a way of return to God. And if just one soul who remembered could show the way to the others, then the chances of their return would be greatly improved.

God also recognized that as a result of this long voyage into matter and error, each soul, if it came back, would be wiser and totally committed to the divine plan of the Father. Each would be fully aware of both its oneness with God and its own individuality. The character of each soul would be enriched with its special and unique experiences and have a maturity enabling it better to fulfill its original role of creativity and companionship with God.

The unfallen souls were full of enthusiasm for the plan and covenanted together to make it succeed. Elder Brother was to be their leader in this mission into materiality. Hereafter they would lovingly refer to him as "Master." In this coming life on earth, however, he would be known as Adam.

The earth had never known such beauty as that which surrounded the unfallen souls when they approached it and prepared for the entry of Adam. The morning stars sang together with the music of the spheres. And the angels of God shouted with joy and promised to help the Master and all the souls seeking to further the will of the Father.

The new body for Adam had been prepared by God from the dust of the earth. It was ready to receive the spirit of God's first-created soul; it would also be the first soul which God had put on earth. For the purpose of companionship and help, God divided the soul; one part entered the male body of Adam, the other the female body of Eve. Together they would work as twin souls in their earth experience.

Everything on earth was now under the control of Adam and Eve and existed to serve them. There never was such a place of beauty as their home, the Garden of Eden. Even the angels in heaven envied Adam and Eve and the paradise of Eden.

The charm, however, would not last.

The fallen angel, Lucifer, plotted how to upset the plan to save the lost souls. He decided to approach Eve disguised as a snake, which then was a gorgeous animal. He told Eve that God's plan was too slow; there was a quicker way to help the lost souls. If she and Adam would eat of the tree of knowledge, they would be equal to God and know the way quickly to help the lost souls. God had not been fair to them by making their mission so difficult; there actually was an easier way.

Eve trusted the snake; after all, it was the wisest of the animals. Surely no harm could come from just eating some fruit of the tree, and maybe they really would become like God.

She ran to Adam to tell him the exciting news. "Adam," she said, "God did not tell us everything. We can be gods as well if we will just eat of the tree of knowledge."

Adam remembered that God had told them not to eat from this tree, and he told Eve that they should obey God. He also reminded her of their important mission to show the lost souls the way back to God.

"But that is why we should eat the fruit," she said. "When we are like God, we can quickly save the lost ones. There is no reason

*why we should make the job more difficult by waiting for God's
plan to unfold."* She was excited about this new-found
opportunity.

Finally, Adam admitted that her logic made sense, and together
they ate of the forbidden fruit.

God soon appeared, but Adam and Eve fled in fear and guilt.
They could not hide from God, however, and were confronted with
their sin.

Adam blamed Eve for the error, and Eve complained that the
snake had misled her. As punishment, God said that they both
would have to suffer death like the lost souls and that they would
be banished from the Garden. For the rest of their lives, they
would have to toil and work the earth in order to obtain food and
the necessities of life. Eve would have to suffer in bringing new
soul bodies into the earth, and the snake would hereafter crawl
upon the ground and be bruised and injured by the feet of men.

As they left the Garden of Eden, they begged for God's mercy
and a second chance. But God's justice is sure and certain, and
their error could not be undone. God did promise Adam, however,
that some day he would be able to overcome his sin and that he
would yet be the savior of the lost souls.

When this promise was made to Adam, God warned that the
journey would be long. Only in patience could Adam regain the lost
glory of his soul. He would have to come to the earth many times
to overcome his errors and, in the process, show the way of return
to all the other souls. He would wander the earth through aeons of
time and rediscover and reveal the mysteries and secrets of the
holy way.

As the other unfallen souls followed Adam into materiality,
they too erred and became involved in the long procession of
earthly lives. They would have to rely on the Master to show them
the way out of chaos, but they would be a comfort and support to
him in the voyage of redemption. Now all the souls who had
entered earth were trapped in it.

After banishment from the Garden of Eden, Adam and Eve
learned to work the earth and live from its produce. They had
children, but even here there was disappointment. One of them,
Cain, was influenced by Lucifer and killed his brother, Abel. Cain
then married one of the souls the sons of God had come to save
and became hopelessly lost in the ways of selfishness and
materiality.

A third son, Seth, maintained the higher spirituality of Adam
and Eve and received from Adam the secrets God had entrusted to
Adam. Through Seth's offspring, the Master would return many

times in the continuing effort to live a perfect life of love.

And the Master did come back. He returned as Enoch, who, according to the Bible, was a very spiritual man. He was respected by all his friends and a source of inspiration to them. After a time, God decided that he would call Enoch up to the heavens and reveal to him all the mysteries of the universe. Enoch had known them once when he was with God in the beginning, but he had forgotten them. So Enoch was taken to heaven, and God revealed all the secrets and wonders of creation to him. God also placed His seal upon Enoch to designate him as the one who would triumph over evil and be the final judge of all souls.

Enoch then returned to earth, and told his family and friends about the things he had learned from God. Many of the souls listened to him and were inspired enough to lead spiritual lives and to seek a return to their Creator. Enoch's fame was great, and numerous nations heard of him and his amazing revelations. The Egyptians called him Hermes. God was so pleased with Enoch and what he had accomplished that Enoch was allowed to avoid death and was taken directly to heaven at the end of his life on earth.

After the departure of Enoch, however, the people forgot what he had said and ceased to follow the ways of love and service. Even the mysteries that he had revealed were lost or were considered to be mere myths.

God and the Master decided to try again. Because of the good life that Enoch had lived, God told the Master he would not have to undergo either a physical birth or death in his next visit to earth. He could enter and leave the earth just as souls originally had been able to do.

This time the Master was known as Melchizedek. He was both a priest of God and king of the city of Jerusalem. He knew Abraham and encouraged him in his spiritual development. The influence of Melchizedek was very powerful and caused many souls to remember their higher selves and return to God. In ages to come, people would look back upon Melchizedek's life and recognize in him a standard of righteousness for proper living and love. As God later talked to His chosen people, the Hebrews, and promised them that one day they would be sent a messiah, some reasoned that it would be someone like Melchizedek.

Yet after Melchizedek was taken to heaven at the end of his earthly life, the people again forgot God and returned to their selfish ways. To them Melchizedek was a god who knew neither birth nor death; he was not like them. They could not do what Melchizedek had done.

God and the Master contemplated a possible solution. Maybe if the Master came to earth the next time through a birth and death, just like the other souls, they would relate to him and remember his ways when he was gone.

So the Master came back to earth as Joseph and was born to Rachel and Jacob after they had despaired of ever having their own children. His half-brothers hated him. Joseph was too good. The brothers were jealous, and they tried to kill him. But God protected Joseph, and he was taken to Egypt where he lived a life of faithfulness and righteousness in the midst of his troubles. God blessed him, and Joseph became a leader in Egypt along with the Pharaoh. Because he listened to God and served others, Joseph saved the Egyptians and others from the starvation of a severe drought. He even forgave his brothers who had tried to kill him, and they came to Egypt to live in prosperity with him. At the end of his life, Joseph realized he had lived a good life that would serve as an inspiration for other souls for generations to come. While they would depart from the true path at times, his life would be an example which they could relate to and follow. After his death, he also knew that he must continue to come to earth until he lived such a perfect life that all would know the way and the separation between God and humanity would be erased forever.

The Master next came back as Joshua, who led the children of Israel into the Promised Land after the death of Moses. Joshua had complete faith in God, but because the people lacked faith, the entry into the Promised Land had to be delayed for forty years. Although Joshua was then in his late years, he served as the military commander who drove out and destroyed the enemy from the land God had promised His people. It was the same land that the Master would come to eventually in his final and triumphant life of love and redemption.

One of the lives of the Master was that of Asaph, a musician in the house of God for King David and King Solomon. He was blessed with the gift of prophecy, and it would be reflected in his writings, including some of the Psalms of the Bible. Asaph was a man of intense faith and love for God and God's Temple. His influence would extend far beyond his lifetime, and a musical or artistic guild would continue for generations and be known as the "sons of Asaph."

The Master had another life as a priest of God. His name this time was Jeshua, and he was instrumental in rebuilding the Temple in Jerusalem after the Jewish people returned from captivity in Babylon. During this lifetime, Jeshua was recognized by a prophet of Israel as the anointed one of God who would one day destroy the devil and his influence and restore the throne of

God to the lost and fallen souls. The Master still bore the seal of
God.

In none of these lives had the Master lived a perfect life, but he
had done much to point the way back to God. Several times, he
had given to the lost souls revelations from God which described
God's mysteries and which should have served as a blueprint for
their salvation. But each time, the meaning of the revelations was
forgotten when the Master departed. There was one revelation,
however, which was not lost and which would continue to serve as
a guide back to God. It was the Jewish Bible, the word of God,
whose parts the Master had either written or influenced
throughout all these lifetimes.

The Master lived other lives and influenced all religions which
believe in the one true God. One of these lives was that of Zend,
the father of Zoroaster. A new religion would bear the name of
Zoroaster, and much of its message was revealed and given
through Zend. It was a religion which quickened humanity's
spiritual thinking and helped prepare for the final entry and
perfect life of the Master.

Before the Master returned again to achieve his goal, God came
to him and spoke lovingly and affectionately: "My dearest son, you
have done well. You do not have to return to earth; you can stay
with Me forever in heaven."

The Master replied, "I thank You, Father, for Your love, but I
also love my brothers and sisters. I want to show them the way,
which I have not yet wholly done. I am ready now to live a perfect
life in materiality. I will not fail this time."

God recognized the commitment and love of the Master for his
brothers and sisters and was pleased. However, God also warned
him: "Although I too think you are ready to complete the task you
began long ago, you should know that your life on earth, even if it
is perfect, will be one of suffering and difficulty. You have set
certain patterns in your earthly record which, if you return, you
must meet and finally overcome. When you lived as Joshua, for
example, you killed many people. If you are to complete your
earthly mission, you must heal and restore life to people in the
areas where you took life before. And you must endure death and
experience some of the agony you inflicted upon others. If you do
all this and do not err, your mission will be complete. You will have
removed the penalty of death which you incurred as Adam. The
way for all to follow will be shown, and they will not forget this

time. The bond will finally be restored between Me and My sons and daughters."

The Master knew what lay ahead, but he praised God and humbly said, "I am ready."

The way was prepared for the Master's entry. Eve returned to be the channel for his birth, and many others who had worked with the Master from the beginning returned to assist him in this epochal venture.

Just as they had done when Adam first entered the earth, the angels sang with joy at the birth of the Master in the Holy and Promised Land which Joshua had entered centuries before. And Wise Men from the East and the religion of Zend came to pay homage to the Master's return. All that had transpired before was now centered in this present life of the Master.

He was called Jeshua this time, which meant "God is salvation." He had had that name before; it was also the same as Joshua in Hebrew. In Greek, it was Jesus.

God and the souls on earth who were close to Jesus watched over him carefully. He was given special training, not only in the Jewish religion but in others which believed in the true God. He traveled to Egypt, Persia, and India and learned much. He and his cousin John completed their final spiritual initiations at the Great Pyramid, which the Master had begun as Hermes.

At the age of thirty, Jesus was ready for his ministry of teaching and healing. He chose a group of twelve disciples to assist him. Each of them had been with him at the beginning and on numerous other occasions in trying to save the lost souls. Each one also brought a special quality and experience to the Master's mission. One was even chosen who would betray him, but who, in so doing, would make possible the Master's final and supreme act of love.

The prophets of Israel had been great, but none had ever taught like Jesus nor performed such miracles. The priests were upset at his condemnations of them and the attention which the people gave him. Some of the Jewish leaders were also concerned about the reactions of the Roman rulers to this young teacher who claimed to have his own kingdom and had so many followers.

For three years Jesus traveled the countrysides of Galilee and Judea. He healed, taught the people, and gave special instructions to his disciples. They would have to carry on after his death and assure that the purpose of the Master's final lifetime was not lost.

Ultimately, in Jerusalem, Jesus was condemned to death and was crucified on a cross. He was buried, but after three days in the grave, left his tomb and appeared again to his followers. He had overcome death. The hopeless circle of material enslavement had been broken; he had shown the way back to the Father. He left one commandment to the world and had exemplified it totally. It was to "love one another."

After Jesus left his followers and ascended to heaven, they began the seemingly impossible task of spreading his message of love throughout the world. Most of the Jewish people rejected this new faith, but the Gentiles were ready for a new religion and eventually embraced it.

As time went on and the pagan nations were converted to the new religion, people began to forget the things that Jesus had said and his one commandment. Instead of loving one another, they continued in the ways of selfishness, and the various factions of the faith began to fight and declare each other wrong. Groups which had been founded by the disciples and knew the mysteries given by Jesus became a minority, and their beliefs were eventually lost in the formalized doctrines of the Roman and Greek branches of the church.

The people forgot that Jesus who became God had been one like themselves. He was a soul who had made the return to God, but they began to remember him as God who could do all kinds of things which they could never do. They forgot that he had said, "Follow me," and had urged them to do the things he had done. They wanted to worship him instead of follow him. The purpose and meaning of Jesus' life was threatened and misunderstood by the brothers he had come to save. It was the same problem the Master had experienced before, especially in his early appearances. The influence of Lucifer was continuing.

The Master had left a promise, however, that there would come a time when his influence would truly return to earth. He would reign as king, and the people of earth would know peace and love for a thousand years. Although Lucifer would thereafter be let loose for a time upon the earth, the ways of the Master would ultimately and permanently prevail. He would then be the judge of the world.

Through long centuries after his death, the world struggled in darkness, selfishness, and a denial of the love Jesus had proclaimed and personified. The church which bore his name was fractured into factions which fought one another, and non-believers were killed in his behalf. And yet there were moments of hope and brightness; there were saints and teachers who appeared from time to time with the memory and true message of the Master's love.

And almost miraculously in recent years, God has allowed the discovery of ancient documents to remind us of the long mission of the Master and the trail back to the Father which he blazed. The writings reflect the thoughts and beliefs of the disciples and other close followers of Jesus. They speak passionately of the secrets of the holy way and the mysteries of the heavens. They tell the story, as did Edgar Cayce from his psychic couch, of the wanderings through many lifetimes of the Master—our Elder Brother—and of his patient and persevering quest to reveal to each of us the path back to our Creator and the way of love.

*   *   *   *   *

In the chapters ahead, this story of the mission and lives of the Master will be examined in the light of these rediscovered documents, of others which had been forgotten or overlooked through the years, and of the Bible itself. The examination will begin with a look at the subject of reincarnation, the belief that souls take on multiple lives—a belief which is the cornerstone of many religions. Its presence and power in the Christian and Jewish faiths may come as a surprise to many.

CHAPTER THREE
Past Lives?

Our birth is but a sleep and a forgetting:
The soul that rises with us, our life's star,
Hath had elsewhere its setting,
And cometh from afar:
Not in entire forgetfulness,
And not in utter nakedness,
But trailing clouds of glory do we come
From God, who is our home:
Heaven lies about us in our infancy!
                              (William Wordsworth)

It is not more surprising to be born twice than
once; everything in nature is resurrection.
                              (Voltaire)

Now when Jesus came into the district of Caesarea Philippi, he asked his disciples, "Who do men say that the Son of man is?" And they said, "Some say John the Baptist, others say Elijah, and others Jeremiah or one of the prophets." He said to them, "But who do you say that I am?" (Matthew 16:13-15)

The finest psychic of modern times answered this question, which Jesus had asked his disciples, as the source speaking through the entranced Edgar Cayce identified a number of prior lives of Jesus who became the Christ. It was a revelation that initially brought consternation to the conscious Cayce, but one which gradually rang true with him and others around him, just as had the information in the medical and other physical readings. The trouble with this new concept as well as the general idea of reincarnation was that, unlike the medical readings or those that could be verified by testing them, this concept had to be taken on faith and could not be proved or disproved.

Edgar Cayce, after searching for Biblical support for or rejection of reincarnation, stated: "I can read reincarnation into the Bible—and you can read it right out again!"

Was the idea of men and women having lived prior lives something that was alien to the Scriptures? Was it a sacrilege to speculate on such a concept, especially in connection with Jesus, the Son of God?

The last question seemingly can be answered with a "no," for as the above quotation from Matthew and similar accounts in the other three gospels indicate, such discussion was common among the people of Jesus' time. Jesus not only failed to condemn it, but asked his disciples to enter into the speculation. It should be noted that Peter answered the question of "who" Jesus was by affirming: "You are the Christ, the Son of the living God." Cayce's psychic information also affirms this proposition. Over and over again, the readings state that Jesus was the Master of masters, the first begotten of God, our Elder Brother, the Christ, the Son of God, the Way, and the pattern for all humanity.

Peter's answer, however, does not negate the possibility of Jesus having been one of the prophets returned or some other previous person. His answer just did not necessarily address the question of what other lives Jesus might have lived or whether such a concept was impossible or wrong. Jesus' response to Peter's affirmation likewise does not deny this possibility nor condemn such an idea. Jesus merely blessed Peter's recognition of the Christ by characterizing it as a revelation from God.

On the contrary, after examining a number of Biblical passages, it seems that at least the possibility of the return of souls for additional lives was accepted and assumed by Jesus and his followers.

The Old Testament closes with this prophecy:

> Behold, I will send you Elijah the prophet before
> the great and terrible day of the Lord comes.
>
> (Malachi 4:5)

Early in the New Testament, Jesus identifies with that prophecy:

> And the disciples asked him, "Then why do the
> scribes say that first Elijah must come?" He
> replied, "Elijah does come, and he is to restore all
> things; but I tell you that Elijah has already come,
> and they did to him whatever they pleased. So also
> the Son of man will suffer at their hands." Then
> the disciples understood that he was speaking to
> them of John the Baptist.   (Matthew 17:10-13)

Not only does this quotation seem clearly to show Jesus giving an example of someone having had a past life, but the fact that the disciples understood the meaning of Jesus' comments without further clarification or explanation suggests that they were familiar and conversant with such a concept.

Jesus' identification of John with Elijah occurred on another occasion. John from prison had sent two of his disciples to Jesus. After they left, Jesus began talking of John and said that he was more than a prophet. He adds (in Chapter 11 of Matthew):

> 10 This is he of whom it is written, "Behold, I send
> my messenger before thy face, who shall prepare
> thy way before thee."
> 11 Truly, I say to you, among those born of women
> there has risen no one greater than John the
> Baptist . . .
> 13 For all the prophets and the law prophesied
> until John;
> 14 and if you are willing to accept it, he is Elijah
> who is to come.
> 15 He who has ears to hear, let him hear.

The cryptic statement, "He who has ears to hear, let him hear," hints at a special meaning and is used elsewhere in the New

Testament in connection with parables and statements which appear to have hidden spiritual import.

Note that in verse 11 above, Jesus states that of those who have been born, none greater than John has "risen." The obvious implication of this statement is that others also have risen, although none of them has been greater than John. Again, such a concept of the dead rising to new life appears to be one that was accepted naturally by Jesus and his disciples.

Similarly, the public's familiarity with such an idea is illustrated not only by the question Jesus asked his disciples, which was quoted at the beginning of this discussion, but also in the following text:

> Now Herod the tetrarch heard of all that was done, and he was perplexed, because it was said by some, that John had been raised from the dead, by some, that Elijah had appeared, and by others that one of the old prophets had risen. (Luke 9:7-8)

A Biblical scholar who has examined the subject of reincarnation states:

> There is a long tradition in mystical Judaism of belief in reincarnation, which can be traced with relative clarity to the earliest periods of this era.[1]

The Jewish historian, Flavius Josephus, who wrote of this period of history, indicates that the Pharisees believed good souls return to earth in new bodies.[2] He also includes the Essenes as believers in the continuity of life by citing their philosophy that the immortal soul occupies corruptible bodies.[3] Josephus himself must have believed similarly, for in an address to Jewish soldiers he said:

> Do ye not remember that all pure Spirits when they depart out of this life obtain a most holy place in heaven, from whence, in the revolutions of ages, they are again sent into pure bodies . . .?[4]

The Bible and historians agree, however, that the Sadducees, unlike the Pharisees and Essenes, believed both the body and the soul to be corruptible and to perish at death.

A Cayce reading confirms that the Sadducees did not believe in the immortality of the soul and adds that this issue was at the

heart of a question presented to Jesus and discussed in three of
the gospels. In these gospels "the Sadducees, who say that
there is no resurrection," asked Jesus to whom at the
resurrection a woman who had been married to multiple
husbands would belong. (See Matthew 22:23, Mark 12:18, and
Luke 20:27.) Jesus' answer appears to be referring to life on the
"other side" and may have been designed to avoid taking sides
in a doctrinal dispute. Cayce said that the term "resurrection"
actually meant to people at that time the incarnating—rising or
resurrecting—into life again. (5749-8) It was the term for the
concept involved in the discussions between Jesus and his
disciples about souls rising from the grave and taking on new
life. Today we call it reincarnation.

The idea that "resurrection" meant the taking on of new life
after death is supported as early as Isaiah 26:19. There, in
discussing the time when Israel would be restored out of its
current bondage, Isaiah promises: "Thy dead shall live, my body
shall rise." (alternate RSV translation)

The Egyptians also, according to James Bonwick in his 1878
book *Egyptian Belief and Modern Thought,* considered the term
"resurrection" to mean being born into new lives. He says, "The
funeral books show us clearly that resurrection was, in reality,
but a renovation, leading to a new existence, a new infancy, and
a new youth."[5]

It might be noted that in Acts 23:8 the term "resurrection"
comes up again:

> For the Sadducees say that there is no
> resurrection, nor angel, nor spirit; but the
> Pharisees acknowledge them all.

Surely this is not a reference to Jesus' resurrection, for the
Pharisees had not embraced such a Christian concept; neither
would the subject of angels and spirits be connected uniquely
with Jesus. If the term "resurrection" here means the concept
of souls' rising from death and taking on new life, or reincarnation, and surely it must in view of what we know historically
about these sects' doctrinal beliefs, then an earlier passage in
Acts 4:1-2 takes on new and significant meaning:

> And as they were speaking to the people, the
> priests, and the captain of the temple, and the

> Sadducees, came upon them, annoyed because
> they were teaching the people, and proclaiming in
> Jesus the resurrection from the dead.

This passage would then seem to be affirming that the disciples, through the authority of Jesus, were preaching a belief in reincarnation or the resurrection from the dead, the doctrine opposed by the Sadducees.

In addition to the instances already cited, there are others in the Bible which seem to imply an acceptance of the belief that souls pre-exist life and may return for additional lives. Following are some examples:

1. The ninth chapter of John begins with this incident:

> As he [Jesus] passed by, he saw a man blind
> from his birth. And his disciples asked him,
> "Rabbi, who sinned, this man, or his parents, that
> he was born blind?" Jesus answered, "It was not
> that this man sinned, or his parents, but that the
> works of God might be made manifest in him."
>   (John 9:1-3)

The disciples obviously believed that blindness was the result of sin by either the man or his parents; inasmuch as the man had been born blind, the sin, were it his, would have had to have occurred in a previous existence. In stating that sin was not involved here, but that the blindness existed so that the works of God could be manifested, Jesus neither refuted nor condemned the logic of his disciples' question. Rather, his answer seems to imply that there was merely a different explanation involved here.

2. In the following passage from Proverbs 8, the author is talking about wisdom, but his comments seem to take on the persona of the soul:

> 22 The Lord created me at the beginning of his
> work, the first of his acts of old.
> 23 Ages ago I was set up, at the first before the
> beginning of the earth.
> 24 When there were no depths I was brought forth,
> when there were no springs abounding with water.
> 25 Before the mountains had been shaped, before
> the hills, I was brought forth;

26 before he had made the earth with its fields, or the first of the dust of the world.
27 When he established the heavens, I was there, when he drew a circle on the face of the deep,
28 when he made firm the skies above, when he established the fountains of the deep,
29 when he assigned to the sea its limit, so that the waters might not transgress his command, when he marked out the foundations of the earth,
30 then I was beside him, like a master workman; and I was daily his delight, rejoicing before him always,
31 rejoicing in his inhabited world and delighting in the sons of men.

(Even if it is conceded that the abstract subject of wisdom is all that is referred to above, the quote still becomes a startling confirmation of the Edgar Cayce creation scenario, which will be discussed later.)

3. Listen to the prayer of Moses to God in Psalm 90 wherein he observes the brevity of life, but acknowledges the requirement of many returns:

1 Lord, thou hast been our dwelling place in all generations.
2 Before the mountains were brought forth, or ever thou hadst formed the earth and the world, even from everlasting to everlasting, thou art God.
3 Thou turnest man to destruction; and sayest, Return, ye children of men.
4 For a thousand years in thy sight are but yesterday when it is past, and as a watch in the night.
5 The span of their life will be as a sleep; in the morning they are like grass which changes.
6 In the morning it flourishes and grows up; in the evening it is cut down and withers.
13 Return, O Lord. How long?

(Lamsa translation)

4. Does not the following quotation suggest that Jeremiah's soul pre-existed his birth and knew God?

Then the word of the Lord came to me saying,

> "Before I formed you in the womb I knew you, and
> before you were born I consecrated you; I appoint-
> ed you a prophet to the nations."
>
> (Jeremiah 1:4-5)

5. The following Biblical statement seems to refer to the pre-existence of the soul and of events which elude the memory of man:

> Is there a thing of which it is said, "See, this is
> new"? It has been already, in the ages before us.
> There is no remembrance of former things, nor will
> there be any remembrance of later things yet to
> happen among those who come after.
>
> (Ecclesiastes 1:10-11)

6. The Cayce readings indicate that by faith, grace, and following the example of Jesus the Christ, we can, like the prodigal son, return to the Father and thus end the cycle of earthly incarnations or lives. Is this not the principle involved in the following promise attributed to Christ?

> He who overcomes I will make a pillar in the
> temple of my God, *and he shall not go out again;* and
> I will write upon him the name of my God and the
> name of the new Jerusalem which comes down out
> of heaven from my God; and I will write upon him
> my new name.   (Revelation 3:12; Lamsa
> translation—Author's italics)

The phrase "he shall not go out again" would seem to mean that further earthly lives are unnecessary for him who overcomes.

7. The concept of going out or forth is contained in an Old Testament prophecy about the messiah who is to be sent to Israel from God:

> . . . yet out of you shall come forth a ruler to
> govern Israel; whose goings forth have been
> predicted from of old, from eternity.
>
> (Micah 5:26; Lamsa translation)

The prophet is saying that the going forth of that one who is to be the messiah is not new, but dates from the beginning.

8. The need for additional lives results from sin. Until we have met our errors and overcome them through right action and grace, we must return to meet the things we have done and try again. Eastern religions call this law of having to face what we have done previously "karma." The principle of the law is stated in the Bible numerous times:

a. "Do not be deceived; God is not mocked: for whatever a man sows, that he will also reap." (Galatians 6:7)

b. "He who leads into captivity shall go into captivity; he who kills with the sword must be killed with the sword. Here is the patience and the faith of the saints." (Revelation 13:10; Lamsa translation)

c. "The point is this: He who sows sparingly will also reap sparingly; and he who sows bountifully will also reap bountifully." (II Corinthians 9:6)

d. "As you have done, it shall be done to you, your deeds shall return on your own head." (Obadiah 1:15)

e. ". . . one who sows righteousness gets a sure reward." (Proverbs 11:18)

It is a matter of historical record that many early Christians believed in reincarnation. The famous translator of the Bible into Latin, St. Jerome, indicates in one of his letters that the concept of reincarnation was accepted by many Christians, especially those in the Greek-speaking areas around the eastern Mediterranean where most of Christianity was centered. Two of early Christianity's greatest spokesmen, Clement and Origen, included a belief in reincarnation as part of their theology. Although Origen lost favor with the established church for a time, he is today revered generally as the finest Biblical scholar of the first six centuries of Christendom.[6] Documents discovered in recent years at Nag Hammadi in Egypt and elsewhere also reveal a belief in reincarnation by various early Christian sects, including the Gnostics.

More important for our purposes, however, may be the fact that several early Jewish Christian groups believed specifically that Jesus had experienced previous human incarnations. The Ebionites taught that his soul had come to the earth first as Adam and later as Jesus. The Church Father Hippolytus of Rome credits the Elkasites as believing that Jesus' virgin birth was not his first birth, but that he had appeared previously and frequently in other bodies. This belief was also shared by the Nazarenes. Even the Clementine Homilies express the view that Christ had appeared as historical personages on various occasions from the beginning of the world. He is therein identified as Adam, Enoch, Noah, Abraham, Isaac, Jacob, Moses, and of course, Jesus.[7]

Some scholars have concluded that the translation "Jesus of Nazareth," which appears frequently in the New Testament, is not correct, but the phrase should have been translated and interpreted to identify Jesus as a Nazarene.[8] There is evidence that the early Christians were called Nazarenes, Nazoraeans or Nasoreans, and Christians are still referred to as "an-Nasara" in the Koran.[9] Matthew 2:23 indicates it was prophesied the messiah would be called "a Nazarene," and in Acts 24:5, Paul is identified as "a ringleader of the sect of the Nazarenes." This sect was the fledgling Christian church at Jerusalem.

The Nazarenes or Nazoraeans were originally a Jewish group. The name could have applied to any strict law-observing Jewish sect, especially if it had secret teachings or mysteries hidden from the uninitiated.[10] The group undoubtedly existed from the earliest times of Christianity and may be an offshoot of the Essenes, whose doctrines are surely older than the Biblical gospels. The Nazarenes believed that Jesus was the divine messenger who had descended and ascended *again* for the salvation of men.[11] John the Baptist is credited with being the founder of this gnostic group, while the Gospel of John and the Johannine Epistles are said to be Christian revisions of the Nazarene beliefs.[12] At least some of the Nazarene theology is very similar to that propounded by Cayce and would support the concept of prior lives of the Christ.

Although early Church Father Hippolytus considered heretical the beliefs of a religious group called Naasseni, which may be a gnostic variation of the Nazarenes, some details he gives of their theology again closely parallel information from Cayce.[13]

If the concept of reincarnation was so prevalent in early Christian thought, why is it not a part of mainstream Christian theology today? Although such a belief has surfaced from time to time in the long history of Christianity, it ceased to be a significant factor in that religion after the Fifth Ecumenical Council of Constantinople in 553 A.D. One of the products of that Council (although apparently added by Emperor Justinian) was *"The Fifteen Anathemas Against Origen,"* in which the doctrines of Origen, including belief in reincarnation, were condemned. Following is typical wording taken from that condemnation of Origenism:

> If anyone assert the fabulous pre-existence of souls and shall assert the monstrous restoration which follows it, let him be anathema.
> . . . If anyone shall say that Christ . . . had pity upon the divers falls which had appeared in the spirits . . . and that to restore them He passed through divers classes, had different bodies and different names, became all to all, an Angel among Angels, a Power among Powers . . . and finally has taken flesh and blood like ours and is became man for man . . . if anyone says all this and does not profess that God the Word humbled Himself and became man; let him be anathema.
> . . . If anyone shall say that the life of the Spirits shall be like to the life which was in the beginning, when as yet the spirits had not come down or fallen; so that the end . . . shall be the true measure of the beginning; let him be anathema.[14]

The teachings of Origen had been affirmed by the Church as recently as the Chalcedonian Decree of 451 A.D. Since the Western or Roman branch of the Church was barely represented at the Fifth Council it refused to accept its legitimacy for some years. And it may never have officially done so. Nevertheless, the Council's pronouncements in 553 eventually became accepted dogma even of the Roman Church. In recent years, however, some Church officials have begun to take a new look at this issue.

> In the light of the references to reincarnation in the Bible, and of statements by the early Church fathers, and now of the position of Catholic scholars in disclaiming the crusade against Origen, it is not remarkable that a growing number

of the Christian clergy and religious writers are
speaking favorably of the new interest in
reincarnation, and are even hoping that this "lost
chord of Christianity" may once more vibrate in
harmony with Christ's teaching of hope and
responsibility.[15]

Edgar Cayce was once asked if early Christian Gnosticism,
which largely accepted the concept of reincarnation, was the
closest parallel to the philosophy of the readings. In answering
this question affirmatively, he also said that this form of
Christianity was the commonly accepted doctrine until "there
began to be set rules in which there were attempts to take
shortcuts. And there are none in Christianity." (5749-14) The
Gnostic *Book of Baruch* (attributed to Justin) supports Cayce's
evaluation of Gnosticism and presents Jesus as the first initiate
into true gnosis. Basilides also concluded that Jesus was the
first true Gnostic.[16]

The question next asked of Cayce and his answer was:

**Q-22. What action of the early church, or council, can be
mentioned as that which ruled [out] reincarnation from Christian
theology?**

**A-22. Just as indicated—the attempts of individuals to accept or
take advantage of, because of this knowledge, see?   5749-14**

We could pursue the question of reincarnation in
Christianity further, but that seems unnecessary. It is not the
purpose of this work to convince anyone of reincarnation in the
Bible or as a necessary tenet of Christian belief but to point to
wording and a historical background that at least allow
discussion and consideration of such a concept. Also from what
we have seen, it would not appear heretical to speculate on the
previous lives of Jesus. Such speculation and belief is not new
to Christianity, and one should be willing to weigh objectively
the pros and cons of such a proposition. It will be the goal in the
chapters ahead to look at various sources which speak to this
question.

The readings of Edgar Cayce indicate that the Jesus soul
lived as many as thirty different lives and from among them
clearly identified the following:

Amilius—an incarnation in spirit form only.

Adam—the first man, described in the opening of the Bible.

Enoch—a man who "walked with God," according to Genesis.

Melchizedek—a priest at the time of Abraham.

Joseph—son of Jacob who was sold into slavery by his brothers.

Joshua—the successor to Moses who led the Israelites into the Promised Land.

Asaph—a musician in King David's court.

Jeshua—a priest who helped re-establish the worship of God after the Israelites' return from captivity in Babylon.

Zend—the father of the religious leader Zoroaster.

Jesus—the Christ.

The readings suggest that Hermes of Egypt may also have been an earlier incarnation of Jesus, and it is so treated herein.

Although the above lives were all that were specifically given, the readings provide these additional profound observations about the appearances of the Jesus soul in the earth plane:

In all those periods that the basic principle was the Oneness of the Father, He has walked with men.   364-8

As has been indicated, the entity [Jesus]—as an entity—influenced either directly or indirectly all those forms of philosophy or religious thought that taught God was One.   364-9

In reading 364-7, a listing of the subsequent lives of Adam included one as Ur. A follow-up question on Ur was included in reading 364-9, and Cayce answered:

Ur was rather a land, a place, a city—and the thought, or intent, or the call was from Ur. Ur, then, as presented or represented in the experience of Jesus, as one that impelled or guided those thoughts in that period, or experience.

No further detail on Ur was given by Cayce. Ur is known to have been a city of Mesopotamia, a few miles from the mouth of the Euphrates River. It is the city from which the father of Abraham is supposed to have migrated and which was inhabited as early as 4,000 B.C.

The name Affa was mentioned in reading 364-8 as an

incarnation of the Master. The only clue on this life is that it may have been Egyptian at a time when Egypt was giving counsel to many nations.

There is elsewhere a hint that Ram or Rama of India, who lived some 2,000 years B.C., may have been an incarnation of the Master.

Similarly, reading 3360-1 seems to suggest that Jesus and Buddha were one and the same, but it is not clear whether the reference is to the individuals or to their philosophies.

Jesus is also identified as "that Son" in the land of the setting sun of Japan and China. It is possible that this reading (2402-2) is linking Jesus with the Oriental religion of Taoism.

Reading 364-9 also states that the "spirit" of the Master walked among men in France, England, and America.

In all these latter cases, the information was so vague or the tie to the Master so tenuous that no attempt has been made to examine the lives and their significance further.

The Cayce readings proclaim that life itself is indestructible; it may change form, but it continues on. This principle is true for all varieties of life, for every living manifestation of God, whether it be of the mineral, plant, or animal kingdoms. Unlike the philosophy of reincarnation which is a part of many Eastern religions, the interpretation described in the readings apparently maintains that life continues in the same form each time; at least it was clearly stated that humans continue as humans in the earth plane: they do not come back as animals or other forms of life. Transmigration was not a part of the philosophy of the Cayce readings.

One further observation on the general subject of past lives: A logical question that might be asked is why such lives are not remembered. As a matter of fact, some people do seem to recall incidents of past lives—a few even with vivid detail. However, for most, if there is any kind of recall, it is a mere glimmer of something that is not a part of the present life. These haunting flashbacks are commonly referred to as "déjà vu" experiences. When Cayce was asked why people do not generally remember past lives, he replied:

The same may be asked of why there is not the remembering of the time when two and two to the entity became four, or when C A T spelled cat. It always did! Ye only became aware of same as it

became necessary for its practical application in the experience!
                                                    2301-4

In a more technical manner, another reading explained:

Birth in the material plane is death in the spiritual-mental plane. Hence the reason that when those physical manifestations began to be impressed upon the brain centers—those portions of an individual entity that are a constant growth from first conception— there were the impressions to hinder rather than aid the memory of other experiences.   **2390-2**

*   *   *   *   *

In reading 2072-4, a request was made for that "information, guidance and direction" which would most help the entity in her spiritual and mental creative efforts. She was told that "parallels might be drawn, lessons gained and instructions given" from the incarnations or lives of "that power given unto man as the ideal"—the Christ Consciousness or the Master Soul, Jesus. In the belief that the study of such incarnations might also offer help to others in their spiritual and mental quest in life, the chapters ahead will attempt to analyze the material given in the Cayce readings and other sources regarding these lives.

How does someone two thousand years after the death of Jesus investigate the possibility that he may have lived prior lives?

There is probably no way to approach this question with the hope of receiving a definitive answer. But certainly the life and sayings of Jesus himself will be an important and significant area to analyze. Biblical prophecy and comment should be relevant. The legends, myths, and ancient writings of the people around Jesus and of those who figure prominently in Jewish history should be of value. Finally, we can look at the legends and history connected with each of the personages whom Cayce identified as prior lives of Jesus and also examine carefully what Cayce had to say about each of them. From all these sources may come something which will support the claims of Edgar Cayce—or else leave Cayce's ideas extremely questionable or untenable.

We hope that as we pursue this search, it will be done with a sense of openness to the outcome. However, there will be times, especially as we reach the later chapters, where the hypothesis of prior lives will be assumed to have been sufficiently substantiated so we need only explore their significance for these later lives. The reader should continue to weigh the legitimacy of any such inferences and make his or her own independent judgments. Possibly, however, as Cayce promised, material will be found in the process of this review which will be helpful to those who are seeking mental and spiritual development.

Even the skeptic is urged to entertain the question of "what if?"—and read on.

CHAPTER FOUR
Amilius

The disciples said to Jesus: Tell us how our end
will be. Jesus said: Have you then discovered the
beginning so that you inquire about the end? For
where the beginning is, there shall be the end.
Blessed is he who shall stand at the beginning,
and he shall know the end and he shall not taste
death.

(Gospel According to Thomas, Logos 18) [1]

Q-6. Please give the important reincarnations of Adam in the
world's history.
A-6. In the beginning as Amilius . . .   364-7

. . . or at the first begotten of the Father that came as Amilius in
the Atlantean land and allowed himself to be led in the ways of
selfishness.   364-8

According to the Edgar Cayce psychic readings, the soul who
became Jesus Christ was the first soul created or begotten by
God. As such, he is our elder brother and beloved of God. After
his creation, he participated with God in further acts of
creation.

This first-created soul had not rushed into materiality and
become lost there, as had many of the souls created after him.
Instead, this first begotten of God led the second wave of souls

into the earth plane who came for the purpose of aiding those who had become entrapped there in matter. The name of this soul then was Amilius, and its sojourn in the earth was in spirit form only.

When souls first came into the earth and entered matter, the configuration of continents and oceans was quite different from today, and the period of time over which the souls' visitations occurred goes far back into antiquity.

In giving such in an understandable manner to man of today, [it is] necessary that the conditions of the earth's surface and the position of man in the earth's plane be understood, for the change has come often since this period, era, age of man's earthly indwelling, for then at that period, only the lands now known as the Sahara and the Nile region appeared on the now African shores; that in Tibet, Mongolia, Caucasia and Norway in Asia and Europe; that in the southern Cordilleras and Peru in the southwestern hemisphere, and the plane of now Utah, Arizona, Mexico of the northwestern hemisphere, and the spheres were then in the latitudes much as are presented at the present time.

... man's indwelling was then in the Sahara and the upper Nile regions, the waters then entering the now Atlantic from the Nile region rather than flowing northward. The waters in the Tibet and Caucasian entering the North Sea, those in Mongolia entering the South Seas, those in the Cordilleras entering the Pacific, those in the plateau entering the Northern Seas.   **5748-1**

... the numbers then of human souls then in the earth plane being a hundred and thirty and three million [133,000,000] souls.

The period in the world's existence from the present time being ten and one-half million [10,500,000] years...   **5748-2**

Another Cayce reading adds:

... in the land of now the Utah and Nevada forces, when the first peoples were separated into groups as families the entity developed much and gave much to the peoples who were to succeed in this land, and in the ruins as are found that have arisen, in the mounds and caves in the northwestern portion of New Mexico, may be seen some of the drawings the entity then made. Some ten million years ago.   **2665-2**

The people were also different from people today. Souls were gradually assuming the density of matter, and the bodies they inhabited were unlike those of modern men and women.

The idea that there were souls in the earth before the entry of Adam may seem to conflict with the Bible. On the other hand, such a concept would reconcile references in Genesis to the "sons and daughters of men" and similar comments about other apparent earth souls at the time of the first family. The *New Catholic Encyclopedia* says: "Neither Scripture nor the teachings of the Church denies the possibility of preadamites."[2]

Amilius' appearance in the earth occurred around 200,000 years ago, and the arrangement and shape of continents still differed from today. One major difference was the presence of a large continent, known as Atlantis, in what is today called the Atlantic Ocean.

The position as the continent [of] Atlantis occupied, is that as between the Gulf of Mexico on the one hand—and the Mediterranean upon the other. Evidences of this lost civilization are to be found in the Pyrenees and Morocco on the one hand, British Honduras, Yucatan and America upon the other. There are some protruding portions within this that must have at one time or another been a portion of this great continent. The British West Indies or the Bahamas, and a portion of same that may be seen in the present—if the geological survey would be made in some of these—especially, or notably, in Bimini and in the Gulf Stream through this vicinity, these may be even yet determined.   364-3

Other readings indicate that certain mountains of Atlantis can be seen above the ocean waters today as islands, not only in the Bahamas, but also in the Azores and Canary Islands. The original continent of Atlantis is described as quite beautiful and fertile.

Although much legend, myth, and fantasy exists in literature today about Atlantis, it was first spoken of seriously by Plato in his dialogues, "Timaeus" and "Critias." They date from the fifth century B.C., and the information about Atlantis was supposedly given to Plato's uncle, Solon, by certain Egyptian priests at Sais based upon historical records maintained by the priesthood.

Cayce says Atlantis was not the first place visited by souls. Other areas, such as Lemuria or Mu, La, Da, and Ur had existed before or during the period of Atlantis and were the scenes of many of the souls' early visitations.

It was the continent of Atlantis, however, that the souls who had not left God's companionship and who were known as the Sons of God chose to enter in a spiritual quest to lead the entrapped souls back to God. This entry marked the spiritual highpoint of the Atlantean civilization, and the Sons of God had as their leader Amilius, the soul first created by God.

In the period, then—some hundred, some ninety-eight thousand years before the entry of Ram into India—there lived in this land of Atlantis one Amilius, who had first noted that of the separations of the beings as inhabited that portion of the earth's sphere or plane of those peoples into male and female as separate entities, or individuals. As to their forms in the physical sense, these were much rather of the nature of thought forms, or able to push out of themselves in that direction in which its development took shape in thought—much in the way and manner as the amoeba would in the waters of a stagnant bay, or lake, in the present. As these took form, by the gratifying of their own desire for that as builded or added to the material conditions, they became hardened or set—much in the form of the existent human body of the day, with that of color as partook of its surroundings much in the manner as the chameleon in the present. **364-3**

The reading describes the souls' process of entering matter and the manner in which, over a period of time, the spirit encasements hardened and became physical bodies more nearly akin to those we know today. A son of Edgar Cayce has given his understanding of how this process occurred:

> I would interpret the readings . . . to mean that the thought forms, who once could move freely in a non-material world (or a different kind of world than is experienced by our fives senses), had projected themselves into material bodies. Once they had done this they were able to experience material sensations—heat, cold, pleasure, pain, etc. However, the more they sought sensual pleasure, through the gratification of selfish desires, the less able they became to move freely in and out of their material bodies. They became encased in them from birth to death and thus subject to all the laws of the physical universe. Evidently they continued to enjoy their material sojourn, and began to

exploit the physical world and pattern it for their
own pleasure and diversion.[3]

Another reading adds that after souls had entered materiality:

. . . there were then—*from* the other *sources* (worlds) the
continuing entering of those that *would* make for the keeping of the
balance, as of the first purpose of the Creative Forces . . . see? and
hence the second, or the *continued* entering of souls into that
known as the earth's plane during this period, for that activity.

364-7

Amilius is described, not only as the leader of those who
entered earth seeking to keep the balance with God but also as
the teacher of those who had covenanted together to keep
"alive in the minds, the hearts, the *soul* mind of entities, that
there may be seen their closer relationship to the divine
influences of Creative Forces." (364-5)

The souls trapped in materiality were known as the sons and
daughters of Men or Sons of Belial.

The Sons of Belial were of one group, or those that sought more
the gratifying, the satisfying, the use of material things for self,
without thought or consideration as to the sources of such nor the
hardships in the experiences of others. Or, in other words, as we
would term it today, they were those without a standard of morality.

The other group—those who followed the Law of One—had a
standard. The Sons of Belial had no standard, save of self, self-
aggrandizement.   877-26

The Sons of God were in the earth in spirit form and as such
had no sexual division. Each such soul was both male and
female, as was the case with Amilius. He observed, however,
that the sons and daughters of Men, in the process of entering
physical bodies, had divided into male and female entities and
were filled with desires for sensual and sexual gratification.

In the process of projecting themselves into a variety of
material bodies, the sons and daughters of Men had in many
cases taken on characteristics of plant and animal life. Some
bodies had plant projections, such as tree limbs or leaves;
others possessed animal legs or hooves, fish scales, furry skin,
or the like. It is from these strange mixtures that our legends of
satyrs, unicorns, mermaids, and other mythological creatures
have come. They have been recalled by man through soul
memory.

Edgar Cayce, in lecturing to his Sunday school Bible Class, gave an interpretation of what he had said while in a psychic state about the activity of early souls:

> These beings were male and female in one; they were images (in spirit) of that God-spirit which moved and brought Light into being. Consequently, they also had the ability to push out of themselves, or to divide into various manifestations. They began to do this for their own selfish gratification, or for the propagation of their own selfishness, rather than for the glory of their Creator.
>
> Unless we can get a glimpse of such a state existing in the earth, it will be impossible to understand the necessity, later, of God creating a perfect man, through which all souls might return to their original source.

The readings indicate that even Amilius succumbed to the evils and selfishness of a material world. Apparently he was not hopelessly trapped, for he continued to work for the freeing of all souls and their return to God. He and other Sons of God could still remember their source and status with the Creator, but the Children of Belial could not. The readings also say that Amilius established "altars upon which the sacrifices of the field and forest" could be made as a religious tribute to God. (364-4)

Amilius reasoned that the animal bodies in which the souls had become entrapped were not adequate for a soul's habitation. He concluded that a new and more perfect body was needed for the Sons of God to enter into for the purpose of helping their lost brothers, the Sons of Belial, recognize their estrangement from God and instilling in them the desire to return to companionship with their Creator.

The Cayce readings indicate that Amilius and the Sons of God working with God were responsible for the planning and development of a new body, which would be the human being or homo sapiens.

... in the Atlantean land ... when one individual [Amilius] first saw those changes that eventually made for that opening for the

needs of, or the preparation for, the Universal Consciousness to bring into the experience what is known to man as the first created man.   2454-3

Another reading says that Amilius "brought into being all that appertains to man's indwelling as man in the form of flesh in this material world." (364-7)

Support from other sources for Cayce's story on the appearance of the Master soul as Amilius is sparse, but not totally lacking. As we shall see in the next chapter, there is considerable authority linking Adam with the messiah and Jesus specifically, and according to the Gnostic Mandeans there was a Mystic or Secret Adam who preceded the human Adam by many myriads of years.[4] The Hermeticists, of whom we will hear much more in later chapters, held similar beliefs.[5] And ancient Jewish mystics claimed that "God first created the Heavenly Man, the Archetype, who filled the universe and served as the pattern on which it was made."[6]

Apparently it was an exciting and glorious period as Amilius and the other Sons of God prepared the way for the entry of physical man into the earth. The readings say that "the morning stars sang together in the glory of the coming of the Lord" (2597-1) and that "the Sons of God came together, and the sounding of the coming of the Man was given." (234-1) This description is echoed in the Book of Job where, in Chapter 38, God asks Job:

> 4 Where were you when I laid the foundation of the earth?
> 7 when the morning stars sang together, and all the sons of God shouted for joy?

It was the period:

... when the Sons of God came together to announce to Matter a way being opened for the souls of men, the souls of God's creation, to come again to the awareness of their error.   2156-2

It was the time when the Amilius soul, the first begotten of God, became fully embarked upon the mission of bringing the lost souls back into the glory of God's presence. It would be a long and difficult journey and one in which this soul would find itself on center stage playing the star role.

CHAPTER FIVE

Adam

I [Jesus] am the Alpha and the Omega, the
first and the last, the beginning and the end.
(Revelation 22:13)

When there was in the beginning a man's advent into the plane
known as earth, and it became a living soul, amenable to the laws
that govern the plane itself as presented, the Son of Man entered the
earth as the first man. Hence the Son of Man, the Son of God, the
Son of the First Cause, making manifest in a material body.

This was not the first spiritual influence, spiritual body, spiritual
manifestation in the earth, but the first man—flesh and blood; the
first carnal house, the first amenable body to the laws of the plane in
its position in the universe.   5749-3

Then, though He were the first of man, the first of the sons of God
in spirit, in flesh, it became necessary that He fulfill *all* those
associations, those connections that were to wipe away in the
experience of man that which separates him from his Maker.

                                                              5749-6

He, that Christ Consciousness, is that first spoken of in the
beginning when God said, "Let there be light, and there was light."
And that is the light manifested in the Christ. First it became
physically conscious in Adam. And as in Adam we all die, so in the
last Adam—Jesus, becoming the Christ—we are all made alive.

                                                              2879-1

For, know that He—who was lifted up on the Cross in Calvary—

was . . . also he that first walked among men at the beginning of
man's advent into flesh! For He indeed was and is the first Adam,
the last Adam; that is the way, the truth, the light!   2402-2

A new body type had been created by God and Amilius—and
possibly the other unfallen souls working with them—for the
use of souls now entering the earth experience. It would first be
inhabited by the soul of Amilius, and as the first man, he would
be known as Adam. It is the same soul that would eventually
and ultimately be known as Jesus, the Christ.

Genesis 1:26 quotes God as saying, "Let us make man in our
image, after our likeness . . ." The use of the word "our" here
has been a problem for Biblical scholars because, for one thing,
it could be interpreted as implying polytheism. The Cayce
readings supply the answer. "Our" refers to God and God's
first-created son—the Amilius soul—who participated in the
creation of the Adamite body.

There is tradition for the concept that Amilius was involved
in the creation of Adam. The Kabbalist Zohar describes two
Adams: the first was "a divine being who, stepping forth from
the highest original darkness, created the second, or earthly,
Adam in His own image."[1]

The initial account of man's creation in the Bible is contained
in the first chapter of Genesis and is referred to by scholars as
the priestly narration. The second account is in Genesis 2 and is
called the "J" or "Yahwist" strand. In the first account,
humanity was created in the image of God and given dominion
over the rest of creation. In the second story, God, after
creating heaven and earth and other life, fashioned a man, or
Adam, "from the dust of the ground, breathed life into his
nostrils, and placed him in the Garden of Eden to be
caretaker."[2]

Edgar Cayce's psychic readings say that the first account of
humanity's creation refers to the original creating of the soul,
while the second account pertains to the creating of the
physical, earthly body. Thus, it would be the soul referred to in
Genesis 1 which was created specifically in God's image and
given dominion over all other creation, including, at least
originally, that of other planets and spheres. And it would be
creation of the earthly man, Adam, that is described in Genesis
2. In support, it should be noted that only in the second chapter
is the created man actually referred to as Adam.

Some early Jewish philosophers had similar points of view on the meaning of the two creation accounts. Philo, for example, believed that Genesis 1 referred to the heavenly man created in the image of God and that Genesis 2 described the earthly man created out of the dust of the earth. The heavenly man is incorporeal, while the earthly man is composed of both corporeal and incorporeal elements of body and mind.[3] Maimonides agreed with Philo in this interpretation.

The book, *2 (Slavonic Apocalypse of) Enoch,* whose date of composition is unknown but probably goes back into the Old Testament period and recounts ancient Jewish tradition, has some relevant comments about Adam and his creation by God:

> From invisible and visible substances I created man.
> From both his natures come both death and life.
> And (as my) image he knows the word like (no) other
>   creature.
> But even at his greatest he is small,
> and again at his smallest he is great.
>
> And on the earth I assigned him to be a second angel,
> honored and great and glorious. And I assigned him to be a
> king, to reign [on] earth, [and] to have my wisdom. And there
> was nothing comparable to him on the earth, even among my
> creatures that exist . . . And I assigned to him four special
> stars, and called his name Adam. And I gave him his free will;
> and I pointed out the two ways—light and darkness . . . [4]

Jewish tradition portrays Adam as a perfect creature. It exalts his beauty and says, "The ball of Adam's heel outshone the glory of the sun; how much more so the brightness of his face."[5] Both Jewish and Islamic legends say that some of the angels were jealous of Adam, although others wanted to pay him homage and worship him. Eventually God pointed out to the angels the limitations of man, and, with the exception of Satan, they accepted him.[6]

The readings indicate that Amilius had been both male and female. As Adam, however, God chose to give him a companion or helpmeet. The Amilius soul was thus divided into male (Adam) and female (Eve) counterparts.

> . . . **this Amilius—Adam, as given—first discerned that from himself, not of the beasts about him, could be drawn—*was* drawn—**

that [Eve] which made for the propagation *of* beings *in* the flesh, that made for that companionship as seen by creation in the material worlds about same.   **364-5**

... this as a being came as the companion; and when there was that turning to the within, through the sources of creation, as to make for the helpmeet ... *then*—from out of self—was brought that as was to be the helpmeet, *not* just companion of the body.
                                        364-7

Genesis 2:21-22 says that God caused a deep sleep to come upon Adam and took from Adam a rib out of which was made woman or Eve.

The Hebrew word for "rib" also means "side," and taking a side of Adam better seems to fit the concept of dividing his soul in the process of creating Eve. According to Cayce, Adam and Eve thus became twin souls; one the male, the other the female. Because of the positive, dynamic role the Adam soul was destined to play in the spiritual evolution of humanity, it may have been necessary that he be cast in the active male gender. The more passive, receptive female soul, Eve, would also have a special and particular assignment ahead for her in complementing and assisting the efforts of Adam.

God blessed Adam and Eve and gave them dominion over the earth—they were to replenish and subdue it. If Adam and Jesus are the same soul, it is not inconsistent then for Matthew in the New Testament to say that all power in heaven and on earth had been given to Jesus. (Matthew 28:18)

The order of creation according to both the Bible and Cayce corresponds to that disclosed by the fossil record of the earth today. Cayce says the Bible used days to show the passing of successive periods of creation and to express the power of the living God; it is not a statement of days as we comprehend them now. Creation in six days would not have been impossible, but rather it was a process of time and patience reflecting the majesty and omnipotence of the Creator. (262-57) He also adds that the human form was a special creation and did not descend from the monkey. (3744-4)

Cayce adds that souls in human form entered earth in five separate places:

Man, in Adam (as a group; not as an individual), entered into the world (for he entered in five places at once, we see—called Adam in

one, see) . . .   **900-227**

The above quotation, together with information from other readings, seems to say that the Biblical Adam was assisted by other Sons of God in leading the entry of souls into the new earth body. The five places of entry each represented a different race of man (red, yellow, white, black and brown) and were located at Eden, Atlantis, the Andes, western America, and India, although the continents and oceans were somewhat different then from today's configurations. (364-9, 364-13) Significantly, there is an Islamic tradition that says Adam was created from red, white, and black clay and that is the reason for the various skin colorings of humanity. The Talmud also says the homogeneity of the multicolored human race results from dust being gathered throughout the whole earth for the creation of Adam's body.[7]

The location of the Garden of Eden has long been a debated question, but traditional Biblical scholars have generally placed it between the Tigris and Euphrates rivers and probably in the northwestern part of Mesopotamia. One Cayce reading described Eden as the "land of the interbetween" and located it "between the Euphrates, or where the Red Sea, the Dead Sea" are now located. (1179-2) Another adds:

In . . . that known as the beginning, or in the Caucasian and Carpathian, or the Garden of Eden, in that land which lies now much in the desert, yet much in the mountain and much in the rolling lands there.   **364-13**

Some versions of the apocalyptic book *2 Enoch* state that Adam was created at Akhuzan, the center of the earth, and that his final grave will be there. (*2 Enoch* 71:34-36) Jerusalem was often referred to in ancient documents as the center of the earth.

The Adam soul, according to Cayce, remained the leader of the Sons of God and set the pattern for those who had entered in the other four areas. It is interesting to note that in the earlier description of Adam from *2 Enoch,* it was said that God "assigned to him four special stars." These four special stars may refer to the souls who entered the other four race groupings. Possibly there is also hidden meaning in the following verse from Genesis 2, which heretofore had not provided Biblical scholars with a meaningful description of an actual place:

> 10 And a river flowed out of Eden to water the garden; and from thence it divided, and became into four heads. (Lamsa translation)

Adam was the primary interface between God and humanity, and it was from him that the other four heads of races branched out into their areas of influence.

The Bible describes how Satan disguised as the serpent tempted Eve and, through her, Adam, to disobey the commandment of God and eat the fruit of the forbidden tree. The serpent used the argument that by eating of this tree "your eyes will be opened, and you shall be like gods, knowing good and evil." (Genesis 3:5; Lamsa translation) Cayce adds further insight into the nature of their error:

> **Do not gain knowledge only to thine undoing. Remember Adam.**
> **Do not obtain that which ye cannot make constructive in thine own experience and in the experience of those whom ye contact day by day.**   **5753-2**

> **. . . knowledge without the practical ability to apply same may become sin. For, it is knowledge misapplied that was the fall—or the confusion—in Eve.**   **281-63**

It was selfish impatience with God's plan and loss of attunement with God's will that was the essence of the error of Adam and Eve.

After confronting the two and receiving their admission of guilt, God pronounced judgment upon them in Genesis 3:

> 16 To the woman he said, "I will greatly multiply your pain in childbearing; in pain, you shall bring forth children, yet your desire shall be for your husband, and he shall rule over you."
> 17 And to Adam he said, "Because you have listened to the voice of your wife, and have eaten of the tree of which I commanded you 'You shall not eat of it,' cursed is the ground because of you; in toil you shall eat of it all the days of your life;
> 18 thorns and thistles it shall bring forth to you; and you shall eat the plants of the field.
> 19 In the sweat of your face you shall eat bread till

you return to the ground, for out of it you were
taken; you are dust, and to dust you shall return."

Cayce explains this punishment further:

**And with error [sin] entered that as called *death*, which is only a
transition—or through God's other door—into that realm where the
entity has builded, in its manifestations as related to the knowledge
and activity respecting the law of the universal influence.**

5749-3

Included in the punishment of Adam and Eve, of course, was
expulsion from the Garden of Eden. There are some interesting
accounts of this banishment in several early Christian Gnostic
documents, most of which have come to light in recent years.
The general theme in these books is that after Adam and Eve
left Eden, they suffered greatly and were most sorrowful for
their error. As an act of penitence, they stood at length in the
Tigris and Jordan rivers. One passage describes how Christ will
baptize Adam in the Jordan river, and others speak of Jesus'
baptism in the Jordan and the reopening of paradise.[8]

Genesis 3:14 and 15 portrays God's punishment of the
serpent but concludes with the statement that the woman's
seed will bruise the serpent's head. This prophecy is considered
to be the first promise of a redeemer or messiah.

Cayce was asked the specific question, "When did Jesus
become aware that He would be the Savior of the world?" The
reply: "When he fell in Eden." (2067-7)

The first sons of Adam and Eve were Cain and Abel, and in
time Cain killed his brother out of jealousy. Genesis 4:16 relates
that Cain went to the land of Nod and knew his wife. Only by
Cayce's explanation, that before the coming of Adam souls
were already in the earth and entrapped in matter, does the
finding of a wife by Cain make sense.

Shortly thereafter, the Bible says that "the Sons of God"
found the "daughters of men" fair and married them. (Genesis
6:2) These very terms, while not explained in the Biblical
account, were identified by Cayce in his narrative of creation.
The "sons and daughters of men" are the lost souls that the
"Sons of God" came into the earth to help save.

**When the Creative Forces, God, made then the first man—or
God-man—he was the beginning of the Sons of God.**

**Then those souls who entered through a channel made by God—
not by thought, not by desire, not by lust, not by things that
separated continually—were the Sons of God, the Daughters of
God.**

**The daughters of men, then, were those who became the
channels through which lust knew its activity; and it was in this
manner then that the conditions were expressed as given of old,
that the Sons of God looked upon the daughters of men and saw that
they were fair, and *lusted!*** 262-119

God then declared that the spirit would not always be with
humanity "for that he is also flesh." (Genesis 6:3) Cayce adds
further detail about this deterioration of conditions:

**. . . we find these as the Sons of Creative Force as manifest in their
experience looking upon those changed forms, or the daughters of
men, and there crept in those pollutions, of polluting themselves
with those mixtures that brought contempt, hatred, bloodshed, and
those that build for desires of self *without* respects of *others'*
freedom, others' wishes—and there began, then, in the latter
portion of this period of development, that [which] brought about
. . . dissenting and divisions among the peoples in the lands.**

364-4

During this period, according to Cayce, there was a variety of
human body forms resulting from the intermarriage of the
"Sons of God" with the "daughters of men." There were giants
as tall as ten or twelve feet, although the ideal stature and form
was that exemplified in Adam and Eve. (364-11) The existence
of giants is noted in the Bible; Genesis 6:4 states:

The Nephilim [giants] were on the earth in
those days; and also afterward, when the sons of
God came in to the daughters of men, and they
bore children to them. These were the mighty men
that were of old, the men of renown.

The Bible records that another son was born to Adam and
Eve—a son in Adam's likeness and "after his image." His name
was Seth, and he would carry on the spiritual lineage of Adam.

Much apocalyptic Jewish and early Christian literature
exists concerning Seth. Nearly all of it agrees that Adam before
his death imparted great spiritual knowledge to Seth. For
example, the *Apocalypse of Adam* relates that at the end of his
life, Adam gave a testamentary revelation to Seth. He tells Seth

of his and Eve's experiences in the Garden of Eden and of special revelations given to him by three angelic informants on the future of the elect race. These disclosures prophesy the future destruction of the earth by flood and fire and the coming of a savior. Seth in turn "taught his seed" about the revelations received from Adam, his father. And the *Apocalypse of Adam* adds that special revelations were also written "on a high mountain, upon a rock of truth."[9]

Similar information is given in *Life of Adam and Eve,* where Eve also tells her children to write the revelations from herself and Adam on tablets of stone and clay. The stone tablets are to survive a judgment of flood, and the clay tablets a judgment of fire.[10] This story is very close to that given by the Jewish historian, Josephus, who states that, at the time of his writing, the stone stele or tablets still survive "in the land of Seiris."[11] It is thought that "Seiris" represents the land of Egypt.[12]

In the *Gospel of the Egyptians,* Seth is pictured as the author of a book on "salvation history," which he placed on high mountains or "in the mountain that is called Charaxio" so it could be used as a revelation in the end-time by the elect. One scholar has suggested that "Charaxio" might be interpreted to mean "mountain of the worthy."[13]

Thus, the spiritual lessons and directions for the future of humanity, as experienced and received from God and His angels by Adam and Eve, were passed on to Seth. According to legend and tradition, Seth put many of these secrets in permanent form in a special place.

Two documents from the Nag Hammadi, Egypt, archaeological find are *Eugnostos the Blessed* and *The Sophia of Jesus Christ.* In both of these Gnostic works, references to Adam appear to identify him as the "Son of Man." Use of this title for Adam by these early Christians must surely evidence their recognition that Adam was the same soul as their Christ, who freely adopted this title as his own.[14]

The First Book of Adam and Eve is a collection of Jewish legends about the first family. It is of unknown antiquity, but dates back as a written document at least to early Christianity, and parts of the work are found in the Talmud, the Koran, and elsewhere. Chapter XLII contains the following statement from God after Adam had requested the Water of Life which he had known in Eden:

> 7 And, again, as regards the Water of Life thou
> seekest, it will not be granted thee this; but on the
> day that I shall shed My blood upon thy head in the
> land of Golgotha.
> 8 For My blood shall be the Water of Life unto
> thee, at that time, and not to thee alone, but unto
> all those of thy seed who shall believe in Me; that it
> be unto them for rest for ever.
> 9 The Lord said again unto Adam, "O Adam, when
> thou wast in the garden, these trials did not come
> to thee
> 10 "But since thou didst transgress My command-
> ment, all these sufferings have come upon thee."[15]

We thus find in a legend important to the literature of several
religions a prophetic promise attributed to God that the Water
of Life Adam had known in Eden would only be attained after
God's blood is shed upon Adam's head at Golgotha. This
prophecy is an obvious reference to the crucifixion of Jesus at
Golgotha, and since it is to be shed upon Adam's head, it would
seem to imply that it would be Adam's crucifixion. It is probable
that this apparent reference to Jesus was either written or
added to the work by zealous Christians. To say from this
document that Jewish tradition attributed a messianic role to
Adam may thus be questionable, but at least early Christian
tradition found such a link between Adam and Jesus.

There is Jewish tradition, however, that does link Adam with
the promised messiah. In the "Notarikon" of the Kabbalah,
Adam, David and the Messiah are all said to be the same soul.[16]

The *Testament of Adam* deserves comment. Originally of
Jewish composition, it was based upon legend and tradition
concerning creation. It was redacted or added to by early
Christians, and in its present form dates from the second to
fifth century A.D.[17] In the section pertaining to prophecy,
Adam tells Seth about the future coming of God who will be
born of a virgin and do numerous other things associated
uniquely with the life of Jesus. Adam continues telling Seth of
his conversations with God:

> He spoke to me about this in Paradise after I

picked some of the fruit in which death was hiding:
"Adam, Adam, do not fear. You wanted to be a god;
I will make you a god, not right now, but after a
space of many years. I am consigning you to death,
and the maggot and worm will eat your body." And
I answered and said to him, "Why, my Lord?" And
he said to me, "Because you listened to the words
of the serpent, you and your posterity will be food
for the serpent. But after a short time there will be
mercy on you because you were created in my
image, and I will not leave you to waste away in
Sheol. For your sake I will be born of the Virgin
Mary. For your sake I will taste death and enter the
house of the dead. For your sake I will make a new
heaven, and I will be established over your
posterity.

"And after three days, while I am in the tomb, I
will raise up the body I received from you. And I
will set you at the right hand of my divinity, and I
will make you a god just like you wanted. And I will
receive favor from God, and I will restore to you
and to your posterity that which is the justice of
heaven."   (Sec. 3:3-4)[18]

God seems to be telling Adam that, after three days, Adam's
body will be raised up by God and that Adam will at that point
reach godhood. Adam, in the last sentence, appears to be
telling Seth that he, Adam, will receive favor from God and
restore to humanity its rightful heritage. The early Christian
editors would thus be identifying Adam with the messianic role
of Jesus and saying, just as Edgar Cayce did, that the Master
soul became aware of this role at the point of his fall in Eden as
Adam.

In one of the earliest documents of the *Pistis Sophia*, a
collection of gnostic writings, a great angel by the name of Jeu
is frequently mentioned. He is referred to as "overseer of light"
and the "arranger of the Cosmos" and is identified as the "First
Man."[19] An identification of Jesus (Jeu) as Adam (and possibly
Amilius) appears to be involved here, and thus another early
Christian writing is equating Adam with Jesus.

The Elkasites are a typical example of early Christians who

believed that Jesus had been Adam. They believed Jesus had previously inhabited many bodies, appearing at intervals to recall humanity to its spiritual source.[20] Early Christian writer Epiphanius said of the Elkasites:

> Some of them, too, say that Christ is Adam, the first-created . . . Others say that he was created before all things, superior to the angels, ruling over all and called Christ. He put on the body of Adam, appeared as a human being, was crucified, arose and went up to heaven.[21]

Even the famous psychologist, Carl Jung, wrote of early Christianity's identificiation of Adam with the Son of God or Christ.[22]

Not only apocryphal and secondary documents but the Bible itself seems to hint that Jesus was Adam. The fifteenth chapter of I Corinthians contains these cryptic statements:

> 22 For as in Adam all die, so also in Christ shall all be made alive.
> 45 Thus it is written, "The first man Adam became a living being"; the last Adam became a life-giving spirit.

The implication of these two verses can reasonably be interpreted to mean that the last appearance of Adam was as Jesus Christ. Romans 5:14 may be even stronger in this suggestion by its messianic reference to Adam:

> Yet death reigned from Adam to Moses, even over those whose sins were not like the transgressions of Adam, who was a type of the one who was to come.

The Christ of the author (probably Paul) is not God; he is God's first creation, Adam,[23] the Archetypal Man.[24]

After a detailed tracing of the geneology of Mary, through David, Luke concludes with this wording:

> . . . the son of Enos, the son of Seth, the son of *Adam, the son of God.* (Luke 3:38) [Author's italics]

The quick explanation of this description of Adam as "the son

of God" is that it is a mere reference to the fact that God created
him. But the question then follows: How many Biblical "son of
God" titles are there? The New Testament is clear in identifying
Jesus as the only-begotten son of God and in reserving the "son
of God" title for him. Is it not possible that the author is here
recognizing the oneness of Jesus and Adam?

In a similar vein, quoted language of Jesus in the last chapter
of the New Testament is worth attention:

> "I Jesus have sent my angel to you with this
> testimony for the churches, I am the root and
> offspring of David, the bright morning star."
>
> Revelation 22:16

The fact that Jesus is the offspring of David is a major theme of
the New Testament and a fulfillment of Old Testament
prophecy. But how is he the *root* of David? An answer is
supplied by a recognition that Jesus had been Adam, the fore-
bear and originator of the Davidic line.

A story from the early Christian era provides another
symbolic tie between Adam and Jesus:

> According to one Christian tradition, Adam is
> buried not in the Machpelah cave at Hebron but
> under the Calvary in the Holy Sepulchre,
> Jerusalem, so that the redemptive blood of Jesus
> shed at the crucifixion, flowed on his grave.[25]

Similarly a Syriac document, *The Cave of Treasures*, tells of a
cave in which Adam lived and was buried. Noah later came to
this cave, took the bones of Adam, and carried them aboard the
ark. After the flood, he reburied Adam's remains at Golgotha.
This theme is also contained in the Arabic book, *Apocrypha
Arabica.*

The book *Life of Adam and Eve* enjoyed wide circulation
among early Christians and dates from between 100 B.C. to
A.D. 200.[26] It hints at a messianic role for Adam:

> And all the angels sounded the trumpets and
> said, "Blessed are you, LORD, who has pitied your
> creature." Then Seth saw the extended hand of
> the LORD holding Adam, and he handed him over
> to Michael, saying, "Let him be in your custody

until the day of dispensing punishment at the last
years, when I will turn his sorrow into joy. Then he
shall sit on the throne of him who overthrew him."

(Par. 47)

Another interesting twist is provided in *Testament of Adam*
3:6:

> And I, Seth, wrote this testament. And my father
> died, and they buried him at the east of Paradise
> opposite the first city built on the earth, which was
> named (after) Enoch. And Adam was borne to his
> grave by the angels and powers of heaven because
> he had been created in the image of God. And the
> sun and moon were darkened, and there was thick
> darkness for seven days. And we sealed the
> testament and we put it in the cave of treasures
> with the offerings Adam had taken out of Paradise,
> gold and myrrh and frankincense. And the sons of
> kings, the magi, will come and get them, and they
> will take them to the son of God, to Bethlehem of
> Judea, to the cave.

The above appears to be saying that Adam was buried near or
"opposite" Jerusalem (which historically had been known as
the first city). Also, Adam's testament or last message was
sealed in a cave of treasures, which will be opened by the Wise
Men who will bring their offerings and the testament to Jesus.
What a beautiful and time-spanning tie is presented here
between Adam and Jesus!

The story of Adam is profound and full of symbolic meaning
for all of us. It assumes even more of these qualities when
viewed in the light of the psychic readings from Edgar Cayce
and the rich legacy of legend and tradition about Adam which
dates from antiquity. This legacy supports the Cayce
revelations, not only as to details in the life of Adam but also in
his future messianic role and identification with Jesus. The
scope and majesty of the Adam story then, as derived from
these sources and the Bible, is probably nowhere better
summed up than in part of a single reading from Edgar Cayce:

**Adam's entry into the world in the beginning, then, must become
the savior *of* the world, as it was committed to his care, "Be thou**

fruitful, multiply, and *subdue* the earth!" Hence Amilius, Adam, the first Adam, the last Adam, becomes—then—that that is *given* the *power over* the earth, and—as in each soul the first to be conquered is self—then *all things*, conditions and elements, are subject unto that self! . . . Hence, as Adam given—the *Son* of God— so he *must* become that that would be able to take the world, the earth, back to that source from which it came, and *all power* is given in his keeping in the earth, that he has overcome; self, death, hell and the grave even, become subservient unto Him *through* the conquering of self in that made flesh; for, as in the beginning was the Word, the Word *was* with God, the Word *was* God, the same was *in* the beginning. The Word came and dwelt among men . . .**364-7**

Adam came into the world to lead the lost souls back to God. At the end of his life, he had not succeeded in subduing and conquering matter as God had directed. In fact, he had lost his battle with the world and materiality. He had defied God's commandment not to eat of the tree of knowledge and had succumbed to the temptation to be as a god, knowing good and evil. And yet, even as he failed, God offered him the promise that a man would some day bruise the serpent's head and that Adam would yet lead his erring brothers back to the paradise of the Father.

Adam was to suffer physical death for his disobedience, but a loving and merciful God would allow him to try again and again until he had met and conquered his failures and shown every soul the way back to the Creator. He would have to do it the hard and difficult way—by meeting and overcoming every sin and obstacle his brothers had encountered. A long earthly journey lay ahead. The Adam soul would have to blaze an uncharted trail, but the first step had now been taken on the road that would lead to Calvary.

CHAPTER SIX

Enoch

By faith Enoch was taken up so that he should not see death; and he was not found, because God had taken him. Now before he was taken he was attested as having pleased God.
(Hebrews 11:5)

And, lo, a voice from heaven, saying, "This is my beloved Son [Jesus], with whom I am well pleased." *(Matthew 3:17)*

Remember those forms which have been given. First, He was created—brought into being from all that there was in the earth, as [Adam] an encasement for the soul of an entity, a part of the Creator; knowing separation in death. Then He was made manifest in birth through the union of channels growing out of that thought of the Creator made manifest, but so expressed, so manifested as "Enoch" as to merit the escaping of [physical] death—which had been the result...of disobedience.

Again it [the soul who became Jesus] was manifested in Enoch, who oft sought to walk and talk with that divine influence; with the abilities latent and manifested in self to find self in the varied realms of awareness, yet using the office of relationships as a channel through which blessings might come, as well as recommendations and warnings might be indicated to others.   2072-4

Enoch occupies a special position in both the Old and New Testaments but is dealt with sparsely in each.

The Old Testament's entire coverage of Enoch is contained

61

in the following verses from the fifth chapter of Genesis:

> 18 When Jared had lived a hundred and sixty and
> two years, he became the father of Enoch.
> 22 Enoch walked with God after the birth of
> Methuselah three hundred years, and had other
> sons and daughters.
> 23 Thus all the days of Enoch were three hundred
> and sixty-five years.
> 24 Enoch walked with God; and he was not, for
> God took him.

The lifespan of Enoch is short in comparison with that of his contemporaries, but the very number of years he lived may be suggestive of the cosmic role attributed to him by Cayce and legend—for the years of his life correspond with the number of days in the solar year.

The phrase "God took him" is generally interpreted to mean that he was taken to heaven by God without suffering physical death, and the reference to Enoch in the New Testament book of Hebrews, quoted at the front of this chapter, supports this interpretation.

The book of Jude in verses 14-15 completes the brief Biblical references to Enoch:

> It was of these also that Enoch in the seventh
> generation from Adam prophesied, saying,
> "Behold, the Lord came with his holy myriads, to
> execute judgment on all, and to convict all the
> ungodly of all their deeds of ungodliness which
> they have committed in such an ungodly way, and
> of all the harsh things which ungodly sinners have
> spoken against him."

Biblical scholars have concluded that this reference to Enoch is drawn from one of the apocalyptic Enochian books which have resurfaced in recent years. They are known to have been in existence in some form during the early Christian era and accorded a position of repute by New Testament writers. The validity of the books of Enoch, of which we now have three distinct and differing versions, is not universally conceded, but it is recognized that they had considerable effect on the content of the New Testament. Prophecy in the Enoch books is thought by the Scofield Bible scholars to be the earliest recorded revelation of the Second Coming of Christ.

Enochian authority Dr. R.H. Charles noted some years ago that "the influence of Enoch on the New Testament has been greater than that of all the other apocryphal and pseudepigraphal books taken together."[1] The *Ethiopian Book of Enoch* is considered to have been Paul's constant reference book; John was quite affected by Enoch, especially in Revelation; and Peter's letters in the New Testament reflect the considerable influence of Enoch.[2] Luke 9:35 was mistranslated by the King James translators; it should read: "This is my Son, the Elect One." The term "Elect One" is used frequently in the Enochian books for Enoch and was apparently borrowed by Luke to identify Jesus.[3] Similarly, the title "Son of Man," often used by Jesus in referring to himself, finds great elaboration in the *Ethiopian Book of Enoch* as Enoch himself was called "Son of Man" by God. And prominent scholars believe it was the Book of Enoch which provided this key term for Jesus.[4]

The apocryphal Epistle of Barnabas quotes the Book of Enoch three times and twice calls it "the Scripture"—a term specifically reserved for denoting the inspired word of God.[5]

A similarity between the story of Enoch and the Mesopotamian legend of Enmeduranna, the seventh king before the flood, has been noted. This king was devoted to the sun-god, to whom his capital city was dedicated, and thus is associated with the worship of a single god. Jewish apocryphal literature has, through similar motifs, connected Enoch, the seventh from Adam, with Enmeduranna.[6] Enoch then may well be a historical figure of archetypal significance common to more than one race or nationality.

Far more is given about the man Enoch in the Enochian books than in the Bible, and any study of Enoch is probably best begun by a review of these books. In discussing the three books of Enoch, the translations, comments, and numbering system of Charlesworth's *The Old Testament Pseudepigrapha*[7] will be used.

The *First Book of Enoch*, sometimes referred to as the *Ethiopian Book of Enoch*, but which we shall call *1 Enoch*, was an important document for both the Jewish Essenes and early Christians. It was used by the authors of Jubilees and other non-Biblical works and, as noted earlier, is quoted explicitly in Jude. It has concepts which are found in various New Testament books, including the gospels and Revelation. A number of other early Christian works were inspired by *1 Enoch*, and several Church Fathers held the book in high esteem. Tertullian, for example, considered this book to be part of the Christian canon.[8] Beginning in the fourth century, however, *1 Enoch* began to lose favor and eventually was relegated to virtual oblivion.

For some reason, *1 Enoch* remained popular in Ethiopia and survived there. It is therefore sometimes referred to as the *Ethiopian Book of Enoch*. It was brought to Europe in 1773 but was not translated until the 1800s, and only in recent years has it generated much attention.

The book *1 Enoch* begins with the story of the fallen sons of God referred to in Genesis 6:1-4 and gives much detail of the plight and corruption of these fallen angels. Its depiction of early man and his spiritual status is very similar to that given by Edgar Cayce. Much discussion then ensues about the messiah, the "Righteous One" or "Son of Man," and he is pictured as "a pre-existent heavenly being who is resplendent and majestic, possesses all dominion" and sits in judgment on all mortal and spiritual beings.[9] The book concludes with the last judgment, the coming destruction of the wicked, and the triumph of the righteous. It is here that the first prophecies of a Second Coming of the Christ or messiah are found.

In *1 Enoch 71* we read:

> Then an angel came to me [Enoch] and greeted me and said to me, "You, son of man, who are born in righteousness and upon whom righteousness has dwelt, the righteousness of the Antecedent of Time will not forsake you." He added and said to me, "He shall proclaim peace to you in the name of the world that is to become. For from here proceeds peace since the creation of the world, and so it shall be unto you forever and ever and ever. Everyone that will come to exist and walk shall (follow) your path, since righteousness never forsakes you. Together with you shall be their dwelling places; and together with you shall be

their portion. They shall not be separated from you
forever and ever and ever."

Enoch is not only called the "Son of Man" but is described as
the one walking a path for others to follow and the one whom
righteousness never forsakes. Peace shall be unto him forever.
Surely, the Prince of Peace, the messianic Christ, is being
depicted.

The significance of the above quotation from *1 Enoch* has
been acknowledged by others:

As is well known, *1 Enoch 71* identifies the son
of man with Enoch himself. This may have some
relevance for the text in Wisdom of Solomon,
because the author of that work denotes Enoch as
the righteous man par excellence. It requires no
stretch of the exegetical imagination to identify
the exalted righteous one in Wisdom of Solomon 5
with Enoch.[10]

And another author adds:

Thus the antediluvian patriarch, Enoch, is given
a revelation which portrays the future redemptive
role of the Son of Man, and which ultimately
equates Enoch himself with that figure![11]

Before Enoch is identified as the Son of Man, he is told by
God of the messianic role of the Son of Man and of mysteries
that will be entrusted only to the Son (and they are eventually
given to Enoch). In him will be hidden all the treasures of
wisdom and knowledge. Then it is said:

For the Son of Man was concealed from the
beginning, and the Most High One preserved him
in the presence of his power; then he revealed him
to the holy and the elect ones.   (1 Enoch 62:7)

Enoch is addressed by both God and the angels or Watchers as
"scribe" or "scribe of righteousness." According to the Cayce
readings, the Jesus soul through numerous incarnations was
responsible for writing much of the Old Testament. The title
"scribe" then would be a most fitting appellation to describe
this same soul.

From *1 Enoch* comes the concept of a pre-existent messiah,

which has been used by Christianity to prove the divinity of Jesus.[12] It is ironical that the concept of a pre-existent messiah is an important part of the Cayce chronicle, which is viewed by many as conflicting with generally accepted Christian theology. The difference, of course, is that Cayce attributes regained godhood to Jesus, whereas conventional Christianity says he was God throughout. This issue was one that divided early Christianity and was the subject of numerous councils and conclaves in the young Church. Eventually the theology that Jesus was and always had been a part of the Godhead became dogma, and the early strongly held opinion by many that Jesus was just man who became God was relegated to heresy.

The next book of Enoch is sometimes called the *Slavonic Apocalypse of Enoch,* but we will refer to it as *2 Enoch.* It is known only from a number of manuscripts in old Slavonic which were brought to the attention of Western Christianity in recent times, having been "lost" for approximately 1200 years. The book probably reached the Slavonic countries many years ago from now extinct Greek texts which were based upon Semitic legends and traditions. There is debate, however, around whether *2 Enoch* originated in Jewish or Christian circles. It could date anywhere from pre-Christian times to the late Middle Ages but probably goes back to the period just preceding Christianity.[13]

In *2 Enoch* is an amplification of Genesis 5:21-32, covering the life of Enoch and extending down to the coming of the flood. The first part of the book deals with Enoch being taken up to the heavens, his experiences there before God, and his return to earth to tell his family what he had learned. The second part covers the lives of his immediate successors. The book generally concentrates upon concepts of creation and represents one of the earliest attempts to reconcile science and Scripture on this subject. Again, there are passages with strong overtones and language reminiscent of the Cayce creation story. Adam, for example, is pictured as an original heavenly creature.

Enoch, while in the heavens, is shown the secrets of the universe by God and told that the information has not even been shared with the angels. Enoch is directed to write of his experiences for coming generations of humanity and to chronicle the history of his forebears back to Adam. We again have Enoch identified with the role of scribe.

After his return to earth and just before his final translation to heaven by God, his earthly family and friends entreat Enoch:

> O Our Father, Enoch! May you be blessed by the Lord, the eternal king! And now, bless your sons, and all the people so that we may be glorified in front of your face today. For you will be glorified in front of the face of the LORD for eternity, because you are the one whom the LORD chose in preference to all the people upon the earth; and he appointed you to be the one who makes a written record of all his creation, visible and invisible, and the one who carried away the sin of mankind and the helper of your own household.   (Enoch 64)

This passage clearly identifies Enoch as a scribe and the messiah or redeemer of humanity.

The language of *2 Enoch* in describing both Enoch and Adam is very similar. As quoted from *2 Enoch* in the Adam chapter, Adam is assigned by God to be a king, to reign on earth, and to have God's wisdom. There is no creature comparable to him. Almost identical language is used for Enoch, and in view of the exclusivity of the wording, the conclusion that the author is saying they are one and the same may reasonably be inferred.

Finally we come to *3 Enoch,* or the *Hebrew Apocalypse of Enoch,* dating from the fifth or sixth century A.D. The text, written originally in Hebrew, is attributed to Rabbi Ishmael, a famous Palestinian scholar who died in A.D. 132. The book was written later than Ishmael but may have been based upon traditions associated with him. It purports to be an account of how Enoch went to heaven, "saw God's throne and chariot, received revelations from the archangel Metatron, and viewed the wonders of the upper world."[14]

We find that *3 Enoch* is strongly corroborative of Edgar Cayce's philosophy on the pre-existence of the human soul before birth and its survival of death. According to *3 Enoch,* the soul survives the body and goes to the heavenly regions—or at least those who have lived a righteous life go there. The soul is portrayed as existing before the body and coming down from the heavenly storehouse to enter bodies at the time of birth. (3 Enoch 43:3)

The angelic hierarchy is discussed at length in *3 Enoch*, and Metatron emerges as the most significant angel. He is called "The Lesser YHWH" and is described as God's vice-regent who, from his throne, presides over the celestial court. Metatron is merged with two other heavenly figures: the archangel Yaho'el and the translated Enoch. In *3 Enoch*, then, Enoch is clearly identified with the archangel titles of Metatron and Yaho'el.

Islamic tradition accords a favorable position to Enoch, identifying him with the righteous Edris or Idris of the Koran.[18] And C.G. Jung concluded that Christ had been Enoch.[19]

The text "Zohar" of the Spanish Jewish Kabbalah also mentions Enoch: "From beneath her feet went forth a youth [Metatron] who stretched from one end of the world to the other . . . and who is called 'Enoch, the son of Jared.' " And according to Jewish folklore, Enoch, during his life on earth, was guardian of the "secret of intercalation" and of the "miraculous rod" which Moses later used to perform miracles.[20]

The *Second Book of Adam and Eve* discusses Enoch and talks about the end of his life:

> When Enoch had ended his commandments to them [the people], God transported him from that mountain to the land of life, to the mansions of the righteous and the chosen, the abode of Paradise of joy, in light that reaches up to heaven; light that is outside the light of this world; for it is the light of God, that fills the whole world, but which no place can contain. Thus, because Enoch was in the light of God, he found himself out of the reach of death; until God would have him die.   (XXII:8-9)[21]

Note that the author of this ancient document does not stop with God's exempting Enoch from death but adds "until God would have him die." Obviously, it was the expectation that Enoch might yet again have to face an earthly death.

There is much tradition then that Enoch was special and exalted by God over all His other earthly and heavenly creations. He was given God's hidden treasures of wisdom and knowledge which were shared with none other, not even the angels. He was so favored by God that he was spared physical death. He was told of a coming redeemer or messiah and identified with him. God's language concerning Enoch is similar to that used for Adam. And these traditions about Enoch were shared by numerous countries and religions.

In short, there is support for the readings of Edgar Cayce which give a special status to Enoch and link him with the soul that became Jesus the Christ.

But there is still more to be said in the next chapter in connection with this man Enoch.

CHAPTER SEVEN
Hermes

The Soul passeth from form to form; and the mansions of her pilgrimage are manifold. Thou puttest off thy bodies as raiment; and as vesture dost thou fold them up. Thou art from old, O Soul of Man; yea, thou art from everlasting.

(Books of Hermes)[1]

The Edgar Cayce readings clearly say that the Master, or the Jesus soul, was in Egypt 10,500 years B.C. at the time of a priest named Ra or Ra Ta. Much detail is given on the activities of Ra, who helped establish and maintain a religious structure based on belief in the One God, but the Master was never specifically identified by name. Notwithstanding this lack of detail, those close to the readings and others who have researched them believe the various references to the Master at this time point unquestionably to his being the legendary figure Hermes. (See reading 281-10.)

The readings definitely place Hermes together with Ra at this period in ancient history. In a reading on the subject of the building and purpose of the Great Pyramid of Gizeh in Egypt, Cayce said:

Then, with Hermes and Ra ... there began the building of that now called Gizeh, with which those prophecies that had been in the Temple of Records and the Temple Beautiful were builded, in the building of this that was to be the hall of the initiates of that sometimes referred to as the White Brotherhood. **5748-5**

Another reading identifies Hermes as the "guide, or the actual (as would be termed in the present) constructing or construction architect" of the Great Pyramid. (294-151) Numerous readings indicate that its purpose was to serve as a Hall of Records or of prophecy and as a place of spiritual initiation.

What is known historically about this man Hermes?

His native Egyptians knew him as Thoth, or Thoth-Hermes, and in time he became deified as Thoth, the Egyptian god of wisdom. As such, he was considered "the scribe of the gods," the "lord of divine words," and "the heart and the tongue of Ra."[2] In Egyptian drawings, "Thoth carries a waxen writing tablet and serves as the recorder during the weighing of the souls of the dead."[3]

> [He] is the personification of Wisdom, he is the
> very intellect of the Great God who formed the
> world. He is not a messenger but a teacher. It is
> true that he is a bearer of divine secrets, but he
> participates fully therein and is in his own right
> both an Initiator and the First Initiate, revealing
> knowledge from his own inexhaustible supply. As
> Lord of the Writing Tablet, as bearer of the Stylus,
> he is frequently depicted as Ibis-headed recording
> the judgments of the dead before the throne of
> Osiris.[4]

The Greeks later called him Hermes Trismegistus, meaning "thrice great." This title meant that he was the greatest of all philosophers, the greatest of all priests, and the greatest of all kings. He is credited by them as being the first and great initiator of Egypt, and various writings on astrology, magic, and alchemy are attributed to him. The well-known Greek god by the name of Hermes may or may not have been the same figure as the Egyptian Hermes Trismegistus. If they are one and the same, and many chroniclers think they are, it is interesting to note that the Greek Hermes was the son of their highest god, Zeus. It is our conclusion here, of course, that Hermes Trismegistus, as an incarnation of the Jesus soul, was the son of the one and only God.

In Arabic traditions, Hermes is presented as the disciple of Agathodaemon, a name usually associated with a supernatural being.[5]

In the infant years of Christianity, some Egyptian gnostic religious sects wrote numerous treatises on cosmology, ethics, and prophecy which they ascribed to the ancient teachings of Hermes. Today these works are known as Hermetic writings or Hermetica.

Early Christian leaders are known to have been interested in Hermes Trismegistus and the Hermetic writings. St. Augustine, for example, believed in the extreme antiquity of Hermes. Lactantius, in the fourth century, taught that the Hermetic writings were based upon the work of an Egyptian seer whose references to a "son of God" were prophetic of Christ. He compared wording in the Hermetica with certain passages in the Gospel of John,[6] and others have noted their striking similarity.[7] Clement of Alexandria cited 42 books written by Hermes. Nearly all of these books were lost, however, in the subsequent burning of Alexandria and its famous libraries.

In one of the few Hermetic texts we still have today, Hermes is called the "shepherd of men" and the redeemer or revealer.[8] A theme found in the Hermetic writings is that of a heavenly Man who descends to earth from time to time to reveal knowledge of the Father, after which he ascends or returns to God the Father.[9]

In a Naassene document cited by Hippolytus of Rome around A.D. 200, Hermes is called the Logos and identified with both Adam and Christ.[10] And according to Carl G. Jung, ancient tradition says that Adam identifies with Thoth, the Egyptian Hermes.[11] He also cites the teaching of the gnostic Naassenes to the effect that Hermes is "the Logos, the interpreter and fashioner of what has been, is, and will be."[12] The term "Logos" is also interpreted by Christians, of course, to mean the Christ.

Text 7 of the "Incantation Texts" from the Dead Sea Scrolls refers to Hermes as "the Great Lord." And the "Habakkuk Commentary" of the Scrolls describes the Essene Teacher of Righteousness as one "to whom God has made known all the mysteries of the words of His servants, the prophets."[13] Such a description fits perfectly with what we know about Hermes and Enoch. As we shall see later, the Essenes expected this Teacher/Soul to return as the messiah and connected him with others whom Cayce said were incarnations of the Master.

Through sources other than Cayce then—in fact by the

Essenes and early Christians—Hermes is identified with the messianic role of redeemer, revealer, Lord, or Christ. They support the thesis that Hermes returned as the messiah or Jesus.

Hermes is also connected by the Egyptians with the building of the Great Pyramid of Gizeh.[14] The Cayce readings date the building of this monument from the period of 10,490 to 10,390 B.C. This dating, however, is approximately 8,000 years earlier than that of conventional archaeology. In referring to the Great Pyramid, Cayce said:

> This, then, receives all the records from the beginnings of that given by the priest, Arart, Araaraart and Ra, to that period when there is to be the change in the earth's position and the return of the Great Initiate to that and other lands for the folding up of those prophecies that are depicted there. All changes that came in the religious thought in the world are shown there, in the variations in which the passage through same is reached, from the base to the top—or to the open tomb *and* the top. These are signified by both the layer and the color in what direction the turn is made.
>
> 5748-5

It is interesting to note Cayce's use of the term "Great Initiate" in connection with the Initiate's return in an apparent messianic role. Hermes was often referred to in ancient documents as the Great Initiate or Initiator.

Finally, a study of the Cayce readings on Hermes and Enoch leads to the very likely conclusion that they are one and the same individual. As indicated earlier, the readings never directly referred to Hermes as an incarnation of the Master soul, Jesus, but placed an appearance of that soul at the same time as Hermes and made other references which seem to point indisputably to Jesus having been Hermes. The reason Cayce did not use the name "Hermes" in linking him specifically with the Jesus soul may be out of a preference for the Biblical name, Enoch.

A conclusive case for connecting Enoch with Hermes probably cannot be made from the readings, but there are other traditions linking the two together. Similarities between *2 Enoch* and the Hermetic literature have been noted, and Duran, in *Heshev Ha-Efod,* specifically identifies Hermes with Enoch.[15]

Arabic Hermeticists believed Hermes was Enoch, and in

excavations in Babylonia, incantation bowls have been found identifying Hermes with the angel Metatron.[16] As we found in the chapter on Enoch, the Enochian books and other material say that Metatron was the name for the translated Enoch.

Although Carl Jung did not quite say that Hermes and Enoch were the same, he says that "Enoch was also considered a pre-figuration of Christ."[17] As noted earlier, he had found evidence that Hermes had been called the Logos, a term for the Christ. He also concluded that Hermes corresponds to Adam.[18]

Many investigators have reached the conclusion that Hermes is the same person the Jews refer to as Enoch, who "walked with God" and was translated to heaven.[19] Similar to Enoch, Hermes has been called the "Second Messenger of God," and Manly Hall opines that "Hermes of all creatures was nearest to God."[20] Hermes is also credited with being the author of the Masonic initiatory rituals.[21] Hermes is given credit for reforming the calendar and increasing the days of the year from 360 to 365. The traditional age of Enoch as given in the Bible as 365 years may thus serve as a further key in identifying him with Hermes.

In an earlier quotation pertaining to Thoth [Hermes], his frequent depiction as an Ibis-headed figure "recording the judgments of the dead before the throne of Osiris [God]" was noted. We learned from the Enochian documents that this was the duty also of Enoch before the throne of God.

One of the still-extant books attributed to Hermes is *Poimandres*, and it has at times been called *The Genesis of Enoch.*[22] The book describes how Hermes, "while wandering in a rocky and desolate place, gave himself over to meditation and prayer." Divine revelations then came to him, and, just like Enoch, he was given information on the mysteries of the heavens and the workings of the universe.

The name "Poimandres" is thought to represent the Greek interpretation of the Egyptian word for "the Knowledge of Ra."[23] This interpretation fits the information in the Cayce readings, for they too mention Ra, and *The Genesis of Enoch* reference strengthens the case for linking Hermes with Enoch.

Note in the portions of the *Poimandres* quoted below the similarity to the revelations received by Enoch and how also the information conforms to that given by Cayce on the subject of creation and the role of Amilius:

> Then the Father—the Supreme Mind—being Light and Life, fashioned a glorious Universal Man in Its own image, not an earthly man but a heavenly Man dwelling in the light of God. *The Supreme Mind* loved the Man it had fashioned and delivered to Him the control of the creations and workmanships.[24]

After describing how humanity was originally both male and female and then became enamored with earth and subject to it, he then discusses how the earthly human being can escape.

> The path to immortality is hard and few find it. The rest await the Great Day when the wheels of the universe shall be stopped and the immortal sparks shall escape from the sheaths of substance. Woe unto those who wait, for they must return again, unconscious and unknowing, to the seedground of stars, and await a new beginning. Those who are saved by the light of the mystery which I have revealed unto you, O Hermes, and which I now bid you to establish among men, shall return again to the Father who dwelleth in the White Light, and shall deliver themselves up to the Light and shall be absorbed into the Light, and in the Light they shall become Powers of God. This is the way of *Good* and is revealed only to them that have wisdom.
>
> Blessed art thou, O Son of Light, to whom of all men, I Poimandres, the Light of the World, have revealed myself. I order you to go forth, to become as a guide to those who wander in darkness, that all men within whom dwells the spirit of *My Mind* (the Universal Mind) may be saved by My Mind in you, which shall call forth My Mind in them. Establish My Mysteries and they shall not fail the earth, for I am the Mind of the Mysteries and until Mind fails (which is never) my Mysteries cannot fail.[25]

Hermes, again like Enoch, then preached these revelations to the people of earth. Some scoffed, but others accepted the message and were "saved."[26] The references to an apparent messianic role of Hermes in the *Poimandres* have been likened to the expressions for Christ in the Gospel of John.[27]

Finally, the Jewish Kabbalah relates that Enoch constructed underground vaults to preserve the secret teachings received by Seth from Adam.[28] This information ties in remarkably well with the information from the Cayce readings concerning Hermes' involvement with the building of the Great Pyramid and the preservation of records there.

One reading describes the Hall of Records:

A record of Atlantis from the beginnings of those periods when the Spirit took form or began the encasements in that land, and the developments of the peoples throughout their sojourn, [together] with the record of the first destruction and the changes that took place in the land, with the record of the *sojournings* of the peoples to the varied activities in other lands, and a record of the meetings of all the nations or lands for the activities in the destructions that became necessary with the final destruction of Atlantis and the buildings of the pyramid of initiation; [together] with who, what, where would come the opening of the records that are as copies from the sunken Atlantis...   378-16

Thus another piece of information is added to the linking of Hermes with Enoch.

As information is retrieved—bit by bit—from the obscurity of time and age, the picture of Hermes gradually comes into focus and assumes shape and meaning. He is recognizable as the Jewish and Biblical Enoch, as the angelic figure Metatron or Yaho'el, as the righteous Idris of the Koran, and as the Egyptian god Thoth. In the process of identification, we find tradition and writings linking this personage with the messiah, the redeemer of humanity, the soul who, according to Christianity, became Jesus Christ.

As the pieces of the puzzle begin to fit neatly together, the credibility of the Edgar Cayce psychic readings—at least as they relate to the lives of the Master—becomes ever more plausible.

CHAPTER EIGHT
Melchizedek

[As to Jesus:] being designated by God a
high priest after the order of Melchizedek.
(Hebrews 5:10)

For as those experiences Jesus . . . came into the earth, the *first*
that were of the sons of God to enter flesh, *there* the first and only
begotten of God. Again, as names would say, Enoch walked with
God, became aware of God in his movements—*still* that entity, that
soul called Jesus—as Melchizedek, without father, without mother,
came—*still* the soul of Jesus; the portion of God that manifests.
1158-5

. . . this entity [Jesus] was that one who had manifested to father
Abraham as the prince, as the priest of Salem, without father and
without mother, without days or years, but a living human being in
flesh made manifest in the earth from the desire of Father-God to
prepare an escape for man . . . 5023-2

Again there may be drawn to self a parallel from the realm of
spiritual enlightenment of that entity known as Melchizedek, a
prince of peace, one seeking ever to be able to bless those in their
judgments who have sought to become channels for a helpful
influence without any seeking for material gain, or mental or
material glory; but magnifying the virtues, minimizing the faults in
the experiences of all . . . 2072-4

Melchizedek is an interesting, yet enigmatic, Biblical figure.
He is first mentioned in the 14th chapter of Genesis after a

77

miraculous victory by Abram (before God renamed him
Abraham) and his household over King Chedorlaomer and the
numerous armies which he commanded. The king of Sodom
along with Melchizedek, king of Salem, went out to meet the
returning and victorious Abram and to offer thanks for his
deliverance.

> And Melchizedek king of Salem brought out
> bread and wine; he was priest of God Most High.
> And he blessed him and said, "Blessed be Abram
> by God Most High, maker of heaven and earth; and
> blessed be God Most High, who has delivered your
> enemies into your hand!" And Abram gave him a
> tenth of everything.   (Genesis 14:18-20)

The phrase "God Most High," or *El Elyon* in Hebrew, is one of
the terms used for God at that time. A typical characterization
was that El Elyon was "maker of heaven and earth." After
paying tithes to Melchizedek, Abram accorded Melchizedek
further respect by addressing the Lord in these terms as "God
Most High, the maker of heaven and earth." (Genesis 14:22)

Melchizedek is involved with two acts which later became
very important Judeo-Christian and religious rites: the
payment of tithes and the symbolic use of bread and wine as in
the Eucharist or Lord's Supper. He received the first Biblical
tithes and was the first in the Biblical accounts to symbolically
use bread and wine. We know from the Dead Sea Scrolls the
Jewish Essenes had a ritual using these elements which Jesus
may have borrowed.[1]

In the Canon of the Mass, the Catholic Church has further
carried forward the pre-eminence of Melchizedek receiving
tithes. The Church prays that the Father will accept its offering
as He accepted "the sacrifice that Your high priest Melchizedek
offered." Some Christian theologians have argued that
Melchizedek's name is placed where Jesus' name should be in
the Mass, for it was Jesus who sacrificed his life to God and is
considered the mediator between us and God. In view of the
special relationship the early Church found between Jesus and
Melchizedek, as we shall see later, the substitution of
Melchizedek's name for Jesus' may have been purposeful.

The only other Old Testament reference to Melchizedek is in

Psalm 110, a prophetic psalm which makes promises about the messiah: "The Lord has sworn, and will not change his mind, 'You are a priest for ever after the order of Melchizedek.'" (verse 4) God thus, under oath, states that the messiah will be linked eternally with the Melchizedek priesthood. This psalm, in the quoted and subsequent verses, uses the term "Lord" to describe both God and the messiah. It is therefore important to Christianity because it provides a validation of the Deity of the messiah and authorizes the title of "Lord" for Jesus.

Melchizedek is next mentioned in the New Testament book of Hebrews. He is described as having been: "Without father, or mother or genealogy, and has neither beginning of days, nor end of life, but resembling the Son of God he continues a priest forever." (Hebrews 7:3)

The author of Hebrews goes into great detail to link the Melchizedek priesthood with Jesus. Chapter 7 acknowledges that Jesus came from the tribe of Judah, "and in connection with that tribe Moses said nothing about priests." (verse 14) The author examines the priesthood of Levi, which had been established by Moses when he named Aaron and his descendants (the tribe of Levi) to minister to the people and to keep charge of the tabernacle of witness. (See Hebrews 8:2.) They were to offer sacrifices for their own sins and the sins of the people, but Hebrews 10:4 points out: "For it is impossible that the blood of bulls and goats should take away sins." Hebrews therefore emphasizes the inadequacy of the Levitical priesthood; a new and better covenant was needed between God and man. "For he finds fault with them, when he says: 'The days will come, says the Lord, when I will establish a new covenant with the house of Israel and with the house of Judah ... '" (Hebrews 8:8) This superior covenant is found through the Melchizedek priesthood in Christ Jesus, "Who has become a priest, not according to a legal requirement concerning bodily descent but the power of an indestructible life." (Hebrews 7:16)

The pre-eminence of the Melchizedek priesthood is arrived at in yet another manner:

> One might even say that Levi himself who
> receives tithes, paid tithes through Abraham, for
> he was still in the loins of his ancestor, when

Melchizedek met him.   (Hebrews 7:9-10)

By this rationale of Levi paying tithes to Melchizedek and by Melchizedek being more than a mere representation between God and man of carnal sacrifices, Melchizedek is recognized in the New Testament as a priest of a higher order than that of Levi. His is a priesthood of sufficient rank to accommodate the Son of God.

Hebrews also recognizes Jesus as the Messiah described in Psalm 110. In first referring to the Levitical priesthood, it is said:

> For they were made priests without oaths; but this one was made a priest with an oath, as it was said concerning him by David, The Lord was sworn, and will not lie, Thou art a priest for ever after the order of Melchizedek. All these things make a better covenant because Jesus is its surety.
> (Hebrews 7:21-22; Lamsa translation)

Verse 21 contains an actual verbatim quote of Psalm 110:4, discussed earlier.

There are a number of interesting parallels between Melchizedek and Jesus:

1. Both were characterized as priests ordained specifically by God, rather than by man. Neither was eligible under Jewish law and tradition to be considered priests: Melchizedek was a Gentile, and Jesus was not of the priestly tribe of Levi. Both represented a dimension above the law with divine ordination.

2. King of Salem means King of Peace, and Jesus was heralded and proclaimed the Prince of Peace.

3. Melchizedek was both a priest and a king. Jesus' priesthood is documented in Hebrews, and he was known by the sign on his cross as "King of the Jews."

4. In giving his blessing to Abram, Melchizedek brought forth bread and wine, traditional memorials of offering and sacrifice. Similarly Jesus, in blessing his disciples before his trial and crucifixion, offered bread and wine as symbols of his body and blood and of the sacrifice he was to make.

5. In tablets excavated at Tell el Amarna dating back to 1400 B.C., Jerusalem is referred to as Uru-Salem, and in Psalm 76:2 (a psalm written by Asaph, who incidentally the Cayce readings

say was another incarnation of the Master soul) Jerusalem is simply called Salem. Most scholars have concluded, as did first-century Jewish historian Josephus, that Jerusalem was originally known as Salem. If so, then Melchizedek was king of the city where Jesus eventually was crucified and ended his ministry. Jesus' lamentation over the error of Jerusalem's ways and its imminent destruction thus takes on special and poignant meaning:

> O Jerusalem, Jerusalem, killing the prophets and stoning those who are sent to you! How often would I have gathered your children together as a hen gathers her brood under her wings, and you would not! Behold your house is forsaken and desolate. For I tell you, you will not see me again, until you say, "Blessed is he who comes in the name of the Lord."   (Matthew 23:37-39)

6. Two Biblical stories stand out as tales with profound symbolic significance for the spiritual evolution of humanity. Each is considered a masterpiece of allegory and esoteric meaning and a complete sermon within itself. One is the parable of the prodigal son in the New Testament; the other, the Old Testament story of Job. The prodigal son parable, of course, belongs to Jesus, and, according to Cayce, Melchizedek wrote the Book of Job. (262-55) Cayce also says that Job was not an actual, historic person, but a symbolic figure—as is the case with the prodigal son. While modern scholars are unsure of the authorship of Job, some do place the book in the historical period of the patriarchs and the Abrahamic covenant—and thus in Melchizedek's time.

Three chapters in the Epistle to the Hebrews (5, 6, and 7) discuss at great length the equality and similarity of Jesus and Melchizedek. The author of Hebrews stops short of saying they were one and the same entity, but he does hint at a mystery. Hebrews 5:10 and 11 states that, although Jesus was "called of God an high priest after the order of Melchizedek," there is more to be said, but it is difficult "seeing ye are dull of hearing." The author continues:

> For though by this time you ought to be teachers, you need some one to teach you again

the first principles of God's word. You need milk,
not solid food; for every one who lives on milk is
unskilled in the word of righteousness, for he is a
child. But solid food is for the mature, for those
who have their faculties trained by practice to
distinguish good from evil.   (Hebrews 5:12-14)

This same language also appears in 1 Corinthians 3:1 and 2,
where Paul indicates his audience is not ready to hear the full
story.

In a similar vein, Cayce stated that the belief in previous lives
of people, or reincarnation, was dropped by the early Church to
create a "shortcut." This deletion was apparently aimed at
simplicity and mass acceptability. The "babes" were not ready
for "solid food" and the learning of the mysteries of the soul.

Some early Christians did apparently understand the full
implication of the connection between Melchizedek and Jesus.
A footnote to Genesis 14:17-26 in the *Jerusalem Bible* states
that several of the early Church Fathers "even held the opinion
that Melchizedek was a manifestation of the Son of God in
person."[2]

The name "Melchizedek" has generally been translated,
from Josephus to modern scholars, to mean King or Lord of
Righteousness.[3] With this meaning in mind, the following
messianic prophecy by the great Hebrew prophet Jeremiah
becomes very significant:

In his days Judah will be saved, and Israel will
dwell securely. And this is the name by which he
will be called: "The Lord is our righteousness."
(Jeremiah 23:6)

Is not Jeremiah identifying the anticipated messiah as
Melchizedek? "The Lord is our righteousness" is the actual,
literal meaning of the name "Melchizedek."

According to esoteric Jewish literature, Abraham received
directly from Melchizedek original teachings, which were then
passed on to subsequent generations as the Hebrew Kabbala.[4]
Melchizedek would thus be the first author of these venerated
teachings.

In the *Jewish Encyclopedia*, Melchizedek is "placed in the
same category [of importance] with Elijah, the Messiah ben

Joseph, and the Messiah ben David."⁵ Christians, of course, recognize Jesus in these messianic references.

Another interesting commentary on Melchizedek is contained in a quote from the *Ethiopian Book of Adam and Eve:*

> . . . Noah tells his son Shem before his death to take "Melchizedek, the son of Canaan, *whom God has chosen from all generations of men,* and to stand by the dead body of Adam after it had been brought from the ark to Jerusalem as the center of the earth and fulfill the ministry before God." The angel Michael then took away Melchizedek, when fifteen years of age, from his father, and after having anointed him as priest, brought him to (Jerusalem) the center of the earth, telling his father to share the mystery only with Shem, the son of Noah, while the Holy Spirit, speaking out of the ark when the body of Adam was hidden, greeted Melchizedek as *"the first-created of God."* [Author's italics]⁶

The words, "whom God has chosen from all generations of men," are the kinds of phraseology generally reserved for Old Testament statements about the messiah and New Testament descriptions of Jesus. And the phrase, "the first-created of God," would seem necessarily to be a reference to Adam. All the wording, of course, pertains to Melchizedek and would appear to identify him as both Adam and the messiah. Although the narrative would differ from both the New Testament and Cayce in seemingly giving Melchizedek an earthly father, it is noteworthy in the above narrative that Melchizedek was taken to stand by the dead body of Adam. According to Cayce, Melchizedek thus would have been standing by the body his soul had previously inhabited. Possibly that was the significance intended by Noah.

The *Encyclopedia Judaica* claims there are other Judaic references to the messianic functions of Melchizedek and that rabbinical sources mention Melchizedek "among the four messianic figures allegorically implied by the four 'smiths' of Zechariah 1:20 and 21."⁷

Manuscripts of the *Slavonic Apocalypse of Enoch (2 Enoch)*

were discovered in recent years in Russia and Serbia. As indicated in the Enoch chapter, it is thought to have been written during the early Christian era and was probably based upon earlier Jewish tradition.

Some of these Slavonic Enochian manuscripts contain a story about Melchizedek having been born miraculously and being in the care of Nir, Noah's brother. An angel appeared to Nir and told him that the archangel Michael would take Melchizedek to Eden, the former paradise of Adam, and that Melchizedek would become the priest to all holy priests. He is to become the head of a line of priests from which the promised messiah will descend. The messiah, who is to be both a priest and a king, is expected also to be an eschatological Melchizedek.

> And afterward, in the last generation, there will be another Melkisedek, the first of 12 priests. And the last will be the head of all, a great archpriest, the Word and Power of God, who will perform miracles, greater and more glorious than all the previous ones. He, Melkisedek, will be priest and king in the place Akhuzan, that is to say, in the center of the earth, where Adam was created, and there will be his final grave. And in connection with that archpriest it is written how he also will be buried there, where the center of the earth is . . .
>
> (2 Enoch 71:34-36)

Jerusalem was traditionally known as the center of the earth, and the quotation seems clearly to identify the last appearance of Melchizedek as that of the messiah. Melchizedek's *final* grave at Jerusalem would be correct if he did, in fact, come back as Jesus. The references to Adam are also intriguing and were referred to in the Adam chapter.

The gnostic Christian manuscript, *Pistis Sophia,* dating from the fourth or fifth centuries A.D., contains mysteries purportedly given by Jesus to the disciples and certain elect after the resurrection and before his ascension. It makes numerous references to Melchizedek as part of the hierarchy of the mysteries and godhead of which Jesus was a part.[8]

Probably the strongest case for corroborating Cayce's

statements that Jesus had previously incarnated as
Melchizedek is the Bible itself. There are a number of Biblical
references, including one of its most quoted verses, John 3:16,
which refer to Jesus as the "only begotten Son" of God.
Webster defines "begotten" as "to bring into being" or
"procreate." Cayce gave a rather obvious definition of
"begotten of God" as "those who have entered into flesh
without that act which man knows as copulation." (1158-5)
Jesus is not the only Biblical son who entered flesh without the
act of copulation. Adam, of course, was created by God rather
than by a human being, and Melchizedek was, according to
Hebrews, without earthly father or mother. Unless Adam and
Melchizedek are the same soul entity as Jesus, as Cayce said,
then the Bible would appear to be contradictory in saying that
Jesus is the *only* begotten son of God.

Even Jesus seemed to imply that he may have been
Melchizedek when he said:

> Your father Abraham rejoiced that he was to see
> my day; he saw it, and was glad. The Jews then said
> to him, "You are not yet fifty years old, and have
> you seen Abraham?" Jesus said to them, "Truly,
> truly, I say to you, before Abraham was, I am."
>
> (John 8:56-58)

These quotations become meaningful in light of the Cayce
information that Jesus was also Melchizedek who, as we know
from the Bible, met and blessed Abram or Abraham. Abraham
thus "rejoiced" to see his (Jesus') earlier day, and he saw it and
was "glad."

Scattered among Christian liturgy are a few prayers which
are thought to be remnants of Jewish synagogal prayers; they
are contained in Books Seven and Eight of the *Apostolic
Constitutions.*[9] One of these, dating from around A.D. 200,
contains the following cryptic wording in a supplication to God:

> You are the one who delivered Abraham from
> ancestral godlessness,
> and appointed him heir of the world,
> AND SHOWED TO HIM YOUR CHRIST;
> the one who appointed Melchizedek a high priest
> in your service . . .[10]

The above emphasized words are thought to be Christian inter-
polations. A reasonable interpretation of the entire quotation
is that it identifies Melchizedek, who was shown to Abraham,
as the Christ.

Most of the documents found in recent years near the Dead
Sea at Qumran are books of the Old Testament and related
materials of the Old Testament period as seen through the eyes
of the Essenes. Cayce provides the interesting insight that the
Essenes grew out of the teachings of Melchizedek as
propagated by prophets, such as Elijah, Elisha, and Samuel.
(254-109) From the documents at Qumran, we know there was
much interest in Melchizedek among these Essenes. This
Melchizedekian influence could be the result of traditions
dating back through the school of prophets to Melchizedek
himself. We also now know that the Qumran Essene priesthood
was modeled after that of Melchizedek.[11] The Essenes' pre-
occupation with Melchizedek may also be the basis for the
detailed discussion of him in Hebrews.[12]

A number of Essenic documents referred to a Teacher of
Righteousness. In the Essene *Commentary on the Book of
Habakkuk,* the Teacher of Righteousness is referred to as one
"to whom God has made known all the mysteries of His
servants the prophets."[13] This Teacher of Righteousness was
expected to return and usher in the Messianic Age and,
according to Jewish tradition, to be Elijah or Phinehas or
Melchizedek.[14] At least one respected Dead Sea Scroll
authority has stated that Jesus in these documents *"appears in
many respects* as an astonishing reincarnation of the Teacher of
Righteousness."[15]

Not all of the documents found at Qumran have yet been
translated or at least been made available to the public. But at
least one treatise now publicly available bears directly on the
question of Melchizedek's relationship to the promised
messiah.

The Last Jubilee: A Sermon "Melchizedek Texts" (also known
as "11Q Melchizedek Text" or "11 Q Melchizedek"), found at
Qumran and considered a part of what is commonly known as
the Dead Sea Scrolls, refers in messianic terms to a future King
of Righteousness. In the text, this King of Righteousness is
described as passing judgment in the time of the tenth or last

Jubilee on Belial and his followers. After the judgment in heaven comes the destruction of those who have followed Belial rather than God. The text states that "the one designed, by God's favor, for the King of Righteousness (which is what, by his very name, Melchizedek prefigures) will come into his dominion." The time of his coming "into his dominion" is identified as the period which Isaiah termed the year of favor (or "acceptable year of the Lord"):

> The Spirit of the Lord God is upon me; because the Lord has anointed me to bring good tidings to the afflicted, he has sent me to bind up the brokenhearted, to proclaim liberty to the captive, and the opening of the prison to those who are bound; to proclaim the year of the Lord's favor, and the day of vengeance of our God; to comfort all that mourn . . .   (Isaiah 61:1-2)

It should be noted here that when Jesus made his first appearance in Nazareth after beginning his public ministry, he spoke at the synagogue there, and the book of Isaiah was handed to him. Luke records that he then found and read the two verses quoted above (Luke 4:17-19), but stopped after the phrase "the year of the Lord's favor" in verse two. Biblical analysts have concluded that by suspending reading without referring to God's day of vengeance, Jesus was distinguishing between his present ministry of grace and the second advent when he would carry out God's judgments. On the other hand, his stopping after that phrase may have been for the purpose of emphasis, for it truly was the "year of the Lord." After Jesus had concluded his reading, verse 21 adds: "And he began to say unto them, 'Today this scripture has been fulfilled in your hearing.' "

Thus in Luke 4:21, Jesus seems to identify himself as the one promised by Isaiah "to proclaim the year of the Lord's favor" when he said, "Today this scripture has been fulfilled in your hearing." And the Melchizedek Texts from the Dead Sea Scrolls identify Melchizedek as the person who will fulfill that prophecy.

The Qumran Melchizedek Texts contain several comments which seem clearly to identify the King of Righteousness as the promised messiah. They discuss the role of this future King in overthrowing Belial and executing God's avenging judgment and clearly state that this King will be "Melchizedek redivivus" (or reincarnated). One scholar has summarized the document thusly:

> In this fragment, written in Hebrew, Melchizedek appears as an eschatological saviour who has a heritage. His mission is to bring back at the end of days the exiles to announce to them their liberation . . . and the expiation of their sins.[16]

A similarity between Melchizedek and Enoch (Metatron) has also been noted:

> A number of clear parallels between the heavenly Melchizedek of Qumran and the Metatron of 3 Enoch at once suggest themselves: both figures hold exalted, if not pre-eminent, positions among the angels; both are heavenly judges . . . and both, apparently, had earthly lives prior to their exalted, heavenly states.[17]

This parallel from ancient documents adds credence to the Cayce proposition that Enoch and Melchizedek are the same soul.

One of the documents found at Nag Hammadi in Egypt in the late 1940s is a text entitled *Melchizedek*. Little is known about its authorship or significance in early Christian theology, but at least one gnostic sect named itself after Melchizedek. The following quote is from this text:

> And you crucified me from the third hour of the Sabbath-eve until the ninth hour. And after these things I arose from the dead. My body came out of the tomb to me. [. . .] they did not find anyone [. . .] greeted me [. . .] They said to me, Be strong, O Melchizedek, great High Priest of God Most High [. . .] [Brackets indicate missing fragments or illegible wording.][18]

There can be little doubt that this quote and the related material—from a group of early Christians—are referring to the crucifixion and resurrection of Jesus.

In commenting on the above text, noted authority Birger A. Pearson states, "Furthermore, the tractate's apparent identification of Melchizedek with Jesus Christ . . . is also documented elsewhere in early Christianity, particularly in Egypt."[19] In the expanded *Nag Hammadi Library*, Pearson adds:

> We are drawn to the conclusion that, in the revelation which the priest Melchizedek has received, he has seen that he himself will have a redemptive role to play as the suffering, dying, resurrected and triumphant Savior, Jesus Christ!
> . . . From what we read . . . it seems that the victory of Jesus Christ is the victory of Melchizedek and that, in fact, they are one and the same.[20]

In correspondence with the author, Pearson adds: "I did and do understand the (very fragmentary!) text of the first tractate to imply that Melchizedek was prophesied to return again, as Jesus."

This tractate contains other material that may be relevant to the lives of the Master. In one section (12, 1), which appears to quote an angelic source, there is a list of several Biblical personages. Because parts of the text are missing, it is not clear what this list purports to be. Scholars have added the names of Noah and Abel to the list, but probably because they were included in some other documents, not because they were a part of the legible text. It has been surmised that the list may be of ancient heroes who also functioned as priests. The listing concludes with the name of Melchizedek, who, as indicated, is identified elsewhere in the document as Jesus Christ. The other two legible names on the list are Adam and Enoch. It may easily be deduced that these names are given as other earlier incarnations of the Master.

As we have seen, there is evidence, aside from Cayce, identifying Melchizedek with Jesus. In fact, a prophecy was made before the time of Jesus that the Christ or messiah would be Melchizedek returned; and another, written by early Christians, actually identifies Christ Jesus as Melchizedek. It should be noted that these documents were not available, however, until after Edgar Cayce's death.

Melchizedek was obviously a very advanced soul. One might logically wonder why it was necessary for this soul to incarnate further, as Cayce states, until reaching Christhood as Jesus. Presumably each intervening life was a learning experience, and, even when entering the earth as Jesus, there was more for this soul to learn. Hebrews 5:8 says: "Although he [Jesus] was a Son, he learned obedience through what he suffered." Thomas Sugrue wrote the definitive biography of Edgar Cayce, *There Is a River.* In compiling the philosophy section of that book, he obtained direct advice and guidance from Cayce through psychic readings. From this section, we get an additional theory as to why the Master soul again incarnated after the experience as Melchizedek:

> The Christ soul helped man. As Enoch, as Melchizedek, it took on flesh, to teach and lead ... Enoch and Melchizedek were not born, did not die. The Christ soul realized after these assumptions of flesh that it was necessary to set a pattern for man, to show him the way back to himself. It assumed this task and was born of woman, beginning voluntarily a new individuality, a new soul record; though behind this new individuality shone the pure Christ soul. But on this the veil dropped, and the Son of God began His pilgrimage.[21]

Thus, the Master soul, after incarnating as Melchizedek, apparently assumed the mission of relating directly to humanity and of becoming the pattern for its return to the Creator through fleshly incarnations and births begotten of human parentage. These lives then should offer special significance and meaning to us, the first of which, according to Cayce, was as Joseph who was sold into slavery by his brothers.

Scattered throughout esoteric religious writings of the centuries, and even the Bible itself, have been references to the priestly order of Melchizedek, as though it were an order of special and high spiritual attainment. Melchizedek established this order, and it was infinitely higher and more perfect than the priesthood of Aaron. The Aaronic priesthood ended with death, but the priesthood of Melchizedek was a spiritual order whose priests were priests forever. The Aaronic-Levitical priests offered sacrifices for the sins of their people; Jesus gave his life as the sacrifice for his people. By resurrecting his body, he made the Jesus-Melchizedek priesthood eternal. This priesthood, according to the *Encyclopedia Judaica's* interpretation of Hebrews, "is excellent, superior to that of Abraham's descent, and transcends all human, imperfect orders."[22]

The author of Hebrews would use Melchizedek as the standard by which to validate the priestly ministry of Jesus and say of Melchizedek:

> See how great he is! Abraham the patriarch gave
> him a tithe of the spoils.   (Hebrews 7:4)

In view of such New Testament and early Christian veneration of Melchizedek and the rich messianic tradition about him which we have found, Christians should in no way find it demeaning to link the soul of Melchizedek with that of Jesus. Certainly both individuals were important instruments of God, and each life marks an historic step in the spiritual evolution of humanity.

CHAPTER NINE

Joseph

I see him, but not now;
I behold him, but not nigh:
a star shall come forth out of Jacob,
and a scepter shall rise out of Israel . . .
(Messianic prophecy in Numbers 24:17)

The story of Joseph as told in Genesis is one of the most favored and beautiful in the entire Bible. It is a story of riches to rags back to riches—in the mold of the Book of Job and the parable of the prodigal son; of good triumphing over evil; of innocence and purity sacrificing itself for others; and of forgiveness and love. Its narrative presages the coming of the messiah or Christ. And Edgar Cayce says that Joseph was in fact an incarnation of that Master soul who became Jesus.

First, in the beginning, of course; and then as Enoch, Melchizedek, in the perfection. Then in the earth of Joseph, Joshua, Jeshua, Jesus.   5749-14

The incarnation of the Master soul in the beginning as the God-created Adam was unique and special, and as Enoch and Melchizedek this soul was in a state of perfection in which physical death was not necessary. But as Joseph, a journey through fleshly incarnations and deaths was begun which culminated in Christhood as Jesus. Apparently such physical births and deaths were necessary in order for the Master to serve as an effective pattern pointing humanity back to the

Father. The life of Joseph takes on special significance then as the first incarnation of the Master soul to which we as earth-bound souls can totally relate.

According to the Biblical story (Genesis 37-50), Jacob, whom God named Israel, had had no children by his favorite wife, Rachel. When Joseph was finally born to her, he was very comely and became Jacob's favorite son. His other sons were jealous and resentful of Joseph, especially when Joseph recited dreams reflecting his brothers' subservience to him. As they saw Joseph approaching them in the fields to deliver a message from their father, the brothers decided to kill him. Through Reuben's intercession, Joseph was placed in a well rather than being killed outright, and when a traveling band of Ishmaelite traders came by, Judah proposed that Joseph be sold. The brothers then sold him and bloodied Joseph's coat of many colors. After showing the coat to their father, they told him that Joseph had been devoured by a wild animal.

The traders took Joseph to Egypt where he became a servant in the household of Potiphar, an official of the pharoah. He soon became head administrator of the household but was imprisoned on a charge of seducing Potiphar's wife, although he had in fact spurned her advances. In prison, Joseph was made administrator over the other prisoners. When the pharoah imprisoned his chief baker and his wine taster, Joseph correctly interpreted a dream for each. Joseph prophesied that within three days the wine taster would return to the king or pharoah and that the baker would be beheaded and hanged from a tree. When both these things happened as predicted, the wine taster forgot to tell the pharoah of Joseph's talent as he had promised to do. Two years later, however, when pharoah had dreams no one else could adequately interpret, the wine taster did remember Joseph.

From pharoah's dreams, Joseph prophesied seven years of feast in the land to be followed by seven years of famine. Pharoah appointed Joseph second in command of Egypt to administer a program for conserving food during the good years, as Joseph had recommended. Seven good years were in fact followed by famine, and the whole area then turned to the rich storehouses of Egypt for relief.

Pharoah gave to Joseph as his wife Aseneth, the daughter of

the priest at On. They had two sons, Manasseh and Ephraim.

Even in Canaan, Joseph's aging father and brothers were affected by the drought, and his brothers, except young Benjamin, came to Egypt to buy grain. Joseph recognized his brothers, but they did not realize they were purchasing food from him. Joseph toyed with them by accusing them of being spies and kept Simeon as a hostage until they should return with Benjamin. Back home, the brothers became concerned because the money used to purchase the grain was found back in their sacks and because Jacob refused to let Benjamin go to Egypt.

Finally, the continuing famine and assurances from Judah forced Jacob to relent, and the brothers went back to Egypt with Benjamin. This time after allowing them to start home and then bringing them back by causing a palace cup to be hidden in Benjamin's sack of grain, Joseph revealed his identity to them. He forgave his brothers and urged them to get Jacob and come to live in Egypt. They did so, and Joseph's family was given choice Egyptian lands in Goshen and other special favors.

Jacob lived for seventeen years and died in Egypt after giving his sons individual blessings. It is from the sons that the twelve tribes of Israel are derived. Before Joseph's death, he predicted difficult times ahead but said that God would eventually deliver the Israelites from Egypt to the Promised Land in Canaan.

Scholars generally concede the historical authenticity of the Joseph story and have found evidence both of great droughts and of Semitic administrators in Egypt. References to seven years of drought in Mesopotamia and in Egypt at Sehel have been uncovered, and it is generally thought that Joseph could have been in Egypt anytime between the Hyksos' reign and that of Ramses II.[1] Joseph's fracas with Potiphar's wife, in which she falsely accused him of seduction, is even paralleled in the Egyptian tale "The Two Brothers." And an ancient waterway to the oasis of Faiyum is known to this day as "Bahr Yusuf," or "Joseph's canal." Arab legends say it was built by the Biblical Joseph.[2]

In a psychic reading for a lady in 1939, Cayce said she had lived at the time of Joseph:

Before that we find the entity was in the land now known as the Egyptian; during those periods when there was the understanding

gained by the ministrations and activities in the days when Joseph ruled in that land.

The entity then was among the princesses of Egypt, and of that king who made for the establishing of that closer relationship to those who had chosen to serve the living God, rather than to serve their own selves.

For the entity was acquainted with and oft associated with Joseph . . .   1825-1

A follow-up reading in 1943 gives added detail:

In those periods when there had been the raising of Joseph from the keeper in the prison to a place of authority close to the king, then the entity—Zerlva—was a princess of the second wife of the king of Egypt in that period. His name is given here in the Exodus itself.

The entity in those periods was acquainted with the family of Joseph's wife; and thus became a worshiper of the one God.

After the famine and the restoration of the princess and the princes of Egypt, and the high priests of the various groups or cults, the entity then interested self in the activities of those peoples that sought gold and silver, and the gems that became a part of the regalia of the princess and prince of the Egyptian people . . .
                                                1825-2

The above readings cause the name of Akhenaton, who was also known as Amenhotep IV or Amenophis IV, to come to mind. He assumed power in 1379 B.C. in the capital of Thebes and reigned there for six years. He then moved his capital nearly 300 miles north and down the Nile River to Akhetaton, now known as Amarna or Tel el Amarna. He established a new religion based upon a belief in one God and denounced the old religious cults of Egypt. His religion was the "closest approach to monotheism that the world had ever seen."[3] He has been credited with the "revolutionary concept of an eternal, absolute, omnipotent, and only God," similar to that of the Hebrews of a later period.[4]

Others, without regard to the Cayce readings, have identified Joseph with the Akhenaton period:

> The marriage of the Viceroy [Joseph] to a Sun-priest's daughter, and Pharoah's acceptance of Joseph's monotheistic religion, both suggest that he was Amenhotep IV, the daring religious reformer who worshipped only Aten, the solar

disk, changed his name to Akhenaten [sic], and
built a new capital at Amarna.[5]

On the other hand, Akhenaton is not known to have had a
second wife, as Cayce said about the king in the quoted reading,
nor is his name in the Exodus (assuming Cayce was referring to
the Biblical book of Exodus). Also, a reading for another
woman would seem to put the period of Joseph at a much
earlier date. This reading (355-1) indicates that Princess
Hatshepsut was the one who retrieved Moses from the
bullrushes of the Nile. She eventually became queen, and her
reign preceded that of Akhenaton by a little over a hundred
years. Inasmuch as Joseph was in Egypt by possibly 400 years
before Moses, the time frame seems to eliminate Akhenaton
and point to the rule of the Hyksos, foreigners who took over
the throne during the period 1720 to 1550 B.C. Most scholars
also seem to favor this dating for Joseph.

One thing the readings do insist is that Joseph's lifetime and
influence aided the belief in one God. This result is one, they
say, that followed whenever there was an appearance of the
Master soul.

Regardless of the time period of Joseph, the similarities and
symbolism between his life and that of Jesus are certainly
impressive:

1. Both were beloved by their father. Genesis 37:3 says, "Now
Israel loved Joseph more than any other of his children . . ."
while in John 3:35 it says of Jesus and his heavenly Father,
"The Father loves the Son, and has given all things into his
hand." Matthew 3:17 adds, "And lo, a voice from heaven,
saying, 'This is my beloved Son, with whom I am well pleased.' "

2. On the other hand, both were hated by their brothers. "But
when his brothers saw their father loved him [Joseph] more
than all his brothers, they hated him, and could not speak
peaceably to him." (Genesis 37:4) And in John 15:25, as to
Jesus for whom all men were counted as brothers: "They hated
me without a cause."

3. Both claimed a status which was rejected and resented. In
Genesis 37:8, Joseph's plight is stated thusly: "His brothers
said to him, 'Are you indeed to reign over us? Or are you indeed
to have dominion over us?' So they hated him yet more for his
dreams, and for his words." Jesus claimed he and his Father, or

God, were one. He was accused of blasphemy and stated, "but now they have seen and hated both me and my Father." (John 15:24)

4. The brothers of both conspired to kill them. In Genesis 37:18, it is said about Joseph's brothers, "They saw him afar off, and before he came near to them, they conspired against him to kill him." Similarly as to Jesus' "brothers": "Then the chief priests and the elders of the people gathered in the place of the high priest, who was Caiaphas, and took counsel together in order to arrest Jesus by stealth and kill him." (Matthew 26:3-4)

5. Joseph was sold for 20 pieces of silver by Judah, and Jesus was sold for 30 pieces of silver by Judas. In a footnote to Jewish historian Josephus' account of the Joseph story, tradition is cited to the effect that it was actually 30 pieces of silver which the brothers received for Joseph, thus even duplicating the exact amount which was involved in Jesus' betrayal.[6]

6. Both Joseph and Jesus forgave the erring brothers and exalted them. Probably the key to the Joseph story and its most compelling theme is Joseph's undying love for his brothers and his readiness to forgive the past and accept it as God's purpose. In Genesis 50:20, he tells his brothers, ". . . you meant evil against me; but God meant it for good, to bring it about that many people should be kept alive as they are today." He also provided his brothers with wealth and glory exceeding their former status in Canaan. Similarly on the cross, Jesus' immortal plea as recorded in Luke 23:34, was, "Father, forgive them; for they know not what they do." And he promised, "And I, if I be lifted up, will draw all men to me." (John 12:32) He made no exception for those who had wrongfully abused him; theirs too was the promise of heaven.

7. Joseph spent three years in prison in Egypt, and Jesus spent three days in the grave before resurrection. (While the Bible is not specific, the *Jewish Encyclopedia* says it is generally accepted that Joseph spent three years in prison.) There seems to be even further symbolism involved in Joseph's sojourn in prison: Joseph interpreted dreams for the pharoah's wine taster and his baker predicting that the latter would be hanged within three days and that the other would be restored to his former position with the king or pharoah within the same period of time. How peculiarly similar this episode is to Jesus'

comments to the two thieves crucified with him to whom he predicted that one of them would join him in paradise or, to put it another way, would be restored to his former position of glory with the king or God. Even the method of death which Joseph predicted for the pharoah's baker—hanging on a tree—seems to be a portent of the manner of death for Jesus. And Jesus' fate would be both crucifixion and a return to his former status with the (heavenly) King—the two things Joseph predicted for his fellow prisoners.

8. Neither Joseph nor Jesus was recognized. When Joseph's brothers, who represent and are the patriarchs of the Jewish people, came to Egypt to buy grain, they did not recognize Joseph. When Jesus came as the awaited messiah, he too was not generally recognized by the Jewish people.

9. The lives of both Joseph and of Jesus were saved by going to Egypt. Joseph would otherwise have died at the hands of his brothers, and Jesus would have been killed as a baby under Herod's death decree had not he and his family escaped to Egypt.

10. And the journey to Egypt in both cases was the result of dreams. Joseph's problems with his brothers were aggravated by his dreams reflecting superiority over them, and it was a dream of Jesus' father, Joseph, which prompted the family to flee Palestine for Egypt.

11. Joseph began his ministry as the pharoah's overseer at age thirty, and at the same age, Jesus began his active ministry for God.

12. Jacob's sons numbered twelve and were the fathers of the twelve tribes of Israel. Jesus, in turn, chose twelve disciples to assist him in his ministry.

13. Joseph went through the pretense of not recognizing his brothers when they came to Egypt. Jesus likewise, on the road to Emmaus after his crucifixion, pretended not to know his friends until he broke bread with them at the end of the day. (Luke 24:13-31)

14. Joseph and Jesus both offered a hope of return to the Promised Land for the faithful or chosen. Before his death, Joseph said to his loved ones: "God will visit you, and bring you up out of this land to the land which he swore to Abraham, to Isaac, and to Jacob." (Genesis 50:24) Jesus made similar

promises to those who would love him: "Fear not, little flock, for it is your Father's good pleasure to give you the kingdom." (Luke 12:32) "I go to prepare a place for you... that where I am, there ye may be also." (John 14:2-3)

15. The "death" of neither Joseph nor Jesus was final, but worked to further God's purposes. Joseph was saved from death in the pit by being sold into slavery, and Jesus' death was followed by resurrection. In both instances, the "death" worked to God's end: Joseph overcame bondage in Egypt and saved the Egyptians and others from famine; Jesus overcame the world and became the example for all humanity, the way out of slavery to the material world and back to the heavenly Creator.

16. Rejected by their own people, both Joseph and Jesus were accepted and exalted by foreigners. Joseph's brothers expelled him from their country; in Egypt he became second in authority to the pharoah. Jesus' death was brought about by his countrymen, but his resurrection and mission were accepted by Gentiles. In time he was recognized as the Son of God by numerous foreign countries, including the powerful Roman Empire.

Although the Bible reflects many similarities between Joseph and Jesus, it does not go so far as to corroborate Cayce's statements that Joseph and Jesus were incarnations of the same soul. There is material in apocryphal books, however, that seems to make such a connection.

The *Testaments of the Twelve Patriarchs* were written between 137 and 107 B.C. by an unknown author or authors drawing apparently from Jewish folklore and tradition. They contain a testament or deathbed statement from each of the twelve sons of Jacob, including Joseph. The early Christians appear to have had great respect for the *Testaments of the Twelve Patriarchs*, and their influence on New Testament writings, such as the Sermon on the Mount and some of Paul's epistles, is very evident. Several of these *Testaments* made predictions, similar to Biblical prophecies, that the Lamb of God or messiah would come from the tribes or descendants of Judah and Levi. Jesus, of course, was born of the tribe of Judah and assumed in his ministry a priestly role typical of the tribe of Levi.

In the "Testament of Naphtali," Naphtali tells of a dream or vision he had while at the Mount of Olives which foretold the coming of the messiah. The symbol of the messiah in the dream was Joseph, who was the only person who could capture a certain winged bull creature that ascended with him on high. The location of the dream—at the Mount of Olives—has special associations with Jesus.

The "Testament of Joseph" contains statements attributed to Joseph which compare favorably with some from Jesus. To his surviving brothers and all of Jacob's descendants, he said, "Do ye also, therefore love one another, and with long-suffering hide ye one another's faults." Jesus frequently admonished his disciples and followers to love one another, and he advised them to forgive their brother, not just seven times, but seventy times seven. (Matthew 18:21-22) Jesus said to return evil with good, and the following statement is attributed to Joseph: "And if anyone seeketh to do evil unto you, do well unto him and pray for him, and ye shall be redeemed of the Lord from all evil."

Joseph said:

> I was taken unto captivity, and His strong hand succoured me.
> I was beset with hunger, and the Lord Himself nourished me.
> I was alone, and God comforted me;
> I was sick, and the Lord visited me;
> I was in prison, and my God showed favour unto me;
> In bonds, and He released me;
> Slandered, and He pleaded my cause;
> Bitterly spoken against by the Egyptians, and He delivered me;
> Envied by my fellow-slaves, and He exalted me.
> ("Testament of Joseph," I:9-17)[7]

How similar are these comments to those of Jesus in Matthew 25:35-36:

> For I was hungry and you gave me food, I was thirsty and you gave me drink, I was a stranger and you welcomed me, I was naked and you clothed me, I was sick and you visited me, I was in prison and

you came to me.

Joseph also made the following prophecy:

> And I saw that from Judah was born a virgin
> wearing a linen garment, and from her was born a
> lamb, without spot; and on his left hand there was
> as it were a lion; and all the beasts rushed against
> him, and the lamb overcame them and trod them
> under foot. And because of him the angels and
> men rejoiced, and all the land. And these things
> shall come to pass in their season, in the last days.
> ("Testament of Joseph," II:74-76)[8]

The most exciting prophecy in the *Testaments of the Patriarchs*, which certainly would seem to corroborate Cayce's connection of Joseph and Jesus, is one from the "Testament of Benjamin." After Jacob was reunited with Joseph in Egypt, Joseph asked Jacob to pray for his brothers, Jacob's sons, that they might be forgiven. Jacob then embraced Joseph and cried out to him:

> In thee shall be fulfilled the prophecy of heaven
> concerning the Lamb of God, and Savior of the
> World, and that a blameless one shall be delivered
> up for lawless men, and a sinless one shall die for
> ungodly men in the blood of the covenant, for the
> salvation of the Gentiles and of Israel, and shall
> destroy Beliar and his servants.
> ("Testament of Benjamin," I:21)[9]

A story of probably Jewish origin tells of Joseph's marriage to Aseneth, virgin daughter of the Egyptian priest, Pentephres. This legend is known simply as "Joseph and Aseneth" and dates somewhere from 100 B.C. to not later than 117 A.D.[10] Some authorities think it may have had an origin with the Essenes, but in any event, it is of sufficient import to have been included in some lists of canonical and apocryphal Christian books.[11]

In the story, Joseph is described as "the mighty one of God," "the son of God," "the blessed one of God," "the firstborn of God" and the "savior" of his people.[12] This language has been taken as evidence of Joseph's identification with the

Redeemer, Jesus Christ.[13] A late sixteenth- or early
seventeenth-century Ethiopian hymn builds upon this
connection:

> Salutation to Joseph, who was called the
>   similitude
> Of the chief of the army of God;
> All my bones sing to this wise man, the bearer of a
>   gem,
> The storehouse of his riches, saying,
> "O Mary, he is thyself."[14]

In the "Joseph and Aseneth" story, Aseneth is a virgin and
quite beautiful. She is surrounded by seven other virgins who
wait upon her and, after falling in love with Joseph, is visited by
a heavenly angel. The angel tells Aseneth:

> For behold your name was written in the book of
> the living in heaven; in the beginning of the book,
> as the very first of all, your name was written by my
> finger, and it will not be erased forever ... Behold, I
> have given you today to Joseph for a bride, and he
> himself will be your bridegroom for ever (and)
> ever.
>   And your name shall no longer be called
> Aseneth, but your name shall be City of Refuge,
> because in you many nations will take refuge with
> the Lord God, the Most High, and under your
> wings many peoples trusting in the Lord God will
> be sheltered, and behind your walls will be guarded
> those who attach themselves to the Most High
> God in the name of Repentance.[15]

This hymn seems to be identifying Aseneth with Eve, whose
name was written in the "beginning of the book" as "the very
first of all." Joseph (Adam) is her bridegroom forever. And she
is promised a special role in the unfoldment of God's plan for
the repentance of humanity. If this soul is in fact Eve, then we
will be hearing more about her in Eve's incarnation, according
to Edgar Cayce, as Mary, the mother of Jesus.
    The events in the narrative unfold at Heliopolis, the home of
Aseneth. (Heliopolis is the Greek name for On, which is the

name given in the Bible.) Heliopolis in Greek means "city of the sun" and was located approximately five miles northeast of modern-day Cairo. As Jesus and Mary seeking refuge in Egypt from Herod's infant death decree, they will return to this very same location.

Legend claims Zeitoun to be one of the places where the Holy Family stayed while in Egypt; today it is a suburb of Cairo. The Church of Saint Mary, a Coptic Orthodox Christian Church, has been built at one of the spots where they are supposed to have lodged. During the late 1960s and into the early 1970s, a series of apparitions above the church, featuring Mary and at times the entire Holy Family, were witnessed by thousands of people. Many photographs were taken of the spectacle, and the event was well documented—including a number of miraculous healings that are alleged to have occurred there. The apparitions ceased after the Egyptian government advertised the event and began charging admission.[16] Possibly, the apparitions were a lingering influence of the souls who lived there as Mary and Jesus, and maybe also as Aseneth and Joseph. These lives were of critical import to humanity's spiritual evolution.

We now know from the Dead Sea Scrolls that the Essenes had a very high regard for Joseph. He was seen by them as an innocent sufferer who was also a prophet and a man of dreams. Of greatest significance, however, was the linking of their True Teacher or Teacher of Righteousness with Joseph.[17] Both of them were connected with the Essene celebration of the Jewish fast, the solemn Day of Atonement. The Essenes believed their Teacher of Righteousness would return as the messiah, and thus, according to them, the Joseph figure came to have messianic significance.[18] As we shall see in the Asaph chapter, this True Teacher was also identified by them as Asaph.

Just before his death, Jacob gave a prophetic blessing to each of his sons. In Genesis 49:22, he calls Joseph a "fruitful bough ...his branches run over the wall." As we shall see in later chapters, the term "branch" will be used by subsequent Jewish prophets in symbolic references to the promised messiah.

How great was this man Joseph?

Jewish tradition considers Joseph a prophet and the representation of a perfectly righteous man. According to

R. Phinehas, "the Holy Spirit dwelt in Joseph from his childhood unto his death."[19]

Joseph is also accepted as a prophet in Arabic literature with a type of manly beauty that engenders the expression "a second Joseph" for anyone who is extraordinarily beautiful. Arabic tradition would also attribute a great many public works in Egypt to Joseph. He is reputed to have been a great mathematician and astronomer, and "some would believe that he built the city of Memphis, and that he was instrumental in building the obelisks and pyramids."[20] One cannot help but wonder here, since there is no other evidence connecting Joseph with the building of the pyramids, if this reputation may not be the result of Arabic legends attributing the building of the Great Pyramid to Hermes (discussed in the chapter on Hermes) and by a recognition of a link between the two.

Joseph was honored by Judaism for his steadfastness against sexual temptation with Potiphar's wife. Potiphar had entrusted everything into Joseph's hand, and Joseph refused to betray this trust. The Fourth Book of Maccabees says:

> This certainly is why we praise the virtuous Joseph, because of his Reason, with a mental effort, he checked the carnal impulse. For he, a young man at the age when physical desire is strong, by his Reason quenched the impulse of his passions. (II:68)

Joseph's trustworthiness was recognized in prison, for even there the keeper "committed to Joseph's hand all the prisoners that were in the prison." And then the pharoah, merely on Joseph's dream interpretations, concluded there was none so wise as Joseph and made him ruler over the land and second only to himself.

Above all, Joseph is considered a highly moral and "innocent victim of jealousy and ill-will, who turns the tables on his persecutors by succeeding despite them and returning good for evil."[21] He exhibited forgiveness, long-suffering, tolerance, patience, and love.

Joseph, however, in spite of all his merit, apparently fell short of perfection. In the resentment of his brothers, there is the suggestion of vanity in the young Joseph. If the account in "The

Testament of Joseph" has any accuracy, Joseph at first had difficulty in forgiving his brothers. Certainly, the Biblical story shows him toying with them when they came to Egypt to buy grain, and he aggravated their grief with his demands regarding Benjamin. Finally, it was Joseph who set up a system of taxes to pharoah by which the surplus grain for the famine became the king's. Eventually the people had to buy it back to survive, and many of them in the process became economic slaves of the pharoah. (See Genesis 47:19-21.) The responsibility for this system was Joseph's, and in his next incarnation as Joshua, it is significant that he himself is enslaved in Egypt and spends his early life fleeing Egyptian bondage.

Edgar Cayce gave other information which makes interesting subplots in the Joseph story.

According to him, Joseph's brother Benjamin had been Seth, the son of Adam. (5148-2 and 281-48) Even though a great and spiritual figure, Seth was not to be compared with his father, Adam, now incarnated as Joseph. And the conditions under which Benjamin was brought into the world were not comparable with those of Joseph:

Also from the same attitude taken by those parents [Jacob and Rachel] when the second son, Benjamin, was conceived—what were the varying characteristics here? The material love was just as great; the satisfying of material desire was completely fulfilled; yet it lacked that desire to *bring* such as was wholly a channel through which the *spiritual* was to be made manifest. But it was a channel that *eventually* brought the material made manifest in Saul, an incarnation of Benjamin.   281-48

Thus, Cayce says Benjamin returned as Saul, who became the first Jewish king.

Another reading implies that Jacob returned later as the disciple John. (3976-15) Thus as Jacob, his beloved son was Joseph; as John, he was the beloved disciple of Jesus, who was formerly Joseph.

In summary, we have seen in Joseph a man of eminent historical and spiritual significance. As with others whom Cayce said were former incarnations of Jesus, there is ancient tradition identifying him with the messiah or savior who would save not only Israel, but the Gentiles as well. He was the "star out of Jacob" who would become the sceptre or king eventually arising out of Israel.

The many parallels between the saga of Joseph and that of Jesus have not gone unnoticed by others.

> The Church has always connected the story of Joseph with the experience of our Lord, who was crucified by his brothers but raised up by his heavenly Father to be the means of blessing and salvation for the world.[22]

If one were to summarize the life of Joseph, it might be said that he exemplified the redemptive work of the people of God, just as did Jesus who brought it to completion. The story of Joseph is a living example of submission to God's will, of paradise lost and of paradise regained.

CHAPTER TEN

Joshua

And Israel served the Lord all the days of Joshua, and all the days of the elders who outlived Joshua and had known all the work that the Lord did for Israel. *(Joshua 24:31)*

. . . Joshua the prophet, the mystic, the leader, the incarnation of the Prince of Peace. 362-1

For without Moses and his leader Joshua (that was bodily Jesus) there *is* no Christ. *CHRIST* is not a man! *Jesus* was the man; Christ the messenger; Christ in all ages, Jesus in one, Joshua in another... 991-1

For Joshua was the interpreter through whom the message was given to Israel. 3645-1

And the answer ever depends upon whether or not there is that choice as was pronounced by another leader [Joshua]—and a prototype of Him who gave His life a ransom for all—"Indeed, let others do as they may, but for me and my house, *we* will serve a living God." 1497-2

. . . the patient Joshua, the one who followed closely in the way that would give to the individual (who would study) the life and interpretation of the Son of man. These in the earth activity were much alike (Joshua and Jesus) not as combative, as in the warrings, but in spirit and in purpose, in ideals, these were one.

Thus . . . may ye use the Son of man, Jesus, the Master, as the ideal in the present, and find a new meaning—if there is the studying and paralleling of the life of Jesus and of Joshua. 3409-1

The Bible is silent regarding details of the early life of Joshua in Egyptian captivity. He is first mentioned some two months after the Israelites had departed Egypt and arrived at a place called Rephidim in the southern part of the Sinai Peninsula. In an attack here by a tribe of Amalekites, Moses sent for the young Joshua to defend the Israelites. Joshua had apparently already demonstrated his leadership capability to Moses, and he was successful on this occasion against the Amalekites.

Hereafter Joshua is often found in the company of Moses, and he is referred to as Moses' "minister" as they approached Mount Sinai. (Exodus 24:13) He presumably accompanied Moses up onto the mountain when Moses received holy revelations and directions from God. As they came down, Joshua alerted Moses to the noise in the Israelite camp, where the people had begun idolatrous worship. And when Moses communed with God in the newly constructed tent or tabernacle, Joshua was there. His recorded presence at such times fits the premise of the Cayce readings that Joshua was Moses' interpreter.

As the Israelites approached the Promised Land, Moses chose a man from each of the twelve tribes to scout the land. Joshua represented his tribe, Ephraim, and, after the return of the scouts, was supported only by Caleb in the recommendation to go on into Canaan. This lack of faith on the part of the Israelites resulted in God's decree that they must wander forty years in the desert and the promise that none of them except Joshua and Caleb would reach the Promised Land.

For forty years, the Israelites were desert nomads. During this period, the people became unified around their hardened determination to establish a nation in the land which lay ahead. As the new generation of people was raised up, it was now ready to enter the Promised Land.

In anticipation of his death, Moses asked God for someone to lead the Israelites, someone "who shall go out before them and come in before them, who shall lead them out and bring them in." (Numbers 27:17) God answered Moses' request and chose Joshua.

After the death of Moses, the Israelites were faced with the task of entering and conquering the Promised Land. Joshua decided to make a thrust into the center of Canaan and drive a wedge between the north and south. In pursuance of this goal, he chose the site to cross the Jordan River and enter the Promised Land—a spot just north of the Dead Sea and approximately five miles southeast of the city of Jericho.

Because of seasonal rains, the river was swollen, and God's intervention was required. He caused a stoppage of the river's flow until the Israelites were safely across. Interestingly, this phenomenon has occurred on other occasions, the latest of which was in 1927. Earth tremors 16 miles upstream caused a collapse of the high clay river banks, and the flow of the Jordan was interrupted for over 21 hours.[1]

After the crossing, they stopped at Gilgal on the west side of the Jordan. Twelve stones had been taken from the river's bed and were set up in a circle at Gilgal as a memorial to the miraculous crossing. The Israelites paused here and performed the ritual of circumcision on all males to symbolize the renewal of their covenant with God and the completion of the delivery from Egypt into the Promised Land. And for the first time in Canaan, the Passover feast was observed.

The city of Jericho lay ahead and appeared impregnable. Following the directions of Joshua, however, the Israelites circled Jericho each morning for six days, with seven priests in their midst carrying the Ark of the Covenant and blowing on rams' horns. On the seventh day they circled the city seven times, the priests blew a long final note, and the Israelites shouted. The city walls are then alleged to have crumbled, with the sacking and destroying of Jericho following. Modern archaeologists have found evidence of an earthquake or similar calamity in ancient times—the kind of destruction which the Bible describes under Joshua and the Israelites.

Now followed a systematic and bloody conquering of many of the cities in the Promised Land. Joshua primarily concentrated on cities in the hills, avoiding the flat ground where the better equipped chariots of the Canaanites would be at an advantage. One by one, the Israelites took Ai, Bethel, Shechem, Gibeon, Aijalon, Libnah, Lachish, Eglon, Hebron, Debir, and Hazor. Although some cities, such as Jerusalem, had been bypassed, the Israelites were now largely in control of the Promised Land of Canaan.

It was time to divide the land among the tribes, and Joshua

required that this division and allocation be done through the casting of lots in order that God's will could be manifested. The people of Israel then began the process of cultivating the land, building homes and towns, assimilating the non-Jewish people into their culture, and becoming a new nation.

At the age of 110, Joshua assembled the important tribesmen together and bade them farewell. He urged them to follow the Lord and resist the temptations of the pagan Canaanites. Shortly thereafter, Joshua died and was buried on Mount Ephraim, probably at Timnath-serath.

Joshua's life could be summarized no better than in his farewell statement to the people: "But as for me and my house, we will serve the Lord." (Joshua 24:15) Based upon this affirmation and the example of his life, the Israelites responded: "The Lord our God we will serve, and his voice we will obey." (Joshua 24:24) Joshua warned the people, however, that if they lost their faith they would lose their land.

A Cayce reading, quoted earlier, indicated that a study of the life of Joshua would help interpret the meaning of the life of Jesus and that in their earth activity—at least in their spirit and purpose—the two were much alike. Because of Joshua's bloody extermination of many of the conquered peoples, the parallel with Jesus seems difficult. The reading, however, did make an exception for Joshua's combative behavior and warrings, but even here there may be parallels worthy of consideration.

First, it should be remembered that the conquest of Canaan was conducted as a *herem* or holy war. Such a war was believed to have been ordered and directed exclusively by God. The victory belonged to the faithful if they obeyed God's commands explicitly. The war against Canaan was waged solely for the purpose of gaining a home for God's people, the Israelites, and it was believed that the land could be purified only by the extermination of the pagans who had lived there.[2] This holy war may have been symbolic of the war ultimately to be waged by the messiah against Belial, Satan, or the devil in behalf of God and God's people. It foreshadowed the role to be played by Jesus.

There may be another significance for Jesus as a result of the wars waged by Joshua in Canaan. Jesus' ministry was performed in the very location of the Canaanite cities which

Joshua conquered. It may have been necessary for Jesus to heal and minister to the peoples of the area where he, as Joshua, had killed and destroyed the earlier inhabitants. God's laws of karmic justice may have been at play here. While not enough historical information is known to allow for a complete comparison of the details of Joshua's campaigns with Jesus' ministries, some interesting observations can be made.

Joshua's final major victory in Canaan was at Hazor over several armies which had united in alliance against the Israelites. After the battle, Joshua captured and burned the city. Hazor had been located near the Sea of Galilee; this is where Jesus spent much of his time and performed many of his miracles. The nearby town of Capernaum was the main base of Jesus' ministry.

One of Joshua's greatest victories occurred in the valley of Aijalon where his army defeated the confederated kings of the area. It was here also that Joshua defied physical laws and commanded the sun and moon to stand still. The Bible says, "There has been no day like it before or since, when the Lord hearkened to the voice of a man." (Joshua 10:14) At the time of Jesus, the city of Emmaus was in this area. Jesus, after his resurrection and triumph over the physical laws of death, appeared here to two of his followers as they traveled on the road into Emmaus.

Joshua had bypassed the city of Jerusalem fearing its strength. As Jesus, however, he ignored the advice of friends and entered and faced the dangers of Jerusalem. It was here, of course, that he met his death.

Fairly early in the military conquest, five kings from territories about to be taken by Joshua hid themselves in a cave at Makkedah, but they were discovered by the Israelites. Because of the haste to pursue the fleeing enemies, Joshua commanded the cave to be sealed until they could return and dispose of the kings. He said, "Roll great stones against the mouth of the cave, and set men by it to guard them." (Joshua 10:18) Subsequently the Israelites returned to the camp at Makkedah. When the cave was opened and the kings brought forth, Joshua directed his captains to put their feet on the necks of the kings and mock them. Thereafter Joshua smote them and hanged each upon a tree until the evening. He then commanded the dead kings to be taken down and put in the cave before sundown and the cave to be sealed by putting great stones in its mouth. The Bible identifies the kings; the first named was the king of Jerusalem.

There can be no stronger parallel between these events and those of the crucifixion of Jesus. They may help explain the necessity of some of the gruesome details of his Passion. The precedent of the dead being removed from the trees before sunset in Joshua's time was still part of the Jewish tradition which resulted in Jesus' being hurriedly taken from the cross and placed in his cave tomb before nightfall.

Another of the five kings was the king of Hebron, a city about 20 miles south of Jerusalem. There is a cave here, although a mosque is built over it today, and non-Moslems are not permitted to enter the premises. This cave of Machpelah may be the one in which the five kings were buried. Some scholars believe it to be the cave where the Jewish patriarchs were supposedly buried[3] and thus where even, according to some legend, the body of Adam may have been laid.

There are other connections.

Joshua's conquest of the Promised Land began with the crossing of the Jordan River. Jesus' ministry began with his baptism in the Jordan. According to tradition, both incidents occurred at the exact same spot.[4] Arculf, a pilgrim to the Jordan in A.D. 670, reports a cross in the middle of the stream at this point near Jericho identifying Jesus' baptismal location.[5]

This is also the same spot where Adam is supposed to have begun his life as an exile from Eden by standing in the River Jordan for forty days and repenting to God.[6] Adam, of course, was an earlier life of Joshua and Jesus, according to Edgar Cayce.

After crossing the Jordan and while encamped at Gilgal near Jericho, Joshua paused for a time before beginning his ministry of conquest. He wanted the Israelites to remember their heritage and renew their vows with God before beginning the struggles ahead. Similarly, after his baptism in the Jordan River, Jesus paused for forty days (that number again!) in the desert wilderness to renew his commitment to God and prepare himself for the mission which lay ahead. According to tradition, Jesus went up on a small mountain at the edge of the Jordan valley overlooking Jericho.[7] This spot would be in the vicinity of Gilgal.

During the period of waiting, the prospect of overcoming the fortified city of Jericho must have been frightening for Joshua. But the Bible records that an angel of the Lord appeared to him. The angel had come as "commander of the army of the Lord" to hearten and encourage Joshua to move forward in his conquests. When Jesus went into the wilderness, he too must have had trepidations about the task which lay ahead of him, for the New Testament records that he was tempted by the devil with easier ways of accomplishing his mission. He overcame the temptations, however, and "the angels came and ministered to him." (Matthew 4:11)

Jesus did not eat during his forty days in the wilderness, and one of the temptations presented by the devil was for Jesus to assuage his hunger by turning the stones into bread. In his reply, Jesus said, "man shall not live by bread alone," and indicated that he had a new food—the word of God. Interestingly, it was here, after the first feast of the Passover during the time of Joshua, that the children of Israel ceased receiving manna. They too had new food: the produce of God's Promised Land.

God had assured Moses on Mount Sinai that an angel would be sent to prepare the way "into the place which I have prepared." God then said:

> Give heed to him and hearken to his voice, do not rebel against him, for he will not pardon your transgression; for my name is in him. But if you hearken attentively to his voice and do all that I say, then I will be an enemy to your enemies and an adversary to your adversaries. When my angel goes before you, and brings you in to the Amorites, and the Hittites, and the Perizzites, and the Canaanites, the Hivites, and the Jebusites, and I [will] blot them out . . .   (Exodus 23:20-23)

As discussed in the Enoch chapter, Jewish tradition identifies this angel as Metatron or Yaho'el, the name for the translated Enoch soul. According to Edgar Cayce, Enoch and Joshua were the same soul. In the above promise to Moses, God would thus be referring to Joshua's angelic counterpart, or possibly Joshua himself—who may simply have been described by God in angelic terms. This "angel" would lead the Israelites into the Promised Land and vanquish their foes. Certainly this is an accurate description of what Joshua accomplished in his years as the leader of God's chosen people.

According to the Cayce readings, Joshua was responsible for the writing, not only of the book of Joshua, but also of the first five books of the Old Testament. Scholars generally concede that the book of Joshua is made up from the same sources as the first five books and was apparently put in final written form at the same time.[8] There also is rabbinical and talmudic tradition that Joshua wrote the book bearing his name and that Eleazar, the son of Aaron, wrote the portion pertaining to Joshua's death.[9]

We have already seen in an earlier chapter similarities drawn in the New Testament book of Hebrews between Jesus and Melchizedek. Preceding the comparisons with Melchizedek, however, parallels are drawn in the third and fourth chapters of Hebrews between Jesus and Joshua. Referring to Jesus, the author says:

> 7 Therefore, as the Holy Spirit says, "Today when you hear his voice,
> 8 do not harden your hearts, as in the rebellion, on the day of testing in the wilderness,
> 9 where your fathers put me to the test and saw my works for forty years."
> 14 For we share in Christ, if only we hold our first confidence firm to the end,
> 15 while it is said, "Today when you hear his voice, do not harden your hearts, as in the rebellion."

It was Joshua, of course, who urged the children of Israel to have faith in God and enter the Promised Land without delay. But the people hardened their hearts and would not listen. The people of a later day are being exhorted not to repeat the error, but to hear Jesus' voice and follow him as they failed to do with Joshua. The Epistle makes no distinction between the voice of Joshua and that of Jesus; they are made to sound as one. Chapter four continues in this same theme:

8 For if Joshua had given them rest [in the Promised Land], he would not speak later of another day.

9 So then there remains a sabbath rest for the people of God.

11 Let us therefore strive to enter that rest that no one fall by the same sort of disobedience.

14 Since then we have a great high priest who has passed through the heavens, Jesus, the Son of God, let us hold fast our confession.

The message here seems to be that another day has been given to God's people to follow the promise of faith given earlier by Joshua and rejected. The new promise and example are found in Jesus.

Early Church Father Irenaeus postulated that Joshua, who led the people into the Holy Land, succeeded Moses as the symbol of the superseded law.[10] That role was assumed—or resumed—by Jesus.

The similarity of the names Yehoshua (Joshua) and Yeshua (Jesus) brought about an early identification in Christian symbolism of Joshua being a "type" or prefiguration of Jesus. Many events of Joshua's life were interpreted by the early Christians as prophetic anticipations of Jesus' life.[11]

The Amalekites, or Amalek, always appear at war with the Israelites in the Old Testament. Thus Joshua, in his first recorded battle, fights and defeats Amalek, the Jewish symbol of the devil.

And the Lord said to Moses, "Write this as a memorial in a book and recite it in the ears of Joshua, that I will utterly blot out the remembrance of Amalek from under heaven."
(Exodus 17:14)

The Amalekites will in fact continue to harass the Israelites for generations to come. It is the devil, for which the Amalekites were mere symbols, that will utterly be put out of remembrance, and it will be done by Joshua when he returns as Jesus. Significantly, God wanted Moses to record this ultimate destruction and "recite it in the ears of Joshua."

While Joshua did the fighting, Moses, who represents the

Jewish nation, watched and stretched out his arms in the "cross" position (cf. Exodus 17:11 and 12). This symbology was noted by early Christians.[12]

The disciples and followers of Jesus believed that his Second Coming was imminent. The lack of faith of those who heard the message concerning the Second Coming may account for its delay. There may have been a requirement for another "forty years" of wandering in the desert—a period which has stretched to the present.

Certainly there is similarity in the spirit and purpose of Joshua with that of Jesus. Each exhibited a total faith in God and possessed a dogged determination and fearless tenacity to hold to his ideals. Each of them also felt that his purpose in life was God's purpose.

The entire life of Joshua has symbolic significance for humanity. Just as we must first find ourselves in the bondage of sin and separation from God, Joshua's life began in slavery in Egypt among a people who recognized their need for escape and delivery. An end to this captivity was not possible without the help of God, just as our salvation is dependent upon God's mercy and grace. The road out of slavery into the Promised Land was most difficult and, if we falter in our faith, it may require delays and detours such as the forty years which the Israelites spent in the desert. Possibly, as with the Israelites, a lapse of faith may mean that we cannot reach the Promised Land in the present lifetime. It may involve a new generation, a new life or lives, before we are ready to enter the glory prepared and promised for us even before we entered material captivity. Or it may mean that a holy war, such as Joshua conducted, may also be necessary to purge us of pagan influences before we are suitable and ready for the Promised Land.

Maybe of utmost importance will be the need for a leader, someone who can show us the way, a Joshua—a Jesus—pointing the direction to this Promised Land. The way will be made clear; it will be based upon faith in God and a complete submission to God's will. And the signpost and guide for each of us to follow will read: "Choose you this day whom you will serve ... but as for me and my house, we will serve the Lord." (Joshua 24:15)

CHAPTER ELEVEN

Asaph

I am continually with thee; thou dost hold my right hand.
Thou dost guide me with thy counsel, and afterward thou wilt receive me to glory.
Whom have I in heaven but thee? and there is nothing upon earth that I desire besides thee.
My flesh and my heart fail, but God is the strength of my heart and my portion forever.
(From Psalm 73 by Asaph)
[verses 25, 23-24, 26]

God was their king, and the elders of each tribe were their several leaders. However, this loose confederation of tribes was no match for the powerful Philistines, and the Israelites pleaded with the prophet Samuel to appoint a king like that of the neighboring countries. Reluctantly Samuel did so, and Saul became king of Israel.

As Samuel had feared, Saul soon lost his orientation toward God and became obsessed with a desire for personal power and a jealousy of a young shepherd named David. Finally, Saul and his sons were killed in battle, and David, the slayer of Goliath and many of the enemy, assumed the throne and began the process of uniting his people. What followed was Israel's most glorious years under King David and his son and successor, Solomon.

Edgar Cayce readings 364-7 and 364-8 indicate that one of

the incarnations of the Master soul was as Asaph, the psalmist and musician of the courts of Kings David and Solomon.

The name "Asaph" in Hebrew means "God has gathered or sustained." Asaph was a descendant of the tribe of Levi and appointed by David to be his chief musician.

Let us look at what the Bible has to say about Asaph and his activities.

In I Chronicles 16, David's return of the Ark of the Covenant to Jerusalem is described. This is the city known as Salem when Asaph lived there earlier as Melchizedek; he was king of the city then. Now Asaph leads the ministry and celebration for the king as the Ark is deposited in the tent at Jerusalem. He begins the ceremony by sounding the cymbals. David then delivers into Asaph's hand a psalm of thanksgiving to be read before the people. Just as Joshua served as Moses' interpreter or mouthpiece to the people, Asaph is performing a similar role for Israel's new leader, King David. After the service, Asaph and the other priests are left to minister continually before the Ark.

In I Chronicles 6 and 15, Asaph is listed again as one of the three whom David set over the service of song in the house of the Lord after the arrival of the Ark. Verse 32 (Chapter 6) indicates these three ministered before the tabernacle tent with singing "until Solomon had built the house of the Lord in Jerusalem." Their ministry then continued in the Temple.

Chapter 25 of I Chronicles gives more information about the duties and composition of the musicians and singers, of whom Asaph was chief. They prophesied through the words of their music, which were presented with the accompaniment of harps, psalteries, and cymbals. Verse 2 indicates Asaph "prophesied under the direction of the king." Just as Joshua had divided the Promised Land through the casting of lots, so also were the duties of the 288 musicians and singers determined. They approached the lottery equally, "the small as well as the great, the teacher as well as the scholar." Verse 9 says the first lot came forth for Asaph and his son Joseph.

Chapter 26 of I Chronicles also includes the duties of porter or gatekeeper for the sons of Asaph. Apparently they were considered a kind of elite spiritual guard.

In II Chronicles 5 is a description of the ceremony for the

dedication of the new Temple built by Solomon. The singers, composed of Asaph, Heman, and Jeduthun with their sons and brethren, were arrayed in white linen and stood at the east end of the altar with their cymbals, psalteries, and harps. One hundred and twenty priests stood with them sounding their trumpets, and the voices of all were lifted up in song of praise for the Lord. It must have been a magnificent and awesome ceremony. Verses 13 and 14 say the house was inundated by a cloud, "for the glory of the Lord filled the house of God."

A specific duty of Asaph's was that of prophecy, and he is listed in II Chronicles 35:15 as one of the king's seers. He apparently was very close to David and an important figure, for in Nehemiah 12:46, there is a reference back to "the days of David and Asaph of old" when "there was a chief of the singers, and there were songs of praise and thanksgiving to God." Just as Joseph had found favor with the pharoah in Egypt, Asaph was now a favorite of King David.

The "sons of Asaph" is a term subsequently used in the Old Testament for a guild of Temple singers named after Asaph and claiming to be descended from him. They will play an important role, for example, in the ceremonies to be discussed in the chapter on Jeshua when the Temple is restored in Jerusalem after the Jewish return from exile and captivity in Babylon.

Little information is given in the Bible about the character of the man Asaph—except what can be discovered in the psalms written by him. Having words and verses created and expressed by one who is alleged to have been an incarnation of Jesus is a rare and unique opportunity. From these literary works we have a window through which to catch a glimpse of the soul of Asaph—and of the Master.

The authorship of 12 psalms is attributed in the Hebrew texts of the Bible to Asaph. They are Psalms 50 and 73 through 83. Let us take a closer look at each of them, beginning with Psalm 73.

In this psalm, Asaph expresses envy of the wicked for whom he sees widespread prosperity. They are not troubled or plagued as are other people, and "they have more than heart could wish." Asaph evidences his own humanity and yet goes on to repent of his folly. He recognizes and acknowledges his error when he enters "the sanctuary of God." Then he can say:

27 For, lo, those that are far from thee shall perish;
thou dost put an end to those who are false to thee.
28 But for me it is good to be near God; I have
made the Lord God my refuge, that I may tell of all
thy works.

He affirms his faith in God as did Joshua when Joshua declared
that he and his house would serve the living Lord. Asaph's
triumphant faith over human doubt also brings to mind the
scene of Jesus in the Garden of Gethsemane where he
questioned God and asked that the cup pass from him, but then
declared: "Nevertheless not as I will, but as thou wilt."
(Matthew 26:39)

In Psalm 74, Asaph again expresses his doubts and asks God,
"why dost thou cast us off forever?" He laments the defiling of
God's sanctuary by the enemy and pleads for God to be
assertive. Although he questions how long these conditions
must continue, he once more exhibits his faith and attests:

12 Yet God my King is from of old, working
salvation in the midst of the earth.

We see Asaph's inherent spirituality coming to the fore, and he
intimates that his commitment to God extends back in time.
We also witness in this psalm his love for God's sanctuary and
can anticipate his anger and force when, as Jesus, he drives the
merchants and despoilers from the Temple.

In Psalm 75, Asaph sees the ultimate triumph of the
righteous and expresses his thanksgiving and praise to the
Lord. He says again in words reminiscent of Joshua:

9 But I will rejoice forever; I will sing praises to the
God of Jacob.

Psalm 76 acknowledges the victorious power of God. Verse 2
helps identify Salem as Jerusalem with the assertion that
Salem is the location of God's tabernacle or Temple. The psalm
concludes with the statement that God will cut off the spirit of
the princes. This reference may be to the ultimate role of the
messiah in destroying Belial or Satan, the prince of this world.

Asaph in Psalm 77 again recounts his human doubts and
complains about God's delay in meting justice to the wicked. He
says his soul refuses to be comforted through the night. But he

finds solace when he meditates upon God's works and wonders of old. We find here a declaration of the value of meditation in the quest for spirituality and attunement with God.

Asaph's concern over the slowness of God's curtailment of the wicked and yet his ultimate expression of the certainty of God's judgment is almost a duplication of Chapter 24 of the Book of Job. Of course, according to Edgar Cayce, both documents were written by the same soul.

Psalm 78 finds Asaph reciting Israel's history of forgetting God and yet being forgiven and sustained by God. He reminds the youth of the country that war, captivity, destruction, and affliction have been brought on by the error of the people. He says it is the same reason Joseph's (Ephraim's) house has been forsaken by God in favor of that of Judah—and the Temple built in the territory allotted to Judah. This lesson may also be one that is personal to Asaph—a reminder that although he was favored by God as Joseph, such status can be lost through lack of dedication to God.

In Psalm 79, Asaph again laments the abominations of the wicked and their defilement of the Temple. In wavering faith, he asks how long this situation must continue and begs that God will pour out wrath on the erring nations:

> 12 Return sevenfold into the bosom of our neighbors the taunts with which they have taunted thee, O Lord!

How much more mature will be his spirituality when, as Jesus, he will tell his disciples they should forgive their brothers seventy times seven—not seek sevenfold punishment.

A plea for the restoration of the people by God is renewed in Psalm 80. Asaph addresses God as "thou who leadest Joseph like a flock." Poetically, Joseph here symbolizes Israel. Asaph also refers to Israel as God's vine or vineyard:

> 15 And the vineyard which thy right hand hath planted, and the branch that thou madest strong for thyself.
> 17 Let thy hand be upon the man of thy right hand, upon the son of man whom thou madest strong for thyself. (KJV)

Who is this right-hand man of God that planted the vine of Israel? In view of Asaph's use of the name of Joseph for Israel, it may be Joseph. On the other hand, historically it was Joshua who planted God's people in the Promised Land. In either case, it would be a prior incarnation of the Master soul. And in the second quoted verse, this right-hand man of God is described in messianic terms. The term "branch" is used in other parts of the Bible in referring to the messiah. As we shall see later, the phrase "son of man" had special messianic meaning. Jesus himself will claim and use this title.

In praying that the hand of God might be upon "the man of thy right hand," Asaph seems simply to be seeking God's guidance and support as his own. By so doing, Asaph may be identifying himself as the son of man or messiah. If there be any doubt about this identification, it would seem to be dispelled by the right-hand terminology of Psalm 73, quoted in part at the front of this chapter. There, Asaph says, God "dost hold my right hand."

Psalm 81 is a call to proper worship. Asaph asks that a musical and joyful noise be made unto the Lord. In pointing out why God deserted Israel for its errors, he says in verse 7: "I [God] tested thee at the waters of Meribah." Meribah is the place where Moses erred, with the result that the leadership of God's people was assumed by Joshua before entry into the Promised Land of Canaan.

In his psalms, Asaph frequently refers to Joseph, and, as indicated earlier, the Bible says one of Asaph's sons is named Joseph. Psalm 81 contains a significant reference to Joseph:

> 5 This [worship of God] he ordained in Joseph for
> a testimony, when he went out through the land of
> Egypt, where I heard a language that I understood
> not. (KJV)

By changing from the third to first person here, Asaph seems clearly to be saying that *he* heard a language in Egypt which *he* did not understand and would appear to be identifying himself as Joseph.

Psalm 82 is short and refers to God's role as judge. Asaph says that "all the foundations of the earth are out of course" and implores all to "defend the poor and fatherless; do justice to the afflicted and needy." These directives are to be echoed centuries later in the words of Jesus. In verse 7, there again is a reference suggesting the ultimate downfall of Satan, the "prince of this world":

> Nevertheless you shall die like men, and fall like any prince.

Verse 6 provides:

> I have said, Ye are gods; and all of you are children of the Most High. (KJV)

We will be looking at this verse again, but for the moment let us examine some of its implications. First, it is in accord with a maxim of the Edgar Cayce readings that we are all children of God and are on the return journey back to the Father and our own godhood. Secondly, Asaph seems to be claiming that he has made this statement before ("I have said"). (The Jerusalem Bible gives his words as "I once said.") If so, where? And what is the significance of noting it here? One possibility is that he said it as Enoch or Hermes and meant to be making that identification. Such a philosophy is contained in both the Enochian and Hermetic literature.

Asaph in Psalm 83 returns to the theme of bemoaning the plight of Israel and even names her enemies. He is without mercy in asking God to:

> 17 Let them be put to shame and dismayed for ever; let them perish in disgrace.
> 18 Let them know that thou alone, whose name alone is the Lord, art the Most High over all the earth.

At least in this plea Asaph has for his purpose the glorification of God, not just the restoration of good for Israel.

Now to Psalm 50. Asaph describes God's judgment when God shall judge the people. He then shifts into the first person and says:

> 5 Gather to me my faithful ones who made a covenant with me by sacrifice.

This soul Asaph, according to Edgar Cayce, had made a covenant in the beginning as Amilius together with other saints or souls who had not yet become entrapped in matter. These Sons of God agreed to make a sacrificial entry into matter in an effort to bring the lost souls back to God. It would be appropriate then for Asaph to be renewing his call to these saints.

Psalm 50 continues by declaring the glory of God's handiwork in earth, and then Asaph says:

14 Offer to God a sacrifice of thanksgiving, and pay
your vows to the Most High;
15 and call upon me in the day of trouble; I will
deliver you, and you shall glorify me.

Again he shifts from the third person to the first and seems to be speaking of himself in a messianic role of delivering his people and receiving their glory. If there is any question about this interpretation, let us go on.

22 Mark this then, you who forget God, lest I rend
and there be none to deliver!
23 He who brings thanksgiving as his sacrifice
honors me; to him who orders his way aright I will
show the salvation of God.

Clearly Asaph is referring to himself as the one to show the salvation of God. This is the unique mission of the messiah and the accomplishment accorded by Christians to Jesus Christ. Asaph is claiming it as his own.

Not only is there language in the Old Testament which seems to identify Asaph with the messiah or Jesus, as we have seen, but Jesus himself identified with Asaph.

In the tenth chapter of John, Jesus asserted his Deity by stating that he and his Father are one. The people threatened to stone him for the blasphemy of making himself an equal with God.

34 Jesus answered them, "Is it not written in your
law, 'I said, you are gods'? . . ."

The only place this kind of statement appears in the law or Old Testament is in Psalm 82, written by Asaph. Jesus elected not to include the words of the psalm indicating we are all children of the Most High—words which would have been germane to the point under discussion. And he did not give a verbatim quote from the psalm, which actually reads: "I have said." (KJV) Jesus dropped the word "have." It can reasonably be argued that the words "I said" were not used by Jesus in a shoddy and inaccurate attempt to quote the psalm, but rather conveyed the literal meaning that he, as Asaph, had made the statement.

Psalm 110 was written by David. It represents a communication from God to one called "my lord" and is an oracle about the messiah. The Psalm preceding it, like several others, is directed by David to his chief musician. If this should be the case with this psalm, then David is calling Asaph his "lord" and thereafter links him with both the messiah and Melchizedek. The New Testament book of Hebrews specifically connects Jesus with Psalm 110.

The Edgar Cayce psychic readings indicate the Master soul was a scribe and wrote parts of the Old Testament. Some portions of the Bible are thought by scholars to date from this period, especially the wisdom literature, the first great literary works of Israel, and even the story of Joseph.[1] It has been noted that the Egyptian names in the Joseph story are those in vogue at the time of David and Solomon.[2]

In the Jewish work *Martyrdom and Ascension of Isaiah*, which may date to as early as the second century B.C., Asaph is referred to in paragraph 6 as the "recorder" and a doer of righteousness in which is the fragrance of the Spirit.[3] Part of the manuscript, *Book of Noah* (traceable to the second century B.C.), refers to Asaph as "the writer and historian of the Hebrews" who explains and teaches the history of the signs of the zodiac but uses the names of the sons of Jacob in referring to the signs.[4]

In the *Pseudo-Philo History of Israel*, a reference is made to prophetic statements about Samuel which are attributed to Asaph.[5] These statements are contained in Psalm 99 wherein the psalmist puts Samuel in the company of Moses and Aaron as priests of the Lord. If this reference to Asaph is correct, then Asaph would be the author of Psalm 99. The psalm's authorship is not known; it is a short and beautiful work praising God and revering the Creator's greatness and holiness.

Recently discovered Essene documents give us a new perspective on Asaph. There has been considerable speculation as to the identity of the Essene Teacher of Righteousness who was venerated as the True Teacher and prefiguration of the messiah. One scholar has applied a form of Hebrew cipher to an otherwise meaningless name (TAXO) for the Teacher of Righteousness in the Essene work known as the *Assumption of Moses.* The name then becomes Asaph. For this reason and others, the scholar is convinced that the Teacher of Righteousness, the True Teacher who would be the messiah, was Asaph.[6] He also finds a link between Asaph and Joseph, whom he too connects with the Teacher of Righteousness. The frequent references to Joseph in Asaph's psalms and the fact Joseph was used by Asaph as a synonym for Israel are noted.[7]

The Biblical Asaph became a legendary figure in both Jewish and Muslim literature. He is presented as master of occult arts, a princely figure, a medical master, the confidant of King Solomon, one who knew the Ineffable Name of God, and one who had the power to perform miracles.[8] An ancient manuscript, variously entitled *Sefer Asaf, Midrash Refu'ot,* and *Sefer Refu'ot,* has been attributed to Asaph, and he therein is referred to as Asaph the Younger, Asaph the Sage, Asaph the Physician, and Asaph the Astronomer.[9]

There has ever been speculation that the fables collected under the venerable name Aesop may actually have been writings of Asaph. Similarities are noted, not only between the names, but also the two historical personages.[10]

In looking at the literary expressions of Asaph—that is, the Biblical Psalms attributed to him—we witness a very spiritual soul. And yet through the heart of the poet, we can observe human frailties such as doubt, impatience, anger, and even vengeance. It is a soul that has not yet reached the spiritual heights of a Jesus, but one in which a positive, dynamic faith in God cannot be denied. There is an awesome reverence for the house or sanctuary of God, which is appropriate for one who guards it and leads the musical service in the worship of the Almighty. The guild which will hereafter bear his name is testimony in itself to Asaph's musical, literary, and prophetic talent and the high esteem in which he was held by his people.

If Asaph was indeed an incarnation of the Master soul, it is one in which we can see growth in artistry and spirituality. It will lead ultimately to completion and wholeness in the man known as the Christ.

EDGAR CAYCE FOUNDATION and
A.R.E. LIBRARY/VISITORS CENTER
Virginia Beach, Va.
OVER 50 YEARS OF SERVICE

CHAPTER TWELVE

Jeshua

For behold, upon the stone which I have set before Joshua [Jeshua], upon a single stone with seven facets, I will engrave its inscription, says the Lord of hosts, and I will remove the guilt of this land in a single day. In that day, says the Lord of hosts, every one of you will invite his neighbor under his vine and under his fig tree.

(Zechariah 3:9-10)

The nation of Israel reached its zenith of power and prestige under the reigns of David and Solomon. Thereafter the people began to lose their dedication and trust in God; pagan influences and worship became acceptable; and the glory of the nation began to recede.

The Jewish people were forewarned, however, about the error of their ways and the consequences that would follow. Through numerous prophets, Israel told of impending disaster unless it returned to its religious heritage and belief in the one God. Although many of the prophets and their messages were not popular in their day, subsequent generations would revere their words and remember their warnings. The writings of these prophets would become an important part of the Jewish scriptures—a feature which would differentiate the Jews from the Samaritans to the north. The names of these prophets include Elijah, Elisha, Isaiah, and Jeremiah.

Eventually the worst of the prophecies came true:
Nebuchadnezzar of Babylon invaded Israel, and Jerusalem was
captured and plundered in 587 B.C. The Temple was razed and
destroyed, and during the next five years, a large number of the
leading Jewish people were deported to Babylon. Those who
remained in Israel were gradually amalgamated into the
cultures of neighboring nations which moved into Judah. Thus,
the dissipation of the Jewish people as a distinct grouping was
begun, and Israel's status as an independent nation was ended
until the twentieth century A.D.

The Jewish captives in Babylon, however, were able to
maintain some semblance of their national life style and
religion. Ezekiel became their chief prophet and religious
catalyst. He reminded them of the warnings of their prophets
and promised that, if the faith were kept, a return to their
country would be possible after the period of national
punishment was over.

In 539 B.C., Cyrus of Persia captured Babylon and was
welcomed as a liberator. The following year, he issued the Edict
of Restoration by which all Babylonian Jews could return to
their homeland and the Temple could be rebuilt in Jerusalem at
the expense of the royal treasury. The return from exile began.[1]

Jeshua is listed in the Bible among the exiles who returned to
Jerusalem from Babylon. His name is given as Joshua in the
books of Haggai and Zechariah, while Ezra and Nehemiah
called him Jeshua. The two names are actually the same;
Jeshua is the Aramaic form of the Hebraic word "Joshua,"
which in effect means "savior."[2] The Greek word is Jesus. To
differentiate him from the Joshua of an earlier period, we will
use the Aramaic name "Jeshua."

According to Edgar Cayce, Jeshua is another incarnation of
the Master soul who became Christed as Jesus. (364-7 and
5749-14)

(... study the Book which tells of Him, Jesus, born in Bethlehem
of the virgin Mary), know this is the same soul-entity who reasoned
with those who returned from captivity in those days when
Nehemiah, Ezra, Zerubbabel were factors in the attempts of the re-
establishing of the worship of God, and that Jeshua, the scribe,
translated the rest of the books written up to that time.   5023-2

Another reading which says he was an incarnation of the

Master soul refers to him as "Jeshua of Jerusalem." (3054-4)

According to the Bible, Jeshua was a high priest and the son of Jozadak. He was a grandson of Seraiah, the last high priest of the old Temple in Jerusalem. Together with Zerubbabel, Jeshua organized the return to Zion.[3] He headed the priestly family of Jedaiah, which returned to Judah and would hereafter be known by Jeshua's name.

Jeshua's leadership in the return to the Promised Land repeated the role he performed for the Israelites as Joshua. Only this time, he would be a man of peace instead of a bloody warrior.

Jeshua and Zerubbabel established the order of sacrifices and helped carry them out. They also planned the reconstruction of the new Temple. The exiles from Babylon began construction of the new Temple, but the native people of Jerusalem refused to help. They had abandoned their old ways and belief in the one true God. The Temple rebuilding therefore languished and had to be abandoned. Jeshua and Zerubbabel rejected an offer of the Samaritans to help in the rebuilding, but the arrival of new exiles from Babylon eventually allowed the project to be renewed. It was completed in 515 B.C. at the beginning of the reign of Darius I.[4]

Jeshua's participation in the decision to reject the offer of Samaritan help should be noted. As Jesus, one of his parables will tell about a wounded traveler accepting help from a Samaritan, and the spirituality and generosity of the Samaritan will be lauded.

The new Temple was not nearly as magnificent as Solomon's had been, but its size, design, and style were the same.[5] The walls of Jerusalem still lay in ruins, however, and were rebuilt only after the intervention of Nehemiah, a Jew who had gained a position of influence in Persia and had come to Judah to serve as an administrator.[6]

After the completion of the walls, a triumphal ceremony was held, and the sons of Asaph played an important role in the services. (Thus influence of a prior life of the Master continued.) Although still under the rule of another country, Israel's national pride and sense of mission began to return.

Another important leader of the time was Ezra, a priest and scholar. Although he was sent to Israel by the Persians, he was instrumental in bringing the Jewish people back to God and away from pagan idolatry. The Bible's historical book of Ezra bears his name.

As indicated in the earlier quote from Edgar Cayce, Nehemiah, Ezra, Zerubbabel, and Jeshua were all involved over a period of time in the attempts to re-establish the worship of God.

A contemporary of Jeshua's was the prophet Zechariah, who also wrote a book of the Old Testament. Zechariah was another who helped push for the rebuilding of the Temple. He writes in the early part of his book about eight mystical visions which he has had and which are full of symbolic images. No Old Testament prophet has more to say in so short a space about the coming of the messiah than Zechariah.

> He predicts the second coming of Christ, His reign, His priesthood, His kingship, His humanity, His Deity, His building of the Temple of the Lord, His coming in lowliness, His bringing of permanent peace, His rejection and betrayal for thirty pieces of silver, His return to Israel as the crucified One, and His being smitten by the sword of the Lord.[7]

What is even more significant for our purposes is Zechariah's actual identification of the messiah.

Chapter Three begins:

> 1 Then he showed me Joshua [Jeshua], the high priest, standing before the angel of the Lord, and Satan standing at his right hand to accuse him.
> 2 And the Lord said to Satan, "The Lord rebuke you, O Satan. The Lord, who has chosen Jerusalem, rebuke you. Is not this a brand plucked from the fire?"

Jeshua had, in a manner of speaking, been "plucked from the fire." His grandfather Seraiah had been killed by Nebuchadnezzar, and Seraiah's children had barely escaped.[8]

As Jeshua is presented to Zechariah, he is dressed in filthy clothes, which is a sign of mourning.[9] After rebuking Satan, the Lord orders the high priest Joshua, or Jeshua, to be clothed with fair raiment. He then says:

7 Thus says the Lord of hosts: If you will walk in my
ways and keep my charge, then you shall rule my
house and have charge of my courts, and I will give
you the right of access among those who are
standing here.
8 Hear now, O Joshua the high priest, you and your
friends who sit before you, for they are men of good
omen: behold, I will bring my servant the Branch.

Scholars are universally agreed that the term "Branch" is a
reference to the messiah or Christ. Isaiah 4:2 described the
messiah as the "Branch." Jeremiah 23:5 has more to say on the
subject:

Behold, the days are coming, says the Lord,
when I will raise up for David a righteous Branch,
and he shall reign as king and deal wisely, and shall
execute justice and righteousness in the land.

Israel, through the throne of David, represents the vine, and the
messiah, or savior, is depicted as its "Branch."

As discussed in the Asaph chapter, Psalm 80, written by
Asaph, refers to "the branch that thou [God] madest strong."
Verse 17 of that psalm also talks about the right-hand man of
God and the son of man. These references in the psalm seemed
to be to Joseph, Joshua, or Asaph—or to all three of them. Here
in Zechariah, the reference is to Jeshua. And, of course
according to Edgar Cayce, all of these names would fit as proper
labels of identification for the "Branch" who is to be the
messiah and the Christ.

At the conclusion of Zechariah's eight visions, the angel of
the Lord says in Chapter 6:11-13:

Take from them silver and gold, and make a
crown, and set it upon the head of Joshua, the son
of Jehozadak, the high priest; and say to him,
"Thus says the Lord of hosts, 'Behold, the man
whose name is the Branch: for he shall grow up in
his place, and he shall build the temple of the Lord.
It is he who shall build the temple of the Lord, and
shall bear royal honor, and shall sit and rule upon
his throne. And there shall be a priest by his
throne, and peaceful understanding shall be

between them both.' "

Jeshua is clearly identified as the messianic "Branch" who shall build God's temple and sit and rule upon God's throne. He is the promised messiah whom Christians will know as Christ Jesus.

As noted in the chapter pertaining to him, Melchizedek has been mentioned as one of the four messianic figures implied by the four "smiths" or artisans of Zechariah 1:20 and 21. According to the Lord, these artisans shall cast out those who have scattered God's people. We thus have an Old Testament authority finding a possible link in the missions of Melchizedek and Jeshua.

The professional duties of scribe were found in earlier lives of the Master soul. According to Cayce, Jeshua again is a scribe who translated all the books of the Bible written up to this time. We again find the hand of the Master upon the written word of God.

Authorities have noted the editorial work of a chronicler which occurred sometime after 561 B.C.[10] The first period covered in this editorial project is from Joshua's entry into Canaan until the middle of the exile. Two key themes which were emphasized were the word of the Lord and the worship of God by the kings and people. A second part of the history of Israel extends through the return to Jerusalem and the rebuilding of the Temple. Whoever the author, he was a devotee of King David, concerned with matters having to do with Jerusalem, and fascinated by the part played by priests and Levites—and by prophecy.[11] These attributes sound like a combination of Asaph and Jeshua, and the dating for the writings fits the time period of Jeshua.

At a time when the fortunes of Israel are at a low ebb—in fact, when many of God's people are again in captivity—we find God showing mercy and providing a way for the restoration of Jewish national honor and pride. And again we find the Master soul playing an important part in the return of his people to the Promised Land, the rebuilding of the Temple, and a revival of faith in the one God.

While little is given in the Bible or other documents about the man Jeshua, he is lauded and anointed by a prophet of God and identified as the messianic "Branch" of the Lord. Just as he participated as priest in the rebuilding of the Temple in Jerusalem, he is prophesied to be the builder of the true temple of God, to bear God's glory, and to sit and rule as priest upon God's eternal throne.

CHAPTER THIRTEEN

Zend

This I ask of Thee, O Ahura Mazda [God];
answer me well:
Who at the Creation was the first father of
Justice?—
Who assigned their path to the sun and the
stars?—
Who decreed the waxing and waning of the
moon, if it was not Thee?—
This I would know, O Wise One, and other
matters as well.
(From Gathas Yasna 44 of the **Zend Avesta***)*

The prophet Isaiah wrote of dark and trying days ahead which Israel and the people of God would have to endure before the dawn of a new era of spirituality. In the tenth chapter of Isaiah, he told how Assyria would overrun the Near East, but also how Assyria in turn would be destroyed. The thirteenth chapter promises that God's "sanctified ones" will come from a far country and bring "the day of the Lord." These people are therein identified as the Medes, who shall bring down the glory of the Assyrian and Babylonian kingdoms.

It is quite unusual for a Jewish writer to call a foreign people God's "sanctified ones" and to say that they will bring "the day of the Lord." Who were these people and what did they believe?

The Medes were a tribe who lived on the Iranian plateau and who were united with the Persians into one kingdom by Cyrus II (the Great) in 553 B.C. As indicated in the Jeshua chapter, Cyrus was responsible for allowing the exiled Jews in Babylon to return to their homeland. His enlightened rule and sympathy for the Jewish people is most noteworthy. He was followed by another progressive leader, Darius, whose reign extended to 485 B.C.

Somewhere around this time period, a great prophet who advocated a belief in one God appeared in the Persian land which is now Iran. His name was Zarathustra, although the Greeks called him by his better known name Zoroaster. The phrase "day of the Lord," which Isaiah used in his prophecy, is generally interpreted to mean here the day when God would reveal Himself to humanity. In other instances in the Bible, such a revelatory "day of the Lord" is accomplished through one of God's messengers or prophets.[1] In view of the historical events after Isaiah, Zoroaster must surely be the prophet and the prophetic faith with which he is connected must fulfill the prophecy of the "day of the Lord" Isaiah had in mind.[2]

The exact dating for Zoroaster is not known. He has been placed by historians anywhere from the first to the tenth century before Christ.[3] Because of the spiritually enlightened reigns of Cyrus and Darius, however, it is probable that Zoroaster preceded them and had a positive effect upon their benevolent leadership. In fact, the following was inscribed on Darius' tombstone:

> A great God is Ahura Mazda, who created this earth, who created these heavens, who created blessings for men . . .[4]

Ahura Mazda is the Zoroastrian name for God and literally means "Lord the Wise One." This inscription, however, may have been added later, so it alone is not proof of Darius' religious persuasion. There is legend, however, that Darius' father, Vishtaspa, was Zoroaster's first major convert.

After an exhaustive study, one scholar has concluded that Zoroaster was born the first day of the year 660 B.C. and died in 583 B.C.[5] Other authority supports this dating,[6] but it is still far from an open-and-shut case.

Several Cayce readings list Zend as an incarnation of the Master soul. (364-7, 364-8) Zend was, according to Cayce, the father of Zoroaster.

There is the one approach to the Father through the Son, who manifested in the earth through the activities which were later, in the son of Uhjltd [Zend], the manifestations of that which eventually became the consciousness in the Nazarene.   2982-4

Q-3. Have I in any experience through the earth plane been associated with Jesus Christ before He became the world teacher: If so, where?
A-3. In this same experience [Persia], that of the brother, the incarnation previous to the Master's entry into the earth's plane, for He became *then* the leader of those lands, and *much* is *still* gained in thought from those of the Persian efforts in this direction; or, as is termed in the *present* day, the Persian philosophy.   993-3

For the entity then was the keeper of the records for what became the Zoroastrian religious purposes.
The entity gained, and the entity should use those religious purposes as comparative experiences in the present—but know that these also from that same one who gave, "I am the way, the truth and the light."   3685-1

Zan [Zend] not in the earth's plane in the present. Came again as those that were the Sons of man, and—the Savior of the world.   538-32

The readings indicate that the philosophy of Zoroastrianism came, at least in part, from Zend.

Q-2. In the Persian experience as San (or Zend) did Jesus give the basic teachings of what became Zoroastrianism?
A-2. In all those periods that the basic principle was the Oneness of the Father, He has walked with men.   364-8

Q-11. Are the truths given by San [Zend] to the people included in the Zend Avesta?
A-11. They were these!   288-29

Cayce is saying here that the *Zend Avesta,* the Zoroastrian bible, contains philosophies and truths which came from Zend.

There is authority for the proposition that the teachings of Zoroaster, which are contained in the *Zend Avesta,* came from an earlier source. Zoroaster is quoted asking God:

O Ahura Mazda, most beneficent Spirit, Maker

of the material world, thou Holy One!

Who was the first mortal, before myself, Zarathustra [Zoroaster], with whom thou, Ahura Mazda, didst converse, whom thou didst teach the religion of Ahura, the religion of Zarathustra?

Ahura Mazda [God] answered:

The fair Yima, the good shepherd, O holy Zarathustra! he was the first mortal, before thee Zoroaster.

Unto him, O Zarathustra, I Ahura Mazda, spake, saying: "Well, fair Yima, son of Vivanghat, be thou the preacher and the bearer of my religion!" [After declining this role, which presumably was assumed by Zarathustra or Zoroaster, God implores Yima further:]

"Since thou dost not consent to be the preacher and the bearer of my religion, then make thou my world increase, make my world grow: consent thou to nourish, to rule, and to watch over my world."

And the fair Yima replied unto me, O Zarathustra, saying:

"Yes! I will make thy world increase, I will make thy world grow. Yes! I will nourish, and rule, and watch over thy world . . ."

Then I, Ahura Mazda, brought two implements unto him: a golden seal and a poniard inlaid with gold. Behold, here Yima bears the royal sway![7]

Note the title "the good shepherd" for the one who preceded Zoroaster. In this quotation, Yima, the good shepherd, also assumed the messianic mission of nourisher and ruler of the world and is given the royal seal and sword of God. The very term "good shepherd" had been used for Hermes. And Jesus identifies himself in John 10:14: "I am the good shepherd." Note also in the role assigned by God to Yima, the similarity in language to the charge God had given Adam: "Be fruitful, and multiply, and replenish the earth, and subdue it."

It might seem unusual that Zoroaster would be asking who this earlier prophet was if, in fact, it was his father. This technique of asking questions, the answer to which is obvious, is employed frequently in the *Zend Avesta*—especially in connection with questions asked of God. The quotation at the beginning of this chapter is an example of Zoroaster asking God a series of questions—apparently for rhetorical purposes—the answers to which are obviously known to Zoroaster.

The identity of this prophet who came before Zoroaster and to whom God taught His religion is not known by scholars. He is considered, however, to have been "a manifestation of God . . . who was divinely commissioned to guide man."[8] According to Edgar Cayce, it would have been Zend, the father of Zoroaster and an incarnation of the Master soul.

It should not be surprising to find Zend authoring the Zoroastrian bible, for after all, Cayce said the Master was involved in the writing of virtually all of the Old Testament. And we have seen numerous lifetimes where he performed the role of scribe in connection with the scriptures or spiritual literature.

Before proceeding with a discussion of Zend, let us look more closely at what is known about the man Zoroaster.

The name Zoroaster has been thought to mean "the golden camel,"[9] as well as "the son of the stars."[10] He was born at Azarbaijan in western Iran. His birth is alleged to have been accompanied by supernatural and occult manifestations.[11] Legend claims that he traveled far in search of his spiritual heritage, going possibly as far as China and India. He began his ministry at age thirty and, like Moses, caused a sea to part so that his followers could pass over on dry land.[12]

Zoroaster initially met with little success in his efforts to reform the primitive religions around him which were based upon animal worship. His first convert is supposed to have been his cousin,[13] although tradition says he eventually won over the chieftain king, Vishtaspa, and his two ministers.[14] Thereafter his ministry seems to have met with great success. According to legend, Turanian invaders killed Zoroaster while he knelt at the altar performing religious rites in the temple.[15]

Zoroaster's life contained many events which are echoed in the story of Jesus, such as the supernatural events at the nativity and the beginning of his ministry at age thirty. His death at the temple altar is similar to the death of Zacharias, the father of Jesus' cousin, John.

Who is Zend?

According to Edgar Cayce, he is the father of Zoroaster and the Master soul whose lives we have been following. Aside from Cayce, however, there is no apparent historical record of Zend. In the readings, he was variously called Zend, Zen, Zan, San, or Sen.

The Cayce story of Zend is very interesting. He was the son of a nomadic chieftain who lived in the plains of Persia. His father, Uhjltd, had married the niece of the Persian king, Croesus, after she helped Uhjltd escape captivity from the king. Uhjltd was a very spiritual and good leader who had been greatly influenced by his mother. She was an initiate of the mystery religions of Egypt. Zend grew up in the city "in the hills and plains" which had been established by Uhjltd and which was named Is-Shlandoen. It had become a very successful trade center for merchants traveling between the East and West. Zend had one brother, Ujndt, who in time became a very effective leader because of his idealistic but practical judgment. Zend also became a strong leader and teacher of his people, but he was more the mystic and prophet. A reading describes this period:

Before that we find the entity was in the land now known as the Persian or Arabian, about that city builded in the "hills and the plains," about that *now* known as or called Shustar in Persia or Arabia.

These were the dwelling places then of the entity with the teacher that had builded there. Hence those teachings that arose through the grandson of Uhjltd, or Zoroastrianism . . .   991-1

The city "in the hills and the plains" also became noted as a healing center with numerous places of refuge or schools for the prophets scattered nearby. The use of psychic talents, healing, hospitalization, bathing, and cleanliness and the teachings of these things were emphasized by the people of Uhjltd, Zend, and Zoroaster. (538, 288)

The influence on Uhjltd of his Egyptian mother and her Egyptian religious beliefs was noted by Cayce. Uhjltd also had had spiritual training in Egypt, which he undoubtedly passed on in the teaching and rearing of Zend. The similarity of Zoroastrianism and Egyptian religions and mythology has been commented upon by scholars.[16]

The readings suggest that Zend was overzealous at times in

his endeavors. (2091-2) The Master soul apparently was not quite ready for Christhood and godly perfection.

If, as Cayce said, Zend's teachings and philosophies are contained in the *Zend Avesta*, what then can be learned about Zend from the study of the *Avesta*?

It may be impossible to know much of the true nature and beliefs of Zend from what is now contained in the *Zend Avesta*. One of the aims of Alexander the Great when he invaded Persia was to stamp out Zoroastrianism and all books dealing with it. Parsi tradition says that the only two complete copies of the *Zend Avesta* were destroyed by Alexander but that the text was reconstructed many years later from fragments that had been saved.[17] Only a portion of the original *Avesta* survives today, and the 17 Gathas or hymns are thought to be the only part that goes back to the original revelation.[18]

Let us look at a few of these Gathas of the *Zend Avesta*.

When the Zoroastrian enlightenment was given by God, the prophet who received it inquired:

> This I ask of Thee, O Ahura Mazda; answer me
> well:
> Is it, that in return for every clear-sighted
> perception which I shall have consecrated,
> The Lord of the Kingdom, even Thou, O Wise One,
> Thou who inhabitest the same dwelling as Justice
> and Good Thought,
> Shalt fulfill to me the promises of Kingdoms
> above?
> (From Gathas Yasna 44 of the *Zend Avesta*)[19]

Zend (assuming it is he to whom the revelations are given) wonders if it is because of good works that he is so honored, and the divulging of the "promises of the Kingdoms above" is language reminiscent of the descriptions of the revelations given by God to Enoch.

The following verse is similar in wording to some of the psalms written by Asaph:

> This I ask of Thee, O Ahura Mazda; answer me
> well:
> (How) shall we relieve ourselves of evil
> In casting it back upon those who, full of

rebelliousness,
Have no care to follow after Justice
And take no pains to consult the Good Thought?
(From Gathas Yasna 44 of the *Zend Avesta*)[20]

Asaph had been impatient for the wrath of God to be brought down upon the rebellious ones, but Zend (if we may so assume this identity here) merely asks, in a manner more spiritually mature, how evil may be turned back. The vindictiveness which often characterized the writings of Asaph is now gone also.

The author of the following lines seems to anticipate a mission ahead for himself and his own eventual Christhood or unity with God:

This I ask of Thee, O Ahura Mazda; answer we well:
Shall I with Thine aid attain to my goal, O Wise
One?—
May I unite myself to Thee, and may my word be
with power,
So that uprightness and immortality may unite
together, according to Thy commandment,
To the champion of Justice.
(From Gathas Yasna 44 of the *Zend Avesta*)[21]

The following passage brings to mind the Book of Job, which Cayce said was written by Melchizedek, an earlier incarnation of the Master; the wording is especially similar to that in chapters 9, 26, and 38 of Job:

Who was the first father of Righteousness at the
birth?
Who appointed their path to sun and stars?
Who but thou is it through whom the moon waxes
and wanes?
Who set the Earth in its place below, and the sky of
the clouds, that it shall not fail?
Who the waters and the plants?
Who yoked the two steeds to wind and clouds?
Who, O Wise One, is the creator of the Good Mind?
What artificer made light and darkness, what arti-
ficer sleep and waking?
Who made morning, noon and night, to remind the
wise man of his task?

Who created Devotion, sacred with the Dominion?
Who made the son reverential in soul towards his
   father?
Thus I strive to recognize in thee, O Wise One, as
   sacred spirit, the creator of all things.
         (From Gathas Yasna 44 of the *Zend Avesta*)[22]

One of the motifs in the *Zend Avesta* is that of farming and
nature. The importance of agricultural matters is shown in the
following quote describing persons who cause "the earth to
rejoice":

It is he who sows most corn, grass, and fruit, O
Spitama Zarathustra! who waters ground that is
dry, or drains ground that is too wet. Unhappy is
the land that has long lain unsown with the seed of
the sower and wants a good husbandman, like a
well-shapen maiden who has long gone childless
and wants a good husband. He who would till the
earth, O Spitama Zarathustra! with the left arm
and the right, with the right arm and the left, unto
him will she bring forth plenty of fruit.[23]

In his parables, Jesus will also talk of the sower of seeds, the
good husbandman, the harvest, and similar agrarian subjects.
   The Zoroastrian religion is often cited for its concepts of
spiritual dualism, but the original teachings are not of this bent.
Rather, they insist upon one true and only God who created the
world and the entire universe.[24] Both good and evil existed, but
God was considered "omniscient, almighty, supreme,
sovereign, good, and merciful."[25]
   Another persistent theme in Zoroastrianism is that of
justice, the personification of which is God. The doing of good is
also of utmost importance, as reflected in part of a Zoroastrian
prayer:

I praise aloud the thought well thought, the
word well spoken, and the deed well done.

Zoroastrianism spread far and wide, with places of worship
reportedly existing in Asia Minor in the West and China in the
East.[26] It was the established religion of Persia prior to the
spread of Islam. Many Zoroastrians fled to India, however, to

escape the zeal of Islam in the seventh and eighth centuries. Today there is a community of a few hundred thousand Zoroastrians in Bombay, where they are known as Parsees, after the land of their origin. There they live as a discrete community noted for their fire temples which contain the sacred flame and their towers of silence on which vultures consume their dead so as not to contaminate the sacred earth, water, or fire. The actual decline of Zoroastrianism began with the advent of another great religion in the Middle East, Christianity.

One of the reasons Zoroastrianism spread so widely and rapidly was its availability to all. Some earlier religions, such as the Egyptian mystery religions, were based upon spiritual attainment and initiation—a proving of worthiness. Zoroastrianism was open to all who would believe, whether it be the traveling merchant from India or the local village farmer. This fluidity and lack of exclusivity may have made it vulnerable to adoption and change by other religions, such as Christianity when it came along.

There is much similarity between Zoroastrianism and Judaism. They had the same basic religious principles and cultural values, and they both denounced mercilessly all idol worshipers and their immoral practices.[27] The rise of Zoroastrianism is credited with creating in even the most staunch Jew of the time a new interest in his nearly forgotten spiritual heritage.[28]

> Many of the Zoroastrian tenets and rituals which have passed down through the ages and are known in the present bear a curious pre-Christian tinge. They practiced baptism, circumcision, and a sacrificial mass with a communion of bread and wine. Their prophecies included the coming of a Messiah.[29]

Not only did Isaiah seem to be referring to Zoroastrianism in his prophecies, but so also did other Jewish writers. Both Zephaniah and Malachi, who wrote near the time of Zend and Zoroaster, are thought to have meant the Persian Zoroastrians in references to the arrival of "the great day of the Lord" and the honoring of God's name by Gentiles.[30]

Cayce was once asked:

Q-6. *In canonizing the Bible, why was the life of Zan [Zend] left out?*

A-6. Called in other names.   262-60

He may have been referring to these Old Testament prophetic statements which do not name Zend, but seem to pertain to the religion begun by him.

As a matter of historical fact, Zoroastrianism had a profound effect upon both Judaism and Christianity, as well as Greek and gnostic thought.[31] Both Mithraism and Manichaeanism are thought to have had their roots in Zoroastrianism. Manichaeanism began about 250 A.D. as a gnostic blend of Christianity, Buddhism, and Zoroastrianism.

One of the strongest tenets of Zoroastrianism was its emphasis upon the coming of a messiah. The Gathas speak of a coming kingdom which is awaited by the faithful. Two more prophets were expected to appear before the final arrival of the messiah "who makes the evil spirit impotent and causes the resurrection and future existence."[32]

According to Acts 2:9, many Medes and Persians were present when Peter addressed the Christians at Pentecost. They probably were Zoroastrians (the religion of the Medes and Persians), who had been affected by the teachings of Jesus.[33]

The Magi were members of the old Persian priesthood who gradually were absorbed into Zoroastrianism. At the birth of Jesus, the Bible records the arrival of Wise Men from the East. They came to King Herod:

> Saying, "Where is he who has been born King of
> the Jews? For we have seen his star in the East,
> and have come to worship him."   (Matthew 2:2)

The term "Wise Men" is from the Greek *magoi*, a "Persian word for men expert in the study of the stars,"[34] or astrology. They were Zoroastrian Magi from Persia. A reading from Edgar Cayce sheds additional light on them:

In those periods that preceded the advent of the Prince of Peace in the earth, we find the entity was among those of the land that would now be called the Persian—as a wise man, a counselor, a sage, that counseled with those peoples; using the mathematical activities of the ages old, as well as the teachings of the Persians

from the days of Zend and Og and Uhjltd, bringing for those peoples
a better interpretation of the astrological as well as the natural laws.

Hence we find the entity was associated oft with those who
looked for the day, the hour when that *great purpose*, that event,
was to be in the earth a literal experience.

Then we find the entity was among those of the fabled as well as
real experience, seeking with the Wise Men that came from the East
during those periods.

We find this entity was the one who brought the incense to the
child Jesus—in the name then Achlar.   1908-1

Readers may remember the reference to the Magi in the
chapter on Adam. In the *Testament of Adam,* dating from the
early days of Christianity, Adam was supposedly buried by God
and the angels. His testament, which he had given to Seth,
received special treatment:

> And we sealed the testament and we put it in the
> cave of treasures with the offerings Adam had
> taken out of Paradise, gold and myrrh and
> frankincense. And the sons of kings, the magi, will
> come and get them, and they will take them to the
> son of God, to Bethlehem of Judea, to the cave.
>
> (3:6)

We have evidence again of the special tie between the
Zoroastrians and Jesus, the high regard the Magi had for him,
and the unfolding of events whose origins date from the first
appearance in materiality of the Master soul as Adam.

From what we have seen, not only of the Wise Men but also of
Zoroastrians at Pentecost, apparently many of that religion
recognized Jesus as the messiah about whom their religion and
legends had foretold. This identification with Christianity may
be the primary reason Zoroastrianism declined dramatically
after the life of Jesus and why the Persian and surrounding
areas were such a fertile ground for converts to the new
religion.

Many early Jewish Christians held the belief that Jesus, the
messiah, and Son of God, "had appeared in or been
foreshadowed by other 'true prophets' or 'prophets of truth.' "[35]
Certainly Zend, a prophet of Zoroastrianism, would fit nicely
into such a concept.

One of the gnostic documents of early Christianity was the

Pistis Sophia. In it there is a reference to Zorokothora Melgisedec. This name is thought somehow to connect Melchizedek with Zoroaster or the religion of Zoroastrianism.[36] Melchizedek would, of course, have been an earlier life of the Master, according to Cayce.

The largest tractate discovered among the ancient documents at Nag Hammadi in Egypt is one entitled "Zostrianos." This name is a variant of Zoroaster and is recognized as such in the tractate itself, as well as by the early Christian Church Father Arnobius and the Neoplatonic author Porphyry.[37] In studying this tractate, scholars have concluded it holds Zoroaster to have been an incarnation of Seth, the son of Adam.[38] Thus, we have another document fitting Zoroaster into a drama enacted ages ago with the Master, and we would have the father-son relationship of Adam and Seth duplicated in that of Zend and Zoroaster.

In the Zostrianos tractate, the recipient of the Zoroastrian teachings from God (presumably Zoroaster in the tractate, but his father Zend, according to Cayce) was taken up into all the regions of heaven and shown the secrets of the universe in a manner similar to Enoch. He then wrote down those experiences in wording echoing the Enochian documents.

There is other information which again harkens back to Seth and Adam. According to Persian legend, the original tablets of Zoroastrian teachings are preserved in "a certain great cavern near the summit of a high peak of the Thian-Shan Mountains." These tablets are expected to be found in some future date "when the world has grown wise enough to interpret the secret mysteries inscribed thereon."[39] As we found in the Adam chapter, the same story exists for Seth who hid in a secret place the teachings Adam had received from God.

At least one other legend about Zoroaster is worthy of comment. According to Greek accounts, at the death of Zoroaster his father descended in a great flame and bore him back to the starry heavens from which he had come.[40] It would thus be the Master soul as Zend, according to Cayce, who is transporting and welcoming Zoroaster back to his spiritual abode.

Zoroastrianism held sway during an important period of humanity's spiritual or religious evolution. It was both a link to

and stimulus for Judaism and Christianity. It was a new
expression of the belief in one God, His goodness and His
omnipotence. And the Master soul, who soon is to reach
Christhood as Jesus, played a vital part in its inception. The
expectancy of a messiah and the recognition of him by at least
some parts of Zoroastrianism will be important to Zend when
he returns as Jesus in the story which lies ahead.

Generally, chapters on the lives of the Master have followed a
chronological order. This chapter may be an exception.
Because of uncertainty as to the exact dates of Zend and
Zoroaster, the story of Zend could not be put into the
chronology of the other reported lives with any degree of
precision or certainty.

If we use the most commonly accepted dating for Zoroaster,
the lifetime of Zend should have preceded that of Jeshua. In
fact, there are some suggestions in the Cayce readings that
Zend goes back in time thousands of years before Jesus, and
there is some Greek support for such antiquity.

On the other hand, reading 993-3, quoted earlier, suggests
that the Zend life is "the incarnation previous to the Master's
entry into the earth's plane." (It is possible, however, that this
language is referring to the incarnation of the person for whom
the reading was given, rather than Zend.) And a number of
readings place Uhjltd in the period of the reign of Croesus. If
this Croesus is the legendary king of wealth who was
overthrown by Cyrus, his reign was roughly 560 to 546 B.C.
Zend's life would have begun sometime near this period and
would thus probably be the incarnation next to that of Jesus.

There is another possibility. The dates of Jeshua's lifetime
are close enough to Zend's so that it is possible Jeshua was the
Hebraic name for Zend and that they were one and the same.
(Remember the reading that said Zend was called by other
names in the Bible.) Jeshua's life began in Babylon, which was
conquered by Persia, but other details do not seem to match.
Zend supposedly grew up in the city of "the hills and plains" in
Persia, not Babylon. Although Judaism and Zoroastrianism
were similar, the identification of Jeshua in the Old Testament
as a priest in the Temple at Jerusalem would seem to preclude
his being the originator of the Zoroastrian philosophy, which
blossomed in Persia.

Regardless of its actual dating, the Zend story is presented last before the life of Jesus because of the closeness in philosophies of Zoroastrianism and Christianity. And there are other factors, such as the Wise Men, which make a smooth transition and bridge between these two epochal lives of the Master.

CHAPTER FOURTEEN

Jesus: His Early Life

And you, Bethlehem Ephratah, though you are little among the thousands of towns of Judah, yet out of you shall come forth a ruler to govern Israel; whose goings forth have been predicted from of old, from eternity.

(Micah 5:2; Lamsa translation)

The psychic readings of Edgar Cayce confirm the details and events given in the New Testament regarding the life of Jesus. They also give much information not contained in the Biblical account. After all, there is much that is not known about the historical man. As one author put it:

> He lived, this man called Jesus, in one of the smallest, most insignificant of the Roman provinces. Although his name is known today throughout all the world, in his lifetime, two thousand years ago, he was virtually unknown outside his own province. He is worshiped today as the Son of God by a very large portion of the world's population, yet he died the death of a criminal. He changed the course of world history

149

as no other man ever has, yet hardly a mention of
him can be found in the history of his own time,
unless the Bible be counted as history. He is the
central figure of the New Testament, yet the New
Testament is strangely silent about most of the
years of his life.[1]

The Cayce readings give much previously unknown
information about the early years of Jesus. Beginning with the
nativity, the Bible's brief narrative is enriched by Cayce with
details about the Holy Family, their friends, and the education
of Jesus. Cayce also provides insight into the preparations for
the messiah, particularly with regard to the involvement of the
Essenes and their expectancy of the one whose entry into the
earth had so long been promised and prophesied.

Let us begin with a look at the times and the role of this
special group—the Essenes.

For the Jewish people, it was a most difficult period. They
were under the rule of Rome with Jewish vassals of Rome in
positions of authority and leadership. Earlier attempts by
Jewish groups, such as the Maccabees, to resist foreign control
had ended in calamity. Herod the Great was now king, although
his family was Jewish in name only. Various cultures met in
Palestine, with the Greek way of life having the greatest impact.
Many Jewish customs and religious practices had been
abandoned by the average Jew. Even the priesthood and
religious leaders were in disarray and disunity.

On the other hand, the severity of the times had caused many
of the Jewish faithful to look for and expect God's intervention
and deliverance. After all, God had come to their rescue many
times before. Some hoped for a political or military leader who
would free them from Roman rule. Others envisioned the end of
the world and were waiting for the promised messiah who
would pronounce and dispense God's final judgment.

As one of the major Jewish religious groups of the day, the
Sadducees represented the priestly aristocracy and accepted
only the Torah (the first five books of the Bible) as law. They
denied the resurrection of the dead (reincarnation according to
Cayce) and the existence of angels and spirits and apparently
had no messianic doctrine. While they did not have
independent political power, they were able to work with the

Roman administration and were often found in the same social circles.[2]

The Pharisees lived a strict life style and conceived Judaism as being centered upon the observance of the law. They were opposed to foreign rule and never took an oath of allegiance to Rome. They believed in the resurrection of the dead, angels, spirits, and the judgment. They worked in close alliance with the scribes and interpreters of the law and were intolerant of the average person who was not a student of the religious rules.[3]

A third group, the Essenes, is not mentioned in the Bible. We know from historical sources (Josephus and Philo), however, that they existed at this time and exerted considerable influence over a portion of the Jewish populace. Cayce said the absence of the Essene name in the Bible is because the chroniclers felt no need to name themselves, and this conclusion has been reached by others.[4] In fact, the relationship of the Essenes to Christianity is now considered so close and vital that one authority states:

> We have to ask whether, without the prior existence and propaganda of the Essenes, their Messianic beliefs, and their organization and discipline, Christianity would have come into existence at all.[5]

There are some things regarding the Essenes about which we can only make educated speculations. Scholars are not united, for example, on their origin. Some have taken the position that they were merely a strict order of the Pharisees; others that they were Zoroastrians; and others that they were Buddhists.[6] The majority view is probably that the Essenes grew out of more traditional Jewish beliefs and existed as a separate and distinct sect along with the Pharisees and Sadducees. It has been argued that both John the Baptist and Jesus were members of the order.[7] John evidently was the more zealous of the two in his Essene convictions. The now famous scrolls found in the area of the Dead Sea are generally considered to have been the product of an Essene group that flourished before and during the time of Jesus.

The Essene way of life was relatively austere. The dedicated Essene lived in a monastic community and followed a strict and regimented routine. He renounced material goods when entering the order, worshiped at sunrise, spent the day in manual crafts, bathed before the common meal, and partook of a restricted diet. The Essenes believed in the immortality of the soul and the foretelling of the future by certain prophets.[8] According to Cayce, they studied the scriptures and other related documents and were students of astrology, numerology, phrenology, and reincarnation. (5749-8) In many respects, their practices were a combination of those of Judaism and Zoroastrianism—placed in a monastic setting.

There were Essene sympathizers who lived a more normal life away from the communal towns. They assisted the efforts of the order and would on occasion travel to the communities to visit relatives or friends and to worship. The extent of Essene influence is not fully known and probably often operated under the surface without public profile.

According to Edgar Cayce, the Essenes played an important part in the preparations for the actual birth of the messiah. The word "Essene," Cayce said, meant expectancy. They were expecting the arrival of the messiah and prepared appropriate "channels" or mothers for his birth. In word and deed, they helped bring about a religious quickening and a new age.

Hence the group we refer to here as the Essenes, which was the outgrowth of the periods of preparations from the teachings of Melchizedek, as propagated by Elijah and Elisha and Samuel. These were set aside for preserving themselves in direct line of choice for the offering of themselves as channels through which there might come the new or the divine origin, see?   254-109

Modern studies of Essenic beliefs confirm the high standing given to Melchizedek. And it seems fitting that the group preparing for the Master's entry had philosophies based upon teachings given earlier by him in his appearance as Melchizedek.

The readings say that Mary was one of twelve young virgins who had been dedicated at an early age to be raised by the Essenes as candidates for the birth of the messiah. Catholic tradition that Mary herself was immaculately conceived is confirmed by Cayce. Her mother's name was Anne. She was a member of the Essenes at Mount Carmel and had given Mary for this spiritual purpose of being a channel for the messiah's entry.

Mary's selection as the one from whom the messiah would be born is described as follows:

> The temple steps—or those that led to the altar, these were called the temple steps. These were those upon which the sun shone as it arose of a morning when there were the first periods of the chosen maidens going to the altar for prayer; as well as for the burning of the incense.
>
> On this day, as they mounted the steps all were bathed in the morning sun; which not only made a beautiful picture but clothed all as if in purple and gold.
>
> As Mary reached the top step, then there were the thunder and lightning, and the angel led the way, taking the child by the hand before the altar. This was the manner of choice, this was the showing of the way; for she led the others on *this* particular day.
>
> 5749-8

Joseph, too, according to Cayce, was a member of the Essenes and, although much older than Mary, had been chosen to be her husband. They were married at the Essene temple on Mt. Carmel, and she lived part of the time before the birth of Jesus with Joseph at his home in Nazareth. It was from there that they went to Bethlehem to register for taxation.

As they approached Bethlehem on this occasion, the readings pick up the story in simple elegance:

> The weather was cool, and there were crowds on the way. For, it was only a sabbath day's journey from Jerusalem. There were great crowds of people on the way from the hills of Judea.
>
> The people were active in the occupations of the varied natures in that unusual land. Some were carpenters—as those of the house of Joseph, who had been delayed, even on the journey, by the condition of the mother. Some in the group were helpers to Joseph—carpenters' helpers. Then there were shepherds, husbandmen, and the varied groups that had their small surroundings as necessitated by the conditions of the fields about Nazareth.
>
> In the evening then, or at twilight, Joseph approached the inn, that was filled with those who had also journeyed there on their way to be polled for the tax as imposed by the Romans upon the people of the land. For, those had been sent out who were to judge the abilities of the varied groups to be taxed. And each individual was required by the Roman law to be polled in the city of his birth.
>
> Both Joseph and Mary were members of the sect called the

Essenes; and thus they were questioned by those not only in the political but in the religious authority in the cities.

Then there was the answer by the innkeeper, "No room in the inn," especially for such an occasion. Laughter and jeers followed, at the sight of the elderly man with the beautiful girl, his wife, heavy with child.   5749-15

The above is an example of Cayce's ability to weave related but previously unknown information into the traditional Biblical account.

He adds an interesting variation about the innkeeper and his family: They were sympathetic with the Essenes and had heard of the unusual events that had already transpired with the holy couple. The innkeeper's statement that there was no room in the inn was made because he felt the raucous nature of the crowd was not an appropriate place for the birth of the messiah. Other Essenes were present who were helping look after Joseph and Mary. The reading quoted previously picks up again:

Thus many joined in the search for some place. Necessity demanded that some place be sought—quickly. Then it was found, under the hill, in the stable—above which the shepherds were gathering their flocks into the fold.

There the Savior, the Child was born; who, through the will and the life manifested, became the savior of the world—that channel through which those of old had been told that the promise would be fulfilled that was made to *Eve*; the arising again of another like unto Moses; and as given to David, the promise was not to depart from that channel. But lower and lower man's concept of needs had fallen.

Then—when hope seemed gone—the herald angels sang. The star appeared, that made the wonderment to the shepherds, that caused the awe and consternation to all of those about the inn; some making fun, some smitten with conviction that those unkind things said must needs be readjusted in their relationships to things coming to pass.

All were in awe as the brightness of His star appeared and shone, as the music of the spheres brought that joyful choir, "*Peace on earth! Good will to men of good faith.*"

All felt the vibrations and saw a great light—not only the shepherds above that stable but those in the inn as well . . .

Just as the midnight hour came, there was the birth of the Master.
                                                            5749-15

Another reading states that Jesus was born "in a grotto which is not marked at present, but is called a stable." (587)

The Master soul had returned again to the earth. This is the soul beloved of the Creator, the only son begotten on earth by God. The Master came this time, as he had done before as Adam and Melchizedek, through divine paternity. He had come to the area where he had lived as Melchizedek, Joshua, Asaph, Jeshua, and possibly Adam. He had returned to complete the mission begun aeons ago, and this time, unlike his earlier efforts, he would finish it. And the soul who began the mission with him, who had been created by God as Adam's helpmeet, Eve, is involved in its completion as Mary, the mother.

As Eve, the relationship with the Master had involved a physical or sexual union, which in and of itself was not unholy. But as Mary, the spiritual evolution can be seen. Her relationship now partook of divine creativity allowing the return of the Master. A Cayce reading expands further upon the spiritual wisdom that is now hers:

. . . seek not for knowledge alone. For, look—*look*—what it brought Eve. Look rather for that wisdom which was eventually founded in she that was addressed as the handmaid of the Lord, and who "pondered those things in her heart," as to how and why Gabriel would speak with her. 2072-10

The readings say the Master had already completed his return to God in other planes or systems when he was born as Jesus but came voluntarily again to earth out of his love for humanity and his concern for its spiritual plight. (5749-14)

He gave up heaven and entered physical being that ye might have access to the Father. 5081-1

There were other spiritual seekers who were awaiting and expecting the arrival of a messianic figure from God.

As indicated by the travels of the Master during the periods of preparation, the whole earth, the whole world looked for, sought the closer understanding. Hence through the efforts of the students of the various phases of experiences of man in the earth, as may be literally interpreted from the first chapters of Genesis, ye find that those that subdued—not that were ruled by, but subdued the understandings of that in the earth—were considered, or were in the position of the wise, or the sages, or the ones that were holy; in body and mind, in accord with purposes. 5749-7

The Wise Men, as they are called in the Bible, are examples of spiritual sages who, though non-Jewish, were aware of the import of the events taking place in Judea.

The name of one of the Wise Men was given by Cayce as Achlar. He brought incense to Jesus and had been guided there through interpretations of both the astrological and natural laws using those mathematical methods taught in Persia by Zend and handed down through the ages. (1908) Jesus' guests were thus influenced by wisdom which he had left years before as Zend.

Cayce said the Wise Men provided needed encouragement for Mary and those about her and that there was more than one visit of Wise Men. The Wise Men recorded in the Bible came from Persia. Others came from Persia, India, Egypt, Chaldea, Gobi, and what is now the Indo or Tao Land. (2067) Apparently a number of religions anticipated the coming of the messiah, this special son of God, and were privy to his arrival. They were directed in part by psychic attunement and by the position of the stars which signaled the beginning of the Piscean Age. (5749-7 and -8)

The Bible records Herod's anger when the Wise Men did not follow his directive to return with information on where the "king of the Jews" had been born. He then ordered all the children in the area of Bethlehem age two and under to be slain. God, however, had forewarned Joseph in a dream to flee into Egypt with Mary and the baby Jesus.

The Cayce readings reveal that a number of Essenes helped with the Holy Family's journey to Egypt. They selected a friend of Mary's named Josie as her handmaid and companion during the trip; Josie also helped in the early training and education of Jesus. As discussed in the Joseph chapter, tradition says the family spent some time in the area of present-day Cairo. It was the place where Jesus and Mary had possibly been together as Joseph and Aseneth. The readings say they also lived "in and about or close to what was then Alexandria." The time spent in Egypt allowed fulfillment of the prophecy in Hosea 11:1 that God's son would be called out of Egypt.

The Holy Family spent five years there and then returned to Judea and Capernaum. (5749-7) The Bible records that the family then lived in Nazareth. Cayce says the family went first to Capernaum because of political reasons resulting from the death of Herod and in order that Jesus' education might be supervised by an Essene teacher named Judy.

Luke states that "the child grew, and became strong in spirit, filled with wisdom; and the grace of God was upon him." (Luke 2:52)

In his twelfth year, on a journey to Jerusalem for the feast of the Passover, he became separated from his parents, and they lost him for three days. He was with the teachers in the temple where the wisdom of his questions and answers amazed all who heard him. To his searching and distraught parents, he simply said, "Knew ye not that I must be about my Father's business?" (Luke 2:49) The love of Jesus for the temple and its activity was surely prompted in part by the lives he had spent in dedication to it as Asaph and Jeshua. A Cayce reading compares the spiritual obedience of Adam to that of Jesus at age twelve:

> In the first we find man listening to those influences which were at variance to God's way. Then in the temple, even at twelve, we find the perfect man seeking, asking, and answering questions as to man's relationship to God . . .
>
> Draw the comparison within thyself as to those experiences indicated in the 1st, 2nd, and 3rd of Genesis and those in the 2nd of Luke—where we find our pattern, our lesson . . . one willfully seeking to know the relationship to the Creator, or the answer, "Know ye not that I must be about my Father's business?" How different from that other, "The *woman* thou gavest me, SHE persuaded me, and I did eat!" 262-125

The Bible gives no further details of Jesus' life until the beginning of his ministry at age thirty. Cayce says Jesus spent these intervening years studying and traveling.

Jesus first went briefly to Egypt. From there he traveled to India and studied with their religious leaders. One of the Indian teachers listed by Cayce was Kshjiar or Kahanja. Jesus learned "those cleansings of the body as related to preparation for strength" in the physical and mental. (1158-9, 5749-2, 5749-7) The readings indicate that in an earlier life the Master had influenced the Buddhist concept of the one God. And now he is back in India studying these teachings.

Jesus then went to Persia and studied the Zoroastrian religion and the "union of forces" under a teacher named

Junner. Of course as Zend, he had been responsible for the original teachings of Zoroastrianism. Cayce says Jesus was called back abruptly to Judea from Persia because of the death of his father, Joseph. He was now approximately sixteen years old. (5749-2, 5749-7)

After the burial of Joseph, Cayce indicates Jesus returned again to Egypt and under a teacher named Zar studied the concept of the crucifying of self in relationship to ideals. He allegedly joined his cousin, John, who was already in Egypt. They both studied there and became initiates in the temple or pyramid, and Cayce says evidence of this training and initiation will yet be found in records set in the pyramid. (5749-2, 5749-7) The construction of the pyramid had been accomplished centuries before when, in an incarnation as Hermes, the Master was already known as the Great Initiate. Supposedly there exist records put there in Hermes' day prophesying the appearance of the Master at the time of Jesus. In this appearance, he was expected to complete his spiritual initiation and earthly purpose.

A century or so ago there would have been no known actual support for Cayce in his chronicles of Jesus' travels and training. In recent years, however, there has been considerable publicity concerning certain writings and findings of Nicolas Notovich, a Russian who traveled throughout Afghanistan, India, and Tibet in the late 1880s.[9] He reported having heard stories and read about a St. Issa (the Buddhist equivalent for the name Jesus) who had visited India at the approximate time of Jesus and who was revered by the Hindus and Buddhists.[10] Although copies were claimed to exist in several Tibetan monasteries, the original manuscript was said to be located at the great monastery on Mt. Marbour, near Lhasa. It was written in Pali (the language of official Theravada Buddhism) about 200 years after Christ and brought later from India to Tibet.[11]

Despite Notovich's call for others to come to Tibet and check the authenticity of the manuscript, it was 35 years before the challenge was accepted. In 1922 Swami Abhedananda went to Himis, saw the manuscript, and, in his Bengali travel book, *Kashmiri O Tibbetti,*[12] confirmed what Notovich had said. The conquest of Tibet by China in 1947 has prevented recent investigation and analysis of the Issa manuscripts; however, a number of religious personages and other people in India and Tibet have made contemporary affirmations about their knowledge of the Issa legend and their belief that documents existed at one time which recorded details of Jesus' visit to India.[13]

Luckily, Notovich translated the manuscript and made a record of its contents in his book, *The Legend of Saint Issa.*[14] According to the translation, Jesus, after his appearance in the temple at age twelve, traveled with merchants to both India and Persia and spent several years studying with their holy men. In chapter IV, verse 1, Jesus' birth is described: "... the moment had come for the compassionate Judge to re-incarnate in human form." The term "re-incarnate" is most significant for us, as it would imply that Jesus had incarnated before in human form.

The account goes on to state that in India Jesus studied the Vedas or prayers of Brahma, learned to cure physical ills by means of prayers, and taught the Holy Scriptures to the people. He also studied the Sutras and sacred scrolls of the Buddha and is said to have preached everywhere "the supreme perfection attainable by man." After Jesus' return to Palestine and his ministry there, merchants are claimed to have brought back the word that "the great and just Issa, in whom was manifest the soul of the Universe," was tortured and murdered.

> The earth trembled and the heavens wept, because of the great crime committed in the land of Israel. (I, 1)[15]

The similarity of Jesus' teachings to the religious philosophies of the countries where he allegedly visited has also been noted.[16] One Indian religious leader has observed:

> The voice of Jesus is, verily, the voice of the eternal being. Through Him is expressed the call of the infinite to the finite, the call of the cosmic being to the individual, the call of God to man. His divine voice is the same, therefore, as the voice of the Vedas and Upanishads, the voice of the Koran, the Zendavesta, Dharmapada and all such scriptures of the great religions of the world.[17]

Even the twice born or "born again" language of Jesus has been linked to India, where the two higher castes among the Hindus are called the twice born.[18]

The important message to be derived from the possibility that Jesus may have visited other lands and studied other religions is a very positive one. It speaks of the universality of all enlightened religious thought which is built upon the belief in one God. If, in fact, Jesus had in earlier incarnations influenced these other religious expressions of belief in God, then his study of them could serve as both a review of their message and an affirmation of his previous involvement with them. Such travels and study at the very least helped prepare him for his Palestinian ministry, for the establishment of a new religion which would shape the coming centuries, and for the ordeals which would result in his death, resurrection, and Christhood.

The pre-ministry years of Jesus then, according to Cayce and others, were not idle ones or merely a period of simple carpentry apprenticeship under Joseph in Nazareth. Rather they were years in which the young Jesus studied a variety of spiritual philosophies built upon faith in the one God. It was a period in which he became aware of his true identity and mission in life. He was involved in refining his skills as a spiritual adept and total initiate in the earthly mysteries of God.

CHAPTER FIFTEEN

Jesus: His Ministry

There has appeared in Palestine a man who is still living and whose power is extraordinary. He has the title given him of Great Prophet; his disciples call him the Son of God. He raises the dead and heals all sorts of diseases.

(Report of Publius Lentulus to Roman Emperor Tiberias) [1]

The Jewish people were expecting their promised messiah. Their oppression mirrored the descriptions of the prophets for the time of his arrival. Almost joyously many of them were enduring the difficulties of the day because of the messianic promise that was sure to follow.

At this time there came a prophet out of the desert proclaiming: "Repent, for the kingdom of heaven is at hand. Prepare the way of the Lord, make his paths straight." (Matthew 3:2-3) Surely this charismatic messenger was the messiah who would deliver God's people from the oppressor.

Huge crowds flocked to the ford of the Jordan River, just north of the Dead Sea, to hear this man named John speak his thunderous message of repentance and deliverance. Many

161

accepted this message and, in a ritual borrowed from the Essenes, were baptized by him in the waters of the Jordan.

John denied he was the messiah, but promised that one would come after him "the thong of whose sandals I am not worthy to untie." (Matthew 3:11)

On one such occasion when a man emerged out of the crowd and entered the shallow water for baptism, John showed signs of recognition. John surprisingly forbade him with the remonstration, "I need to be baptized by you." The stranger persisted, however, saying, "Let it be so now." And John placed his hands on the man's shoulders and immersed him in the water.

> And, behold, the heavens were opened and he saw the Spirit of God descending like a dove, and alighting on him, and, lo, a voice from heaven, saying, "This is my beloved Son, with whom I am well pleased."   (Matthew 3:16-17)

This baptism of Jesus formally heralds the beginning of his ministry and his public commissioning by God. It occurred at the spot in the Jordan River where tradition says Adam stood and pleaded for God's mercy after his fall and banishment from Eden. It is also where Joshua chose to cross the Jordan and enter the Promised Land with the Israelites centuries before. These had all been acts of the same soul and were symbolic portents of the reasons for Jesus' present ministry: the original fall and, through redemption, the final entry of God's people into the Promised Land.

According to both John the Baptist and Jesus, baptism was to be done in token of repentance for commission of sins. Why then did Jesus, if perfect, need baptism? This question has long been a problem for theologians. It may well be answered in the premise of his past, imperfect lives.

The New Testament story indicates that Jesus, at the prompting of the Spirit, then went into the nearby wilderness for a period of solitude that lasted for forty days. Instead of a forty-year wait which he had endured as Joshua because of the Israelites' lack of faith, Jesus now must wait for forty days while his faith is tempted and proved.

In the wilderness area near Gilgal, where Joshua had paused and camped before beginning his military conquest of the Holy

Land, Jesus too pauses before marching forward with his ministry. In a similar manner, Enoch and Hermes had gone into the desert or a high place to pray and meditate before receiving divine revelation.

The Bible records three temptations presented by Satan with which Jesus had to wrestle. As he had fasted and not eaten during his forty days in the desert, he was tempted first to turn the stones into bread. The second temptation was to jump unharmed from a high pinnacle and prove that he was the son of God. The third was to bow down and worship Satan, who in return promised to give Jesus all the kingdoms and glory of the world. With all three temptations, Jesus persevered over the devil and his own inner doubts and desires. Thereafter the devil departed, and the angels came and ministered unto him.

Jesus had to face and subdue physical, mental, and spiritual temptations. The food appealed to his physical desires; the public spectacle of jumping unharmed was directed to his mental ego; and the offer of submission to the devil in order to conquer the world was an attempt to subvert his spiritual mission. Where he had failed before, he now succeeded. His original temptation in the beautiful Garden of Eden—to obtain knowledge before he was ready for it and in defiance of God's plan—had now been met and conquered in the bleak Judean wilderness near Jericho. He had "to meet that which had been His undoing in the beginning" as Adam. (2067)

Jesus' actual ministry began shortly thereafter when he heard that John had been imprisoned by Herod. He went to Capernaum and the seacoast of Galilee and began preaching that the kingdom of heaven was at hand.

The first recorded miracle of Jesus occurred at a wedding in Cana of Galilee. Jewish weddings were festive and often lasted for an entire week. A Cayce reading adds detail to the Biblical account of Jesus' turning water into wine when the supply ran low:

The girl to be wed was a daughter of the cousin of Mary, a daughter of a younger sister of Elizabeth, whose name was also Mary. And she was the one spoken of as "the other Mary," and not as some have supposed.

The customs required that there be a feast, which was composed of the roasted lamb with the herbs, the breads that had been

prepared in the special ways as were the custom and tradition of
those who followed close to the faith in Moses' law, Moses' custom,
Moses' ordinances.

The families of Mary were present, as well as those of the groom.

The groom, in the name Roael, was among the sons of Zebedee;
being an elder brother of James and John who later became the
close friends and the closer followers of Jesus.

The Master, returning with those who were hangers-on, naturally
sought to speak with His mother. Learning of this happening He,
too—with the followers—were bid to remain at the feast.

Much wine also was part of the custom. The day was what ye
would call June third. There were plenty of flowers and things of the
field, yet only a part of those things needed. For, the custom called
for more of the meats prepared with certain herbs, and wines.

The day had been fine; the evening was fair; the moon was full.
This then brought the activities with the imbibing more and more of
wine, more hilarity, and the dance—which was in the form of the
circles that were part of the customs, not only of that land then, but
that are in your own land now and then being revived.

With those activities, as indicated, the wine ran low. Remember,
the sons of Zebedee were among those of the upper class, as would
be termed; not the poorer ones. Thence the reason why Mary served
or prepared for her relative the feast.   5749-15

Capernaum became the center and home base of Jesus'
ministry. The town was noted for its commerce and fishing
industry; it lay on the northwest shore of the Sea of Galilee. In
this area, he gathered his twelve disciples, although Cayce
indicates Andrew had been with Jesus at the Jordan and was
close by during the temptation. (341-19)

One can only wonder at the significance of the disciples'
selection and what past relationships Jesus may have had with
each. As indicated in the Joseph chapter, there is the
implication in one of the Cayce readings that the young disciple
John, of whom Jesus was quite fond, had been Joseph's father,
Jacob. The readings also suggest that Andrew had been with
the Master when he was Amilius and Hermes. (341-1) It is
tempting to speculate further on past involvements with the
other disciples.

As it was the time for the Jewish Passover, Jesus and the
disciples traveled to Jerusalem for the observance. While there,
his great love for God's house came to the fore when he drove

out the moneychangers. They had desecrated the house of prayer by making of it a commercial enterprise or "den of thieves." Surely the influence of his experiences as a priest, guardian, and rebuilder of the Temple in the lives of Asaph and Jeshua was now being exhibited. There also is symbolic meaning to Jesus' aggressive overthrowing of the money-changers. According to him, our bodies, which house the soul, are temples where we can meet God. To do so, it is necessary to physically subdue and control material desires and activities.

Jesus' conduct at the Temple may have approached unwarranted aggressiveness, however. John 2:17 states that, after Jesus had thrown out the moneychangers and merchants, the disciples remembered that it had been written, "Zeal for thy [God's] house will consume me." The quotation is from Psalm 69, where King David writes to the chief musician—Asaph— about the house of God:

> For zeal for thy house has consumed me, and the
> insults of those who insult thee have fallen on me.
>
> (verse 9)

Apparently the disciples connected this quotation with Jesus— and possibly because of a recognized tie between him and Asaph.

After a brief ministry in Judea, Jesus returned to Galilee. On the way, they passed through the Samaritan countryside and stopped at a well near Sychar, which formerly had been known as Shechem.

Jesus remained at the well while the disciples went into town to obtain food. As he rested here, a Samaritan woman approached the well to draw water from it. Much to her surprise, Jesus requested a drink of water from her. She was a Samaritan, and the Jews looked down upon them as inferior. She responded to Jesus' request, however, and gave him a drink from the deep well. Jesus promised to give her "living water" from which she would never thirst. Unable to comprehend the meaning of his words, she was stunned when he recounted details of her personal life. Jesus then revealed to her that he was the messiah who had been promised by God.

When the disciples returned with food, they were surprised

when Jesus declined to eat. Jesus explained, "My food is to do the will of him that sent me, and to finish his work." He must finish the work begun aeons ago of returning humanity to the Father.

When the woman returned to the city, she spread the good word of this strange man, and Jesus and his disciples were welcomed and stayed there several days teaching the people. Many of the Samaritans believed in Jesus as a result of his teachings. This non-Jewish ministry would serve as an important precedent and example for the early Christians in spreading the gospel of Jesus to the Gentiles.

The Shechem well had originally been dug by Jacob, the father of Joseph. Thus Jesus probably had drunk from this well years before as Joseph. He had been sent here specifically by his father, Jacob, to check on the welfare of his brothers. When he arrived at Shechem, he learned that they had left and gone to Dothan. When Jesus was sent to earth by his heavenly Father to check on the welfare of his brothers, he found that they too had gone astray from the directions and knowledge of the Father. It is interesting to note that in his final gifts to his sons, this well and surrounding territory were bequeathed by Jacob to Joseph.

The prior life of Joshua also provides parallels with Jesus' visit. For at this very city of Shechem, the Master had, as Joshua, convened the tribes of Israel to pledge their covenant with God. Joshua had also proclaimed his personal faith in God here with the ringing affirmation: "As for me and my house, we will serve the Lord." How appropriate then, that on this final visit to Shechem, the Master's thirst is quenched by a stranger, and he and his party are accepted and welcomed into the city. Thus the living water offered by Jesus is predicated upon a covenant of faith or commitment to God similar to that which had been pledged by Joshua.

When Jesus returned to Galilee, huge crowds flocked to hear him as he traveled the hills and green valleys. In a gentle and persuasive manner, he delivered a joyous message about the availability of the kingdom of God. Often in the evenings or on the Sabbath, he would speak in the local synagogue to throngs of people hungry to hear his words.

When he came to his hometown of Nazareth, he spoke in the

synagogue on the Sabbath. It was here, as was discussed in the Melchizedek chapter, that Jesus read certain passages from the book of Isaiah. In the selection of the passages and his affirmation that the scripture was that day being fulfilled, he made a possible identification with the life of Melchizedek. According to ancient messianic prophecy, Melchizedek "redivivus" or reincarnated was the one expected to preach "the acceptable year of the Lord" of the Isaiah quote, which Jesus said he was that day fulfilling.

Jesus told his audience at Nazareth that, like the prophet Elijah who was selective in the cities to which he was sent, he too was not free to minister everywhere. The lack of faith of the people in his own country or town limited his performance of miracles there; therefore, he returned to Capernaum and resumed his ministry of healing. So now in the very areas where before, as Joshua, he had fought and killed, Jesus found himself teaching and serving the physical comfort and well-being of the people around him.

Much of Jesus' teaching consisted of simple parables which illustrated points for the least educated, yet confounded his most learned opponents. In these parables Jesus often used agrarian subjects and stories. Subjects such as sheep, wheat, seeds, and the harvesting of grapes in vineyards were things to which the simple rural people of Galilee could relate. It was also a style similar to the agricultural motif found in the Zoroastrian bible, the *Zend Avesta,* whose concepts Jesus had provided in an earlier incarnation as Zend.

Jesus truly loved the children and often spoke to them. Edgar Cayce gave an explanation for Jesus' statement, "Except ye become as little children, ye shall in no wise enter in": The kingdom of God is achieved by our being as forgiving, as generous, and as dependent as little children. (1532)

Soon the popularity of Jesus and some of his statements began to spark controversy. The strict and learned Pharisees resented the free access into the kingdom of God Jesus promised to the people.

According to him, ritual observance of the laws was not necessary. He claimed that sin could be forgiven, and he himself associated with social outcasts. His crowning insult was public mockery and condemnation of the Pharisees' self-professed piety.

Sometimes in his healings, Jesus forgave the sins of those he healed. Immediately the priesthood challenged Jesus' authority and power to forgive sins. The Bible records that Jesus silenced these critics by asking whether it was easier to forgive sins or to heal. Cayce adds an important element to the logic of Jesus' rebuttal: "The recognition was that *sin* had caused the physical disturbance." (5749-14) Thus, the law of karma was at the core of the question and answer and was apparently accepted by both Jesus and the religious authorities of the day. Cayce also explained why the Master forgave sins in some cases of healing and not in others.

Sins are of commission and omission. Sins of commission were forgiven, while sins of omission were called to mind—even by the Master.   281-2

Jesus often had special sessions with his disciples, because he recognized that the multitudes were not ready for the true meaning and spirituality of his teachings. At least part of his famous "sermon on the mount," for example, was delivered privately to his inner followers. After Jesus' death, so-called "secret gospels" were attributed to various of the apostles and were purported to be teachings and interpretations given by Jesus to the select few. A number of these "secret gospels" and other such works are still available today, although they were not canonized into the New Testament. Many of them contain concepts, such as reincarnation, which, as we have already seen, are closely akin to the philosophies and interpretations of Jesus' teachings as given by Edgar Cayce.

While in some ways Jesus' rules seemed easier than the strict observance of the old laws as advocated by the orthodox priesthood, they called, on the other hand, for a very high standard of individual and corporate conduct. They stressed the spirit, rather than the letter, of the law and insisted that love should be the controlling motive in human relationships. There was no limit on how many times one should forgive another, and each person is forgiven by God as he or she forgives others. According to Jesus, more important than one's outer conduct is that person's inner thoughts and intents. These standards were not necessarily in conflict with the

Mosaic laws; primarily they represented an emphasis different from that of the conventional priesthood.

The ministry of Jesus in Galilee lasted nearly three years. Toward the end, his confrontations with religious leaders and government officials became more bitter and extreme. Jesus received word of the beheading of John the Baptist by Herod Antipas, and he must have recognized the grave difficulties which lay ahead for him. Increasingly, he gave private instruction to his disciples, much of which anticipated the time when he would no longer be with them. He even told them that he would be killed but would arise after three days.

Jesus felt John's death deeply. The scriptures relate that after hearing the news, he went to a desert spot outside of Bethsaida, where presumably he meditated and prayed to God. After all, John had been Jesus' cousin, his fellow student and initiate at the Great Pyramid in Egypt, the one who had baptized him, and the great prophet Elijah who had re-entered the world to prepare the way for Jesus.

It was during this period that Jesus talked to his disciples about the public speculation on prior lives he himself had lived. He frequently identified himself as "the son of man." It was a term used by the Essenes, Nazarenes, and others for the messiah who had come to earth many times to help further humanity's spiritual evolution. Its use by Jesus in view of this contemporary meaning has to be significant and an apparent affirmation of his own multiple lives on earth.

On a short visit to Bethsaida, three miles east of Capernaum, Jesus spoke to a captivated audience and then miraculously fed the crowd of 5,000 with but five loaves of bread and two fish. According to Edgar Cayce and the New Testament, such a miraculous feeding actually occurred on two different occasions, although the other feeding involved only 4,000 people. (1532 and Mark 6:34-44, 8:1-10)

Shortly thereafter, Jesus took Peter, James, and John to a high mountain. There he was transfigured before them. His face shown like the sun, and his raiment was as a white light. With him appeared Moses and Elijah, and God identified Jesus as his Elect or Beloved Son. Symbolically, both Moses and Elijah had been essential predecessors of the Master. Moses had been with Jesus when he was Joshua and had prepared the

way for Joshua to lead the Israelites into the Promised Land of
Canaan. Elijah had returned as John the Baptist, the
Forerunner, who had prepared the way for Jesus to show the
way to the Promised Land of the Father.

Friends now warned Jesus that he must leave the area, and
he left Galilee for the last time, heading with his disciples for
Judea where he had already predicted he would meet his death.
He would spend the last seven months before his crucifixion on
this journey. His final ministry would be conducted along the
way.

Rather than taking the direct highway south through
Samaria, Jesus and his group traveled eastward around the
central hills of Samaria before turning south toward the Jordan
valley into Jericho. As he traversed this route, he may have
recalled his reverse journey centuries before as the conquering
military commander, Joshua. Near the culmination of Jesus'
trip, he too would be welcomed as a hero by the crowds in
Jerusalem, but ultimately he would suffer public denigration
and humiliation there. Joshua had chosen to avoid the military
power of Jerusalem and had marched around it. He had,
however, captured its king and personally hanged him from a
tree.

When they arrived at Jericho, Jesus healed a blind man and
spoke to huge crowds. His fame had preceded him, and even
the chief tax collector, Zaccheus, came to hear him and
permitted Jesus to stay in his home. When Joshua had first
approached the city of Jericho years before, his two spies and
representatives had been sheltered and lodged there by a
woman of questionable vocation, Rahab, the prostitute. Now
Joshua as Jesus is given lodging by Zaccheus, whose vocation of
tax-collecting was also considered improper by many. Rahab's
house had been built up into the Jericho wall, thus providing an
excellent spot to view the city's activity. Zaccheus too obtained
a good vantage point to view the Master by climbing up into a
sycamore tree. And just as Rahab and her household were
saved by Joshua after the destruction of Jericho, Jesus
promised Zaccheus: "This day has salvation come to this
house." (Luke 19:9)

Jesus and the disciples spent nearly seven months in the
area of Jericho, although they made several visits to Jerusalem

to participate in major religious festivities.

While in Jerusalem, Jesus taught in the Temple about the nature of God's kingdom. The simplicity and wisdom of his words astonished those who heard him, and his following grew. However, both the Pharisees and Sadducees became united in the conviction that Jesus must be silenced.

They tried unsuccessfully to trap him in his words. An adulteress was brought to him, and he was asked if she should be stoned according to the law of Moses. The Bible records that he wrote on the ground and said, "He that is without sin among you, let him cast the first stone at her." (John 8:7) As her accusers left and there was no one to condemn her, Jesus added that he did not condemn her either. The Cayce readings indicate there were two separate but similar cases of an adulteress being brought to Jesus. Cayce was asked specifically what Jesus wrote upon the ground. In one case, which he said involved Mary Magdalene, the words were: "That which condemned each individual, as each looked over His shoulder as He wrote." (295-8) For the other, Cayce said Jesus wrote: "'Medi, Medici, Cui,' or the expression of mercy and not sacrifice." (1436)

During his visits to Jerusalem, Jesus and his disciples usually stayed overnight in the nearby village of Bethany with the family of Mary, Martha, and Lazarus. The Cayce readings indicate that this Mary is the same as Mary Magdalene and that she had been a harlot in the Galilean city of Magdala. (295-6) Roman Catholic tradition has sometimes associated these two Marys together, but the Biblical account does not make such a clear connection. After her confrontation with Jesus, she returned to the family home in Bethany and was probably the key to Jesus' identification with this family.

Jesus had developed a close association with them and on one occasion was summoned to come and heal Lazarus who had become ill while Jesus was preaching on the other side of the Jordan River. Before Jesus arrived, Lazarus died, and Jesus wept when he learned of his death. One of Jesus' greatest miracles occurred then, when he raised Lazarus from the dead after he had been in the tomb for four days. Cayce indicated that Lazarus had died from the disease we today call typhoid fever and that many who witnessed his return from death were profoundly moved and became dedicated followers of Jesus.

Some people have tried to paint romantic ties between Jesus and Mary Magdalene. Cayce was once asked about this possibility and whether Jesus ever had such a relationship with anyone. He replied:

Mary, the sister of Martha, was an harlot—until the cleansing; and not one that Jesus would have loved, though He loved all. The closer associations brought to the physical or filial love, were with the children—and not with those the age of the Master. 2067-7

As the time for the feast of the Passover approached, Jerusalem was alive with news of Jesus' having raised Lazarus from the dead and speculation that he must be the messiah. The chief priests and Pharisees decided in council that Jesus had to be put to death so that the Romans would not become alarmed at his power and popularity and punish the whole Jewish nation.

When Jesus entered Jerusalem from Bethany a few days before Passover, he rode a lowly donkey but was welcomed by huge crowds waving palm branches. Cayce describes this event:

And when there were the cries of "Hosanna!" and there were the processions, these brought strange feelings to the entity . . . and the wonder became rather that of a worshipfulness.

For, even as He gave on that memorial day . . . if the people had not cried "Hosanna!"—the very rocks, the very trees, the very nature about, would cry out *against* those opportunities lost by the children of men—to proclaim the great day of the Lord!

. . . can ye not see the place . . . the city of the many strange noises, the many strange lights, the many unusual customs . . . and then this new experience of He that brought hope and cheer to those . . . ill in body, those that had lost hope through the holding to material things and to the old tenets of tradition? And can you not see the great throng as they spread their garments—yea, those of high and low estate or position . . .   1468-1

In a triumphal procession, the throng followed Jesus through the city to the Temple.

Every time Jesus approached Jerusalem from the east, he viewed a majestic city whose skyline was dominated by the gleaming, gold-embellished Temple. A different city from David's day, Jerusalem had been destroyed, rebuilt, and completely transformed by Herod with palaces, viaducts, theaters, and other public monuments. The city was a source of Jewish national pride and a showplace even for the Romans. As Jesus observed Jerusalem in his last days, he foresaw its coming destruction, and he sorrowed.

As he contemplated the doom of Jerusalem, he must have been overwhelmed with soul memories. Tradition says that as Adam he had spent part of his life in Jerusalem and that his body had ultimately been buried on Golgotha. As Melchizedek, he had been king of the city. Joshua had not conquered Jerusalem but had surrounded it with the new Israelite nation. Asaph played and sang there for Kings David and Solomon, and Jeshua had returned to Jerusalem from captivity in Babylon to restore the city and its temple. There is little wonder then that Jesus lamented over Jerusalem's fate and that in his prophecies about the coming kingdom of God, he talked in terms of a new Jerusalem.

The traditional ministry of Jesus had now been completed. He had advocated and demonstrated a new order of love and service for one's fellow man. His message had been delivered in settings and events which, in poetic fulfillment, mirrored his earlier lives. The seeds of a new religion had been sown, and an inner core of followers—weak, untested, but carefully chosen—had been given special and even secret directions for the dissemination and spread of the word of God. Jesus' ministry had been punctuated with parables of profound symbolism and meaning and with miracles—miracles which exceeded all those of Israel's earlier prophets.

The stage was now set for Jesus' Passion and for the final and most important miracle of all.

CHAPTER SIXTEEN

Jesus: His Death and Resurrection

But we impart a secret and hidden wisdom of God, which God decreed before the ages for our glorification. None of the rulers of this age understood this; for if they had, they would not have crucified the Lord of glory.
(I Corinthians 2:7-8)

The first day of Passover is marked by a customary ritual feast. At sundown, Jesus and his disciples met in the home of a friend to partake of this meal. It was an event which would hereafter be known to Christianity as the "Last Supper."

Following a psychic reading in 1932, Edgar Cayce did not wake up after the usual suggestion to do so had been given three times. He then began describing the Last Supper spontaneously and in beautiful detail. Because of its unusual quality, it is quoted in its entirety:

The Lord's Supper—here with the Master—see what they had for supper—boiled fish, rice, with leeks, wine, and loaf. One of the

pitchers in which it was served was broken—the handle was broken, as was the lip to same.

The whole robe of the Master was not white, but pearl gray—all combined into one—the gift of Nicodemus to the Lord.

The better looking of the twelve, of course, was Judas, while the younger was John—oval face, dark hair, smooth face—only one with the short hair. Peter, the rough and ready—always that of the very short beard, rough, and not altogether clean; while Andrew's is just the opposite—very sparse, but inclined to be long more on the side and under the chin—long on the upper lip—his robe was always near gray or black, while his clouts or breeches were striped; while those of Philip and Bartholemew were red and brown.

The Master's hair is 'most red, inclined to be curly in portions yet not feminine or weak—*strong*, with heavy piercing eyes that are blue or steel-gray.

His weight would be at least a hundred and seventy pounds. Long tapering fingers, nails well kept. Long nail, though, on the left little finger.

Merry—even in the hour of trial. Joking—even in the moment of betrayal.

The sack is empty. Judas departs.

The last is given of the wine and loaf, with which He gives the emblems that should be so dear to every follower of Him. Lays aside His robe, which is all of one piece—girds the towel about His waist, which is dressed with linen that is blue and white. Rolls back the folds, kneels first before John, James, then to Peter—who refuses.

Then the dissertation as to "He that would be the greatest would be servant of all."

The basin is taken as without handle, and is made of wood. The water is from the gherkins, that are in the wide-mouth shibboleths that stand in the house of John's father, Zebedee.

And now comes "It is finished."

They sing the ninety-first Psalm—"He that dwelleth in the secret place of the Most High shall abide under the shadow of the Almighty. I will say of the Lord, He is my refuge and my fortress: my God; in Him will I trust."

He is the musician as well, for He uses the harp.

They leave for the garden.   5749-1

The authorship of the 91st Psalm is not given in the Bible. One cannot help but wonder if it might not have been written by Asaph, David's chief musician and an earlier incarnation of the Master. The wording and message are very similar to that of other psalms which are attributed to Asaph. Surely, as a

musician now playing the harp, the influence of the Asaph life
may be seen in Jesus.

Jesus gave symbolic meaning to this supper by saying that
the bread represented his body and the wine his blood which
would be given as a ransom for many. This symbolic meaning
may have been borrowed in part from the Essenes, who gave
special symbolic emphasis to bread and wine. As the ceremony
was concluded, Jesus said he would drink no more of the fruit of
the vine "until that day when I drink it new in the kingdom of
God." (Mark 14:25)

Another reading describes the significance and meaning of
Jesus' washing the feet of his disciples.

**Though He was their leader, their prophet, their Lord, their
Master, He signified—through the humbleness of the act [washing
of the feet]—the attitude to which each would come if he would
know that true relationship with his God, his fellow man.**

5749-10

At the conclusion of the supper, Jesus prayed to God:

"Father, the hour has come; glorify thy Son that
the Son may glorify thee, since thou hast given him
power over all flesh, to give eternal life to all whom
thou hast given him . . .

"I glorified thee on earth, having accomplished
the work which thou gavest me to do. And now,
Father, glorify thou me in thine own presence with
the glory which I had with thee before the world
was made."   (Excerpted from John 17:1-5)

In this prayer, Jesus refers to his power over all flesh; it is the
charge God had given to Adam. He also asks for the glory which
he had with God before the world was, not the glory he had
before he entered the earth as Jesus. The implication here may
be that he had not yet achieved this complete glory when he
came as Jesus. His prayer and plea is consonant with the
picture of the Master as given by Cayce—one in which the
Master's mission had stretched from the beginning through
numerous lives until its completion in Jesus.

Jesus prayed specifically for his disciples and noted that he
had lost none of them except "the son of perdition." (John
17:12) Cayce was asked the meaning of this wording; his

answer is a warning to each of us.

Hence that spoken of him that rebelled against the throne of heaven, and manifested in the flesh and in the one who betrayed Him.

Then, all are sons of perdition—or allow that force to manifest through them—who deny Him, or who betray Him, or who present themselves to be one thing and—under earthly environment or for personal gain—or for reasons of gratification—do otherwise; for they do but persecute, deny, betray Him.   **262-93**

After the departure of Judas and the singing of the 91st Psalm, Jesus and the disciples walked to an olive grove or garden called Gethsemane. They had in the past frequently met here at the foot of the Mount of Olives.

Jesus predicted his disciples' lack of faith during the night and told Peter he would deny the Master three times before the cock should crow. Taking Peter, James, and John, he went a little further into the garden to pray. The weary disciples soon fell asleep, and three times Jesus returned to them and found sorrowfully that they had not kept the watch.

In this lonely and critical hour, Jesus faced the temptation to avoid crucifixion. The Bible records his sweating drops of blood in anguish and doubt. He pleaded with God that "this cup" might pass from him, but in glorious victory and surrender of self proclaimed to God: "Not my will, but thine, be done." *The final battle of the soul had been won.* The Gospel of Luke records the appearance of an angel from heaven then to strengthen him.

This surrender of self is undoubtedly the most eloquent message of Jesus' entire ministry. It was the putting of self ahead of God's will that had been Adam's transgression in the beginning—and the sin of each of us. The Cayce readings challenge us all to the same standard of selflessness and vision exemplified by Jesus:

Pray ye, then, that ye be ready in the hour of trial or temptation; that ye may say, even as He, "Not my will but Thine, O God, be done in and through me; that I may have that estate with Thee that was before the worlds were—and be conscious of same."   **3188-1**

. . . for He has promised that we *shall* not be chastened beyond what we are able to bear, and he that endureth unto the end shall *wear* the crown of *eternal* life!   **2466-1**

When Jesus returned to the sleeping disciples the third time, he said:

> It is enough; the hour has come; the Son of man
> is betrayed into the hands of sinners. Rise, let us
> be going; see, my betrayer is at hand.
>
> (Mark 14:41-42)

Judas and a crowd of followers then approached the group. Judas addressed Jesus as "Master" and kissed him in recognition, identification, and betrayal. Guards seized Jesus and dragged him away to the palace of Caiaphas to be tried for blasphemy before the 70 members of the Sanhedrin. Cayce gives a little different perspective as to the charge:

These were the conditions when this man, this prophet, this master, was presented to those in authority for civil consideration; *claiming* by the ones in authority that there had been a neglect to pay tribute, or that there had been first that attempt upon the part of those that were as the followers of same to prevent the tax, the levies to be paid. *This* was the manner of presentation rather than much of that as ye have recorded even in Holy Writ.   1151-3

The Sanhedrin was composed of the chief priests, elders, and scribes. They were the descendants of ancient ruling families whose position had been determined centuries before, after the return from Babylonian captivity. They had considerable power, but not the authority under Roman rule to carry out a death sentence.

A reading identifies one of the Sanhedrin members:

The entity then was among those that were the scoffers, among those of the Sanhedrin itself; for the entity then, in the name Samaleuen, represented the tribes of Reuben, and was of the household of those of that particular people. For it represented same in those experiences in the beginning of the separation of the house, for the entity was itself Reuben!   693-3

As Reuben, this soul previously had been involved in judgment and punishment of the Master. The Master soul, as Joseph, had been betrayed and disposed of by Reuben and his other brothers. It should be noted, however, that Reuben had objected to the killing of Joseph. He had proposed that Joseph be cast into a pit. No detail is given about his words now before the Sanhedrin regarding the disposition of Jesus.

In the Cayce readings, Jesus is depicted as cheerful through this ordeal and even on the way to the cross.

The trial—that was not with the pangs of pain, as so oft indicated, but rather glorying in the opportunity of taking upon self that which would *right* man's relationship to the Father—in that man, through his free will, had brought sin into the activities of the children of God. Here *His Son* was bringing redemption through the shedding of blood that they might be free.   5749-10

For, know—only in those that God hath favored is there the ability to laugh, even when clouds of doubt arise, or when every form of disturbance arises. For, remember, the Master smiled—and laughed, oft—even on the way to Gethsemane.   2984-1

Throughout the night, Jesus was ridiculed, blasphemed, and beaten.

The next morning, he was brought to the Roman governor, Pilate, for trial on charges of failing to give proper tribute to Rome and Caesar. After questioning Jesus and learning that he was a Galilean, Pilate sent him to the visiting Herod, who had jurisdiction over Galilee. Herod found Jesus guilty of nothing worthy of death and returned him to Pilate, who then sought to release him. The crowds demanded his crucifixion, however, and urged that Barabbas, not Jesus, be released under the holiday tradition of forgiving one criminal. Bowing to public pressure, Pilate sentenced Jesus to death by crucifixion but symbolically denied responsibility for the act by washing his hands.

The Master had, as Adam, avoided responsibility for his action by saying to God that the woman God had given him had beguiled him: The fall was her doing. Now Jesus, in his final test, is facing and must endure that same avoidance of responsibility and passing of blame by Pilate.

After Jesus' condemnation by the Sanhedrin, the Bible records that Judas returned the thirty pieces of silver to the chief priests and renounced his act of betrayal. Thereafter, he went out and hanged himself.

Just as Jesus was sold for thirty pieces of silver, the Master had as Joseph been sold for twenty pieces of silver (although the Jewish historian, Josephus, records the actual amount as thirty pieces also). The sale of Joseph had been proposed by his brother, Judah. The similarity of names and the incidents in which each was involved raises the spectre of speculation that Judah and Judas may have been one and the same soul.

The reason for Judas' betrayal of Jesus has been the subject of conjecture throughout history. Edgar Cayce was asked the following:

Q-27. *Was Judas Iscariot's idea in betraying Jesus to force Him to assert Himself as a king and bring in His kingdom then?*

A-27. Rather the desire of the man to force same, and the fulfilling of that as Jesus spoke of same at the Supper.   2067-7

Another reading indicates that Judas' friends sought to proclaim Jesus as the people's deliverer from bondage. (1179-7) The impatience with God's plan, which Jesus exhibited in the beginning as Adam, is now being met by him in the same trait of Judas and his friends.

The soldiers put a crown of thorns on Jesus' head and a reed in his right hand and then mocked him as the "king of the Jews." Around nine o'clock in the morning, Jesus was led through the streets to a hill outside the walls of Jerusalem known as Calvary or Golgotha. It was here, according to some tradition, that the bones of Adam had been buried and given their final rest.

With two other prisoners on crosses on either side of him, Jesus was nailed to his. When the cross was raised to its vertical position, Jesus was thus suspended between the earth and sky.

. . . so that those who looked, those who beheld, might know that they—themselves—must pass along that road, *crucifying* in their bodies that which would make for the gratifying of desires, that which would make for an exaltation of self rather than those tenets as He gave: "The new commandment I give, that ye love one another."   897-1

Even in his hour of extreme anguish, Jesus recognized the statement of faith and forbearance of one of the thieves on the cross and promised him: "Truly I say to you, today you will be with me in paradise." (Luke 23:43)

He also was concerned about the welfare of his mother and even his enemies. He asked his disciple John to look after his mother, and in an act of supreme and sublime charity prayed: "Father, forgive them; for they know not what they do." (Luke 23:34)

Jesus had been deserted at the cross by all but one of his own disciples, and yet the power and value of patience can be seen in his tolerance with them. In the years ahead, they would return to testify to the works and resurrection of Jesus and would eventually suffer their own martyrdom. It is an eloquent demonstration of the importance of patience, tolerance, and forbearance by each of us in our dealings with our fellow human beings.

Cayce indicates that the women at the cross were those of Jesus' own household, the mother of John and James, Mary Magdalene, and other women of that grouping. (5749-10)

As Jesus hung on the cross, he asked, "My God, my God, why hast thou forsaken me?" The Cayce readings state that Jesus endured God's temporary absence so that the rest of us would not have to experience such a forsaking. (2466) A possible translation of Jesus' words from the original Aramaic could be: "My God, my God, for this I was spared."[1] Truly for this moment the Master had been spared, even from the time when as Adam he had erred and been banished from Eden.

Jesus was asked why, if he was the Son of God, he did not save himself. The answer is supplied by the readings thus:

Though ye know He had the power within Himself to come down from the Cross, though He had the power to heal, though He had power to rid the very taking *hold* upon death, it had no claims upon Him. Why? *quickened* by the Father because the life *lived* among men, the dealings among *men*, brought *only* hope, *only* patience, *only* love, *only* long-suffering!

This then being the law of God made manifest, He *becomes* the law by manifesting same before man; and thus—as man, even as ye—becomes as one with the Father.

For until ye become in purpose, in activity, a savior—yea, a god—unto thy fellow man, ye do not take hold upon that *personality*, the *individuality* of GOD—that is the life . . . eternity, hope and love!

1158-12

The Bible indicates that from the sixth to the ninth hour there was darkness, and an earthquake occurred at the time of Jesus' death. The Cayce readings confirm these unusual natural phenomena and describe great fear and panic among the people. (333, 1747)

Jesus expressed his thirst, but refused an offer of vinegar and gall which would have assuaged his pain.

The Gospel of John says that just prior to his death, Jesus knew "that all things were now accomplished." (John 19:28) Shortly afterward, he cried, "It is finished," or "It is fulfilled" (John 19:30) and gave up the spirit. The first begotten of God, our Elder Brother, the Good Shepherd, the Master, the Way— and now the Christ—was dead. The mission begun aeons ago and carried through numerous lifetimes was now fulfilled.

To be sure that Jesus was dead, one of the soldiers "pierced his side, and immediately came there out blood and water." (John 19:34) Edgar Cayce was asked to explain this verse.

The fulfilling of "Without the shedding of blood there is no remission of sins." Hence His blood was shed as the sacrifice of the just for the unjust, that ye all may stand in the same light with the Father. 5749-10

According to Matthew and Luke, the veil of the Temple was torn from the top to the bottom at the death of Jesus. The veil traditionally separated the Holy of Holies from the rest of the Temple and was lifted once a year by the High Priest when he made a sacrificial propitiation for the sins of the people. Jesus' death served as the permanent sacrifice to God for the sins of humanity. The veil symbolically separating humanity from God was torn because the separation no longer existed; people now had direct access to God.

The Bible relates that Jesus was hurriedly taken from the cross so that he would not remain there on the Sabbath day. One author, after examining the *Secret Gospel of Peter,* suggests that the precedent of being taken down before sundown had been set years before by Joshua (the Master) when he insisted that the kings whom he had hanged be removed from their trees before sunset.[6] This earlier experience of Joshua in hanging five alien kings, including the king of Jerusalem, may possibly explain why Jesus' death was one of hanging or crucifixion from a tree or wooden cross.

The body of Jesus was put into the new tomb of a friend, Joseph of Arimathaea. And just as Joshua had done before with the kings, the cave tomb or sepulchre was sealed with a stone. Roman guards were placed in front of it.

The Cayce readings tell of one woman who helped prepare

"the linens about the head of the Master when He was buried
by Josephus and the friends," (1081) and of another who:

. . . aided in preparing . . . the wrappings for the last of the
anointing of the body of the Holy One—rather the wrappings than
the spices, for Magdalene and Mary and Jose [Josie], and the
mother of the Lord prepared these. The napkins that were about His
head, and with those seals that were later made as raised figures . . .
                                                        649-1

[She prepared] The seals of the Holy One, as the seals of the son
of David; the pear with the bell, with the pomegranates on either
side.   649-2

In previous chapters, legend was encountered suggesting
that the spot of Adam's creation had been at Jerusalem and
that the final grave of Adam and Melchizedek would be here. If
so, the story has come full circle, and the Garden of Eden has
become the Garden of Gethsemane.

The Bible records that Jesus was in the tomb for three days.
On the morning of the third day, Mary Magdalene (and possibly
also Mary, the mother of Jesus) came there to complete the
customary burial preparations but found the stone rolled away
and the grave empty. Mary Magdalene then ran to Peter and
John, and together they found the tomb as she had described it.
Peter and John left, and weeping, Mary saw an angel within the
tomb. As she turned away, Jesus appeared before her.

Hence when those of His loved ones and those of His brethren
came on that glad morning when the tidings had come to them,
those that stood guard heard a fearful noise and saw a light, and—
"the stone has been rolled away!" Then they entered into the
garden, and there Mary first saw her *risen* Lord. Then came they of
His brethren with the faithful women, those that loved His mother,
those that were her companions in sorrow, those who were making
preparations that the law might be kept that even there might be no
desecration of the ground about His tomb. They, too, of His friends,
His loved ones, His brethren, saw the angels.   5749-6

Jesus appeared first to one who had been an adulteress but
one who had been forgiven by him and whose life had been
changed. Jesus had also once commended Mary Magdalene's
attention and faithfulness over that of her sister, Martha, who
was more concerned with household duties. Mary Magdalene
had apparently become an important factor among the

followers of Jesus.

> ... [she] was the same to whom the Master first appeared upon
> the resurrection morn; the same to whom many of the apostles and
> leaders during that experience went for counsel, in the ways and
> manners that are spoken of in the various accounts that are kept in
> the present . . .
> ... she thought He was the gardener. This indicates all the hope-
> lessness, all the sorrow that is possible to be indicated in hopeless-
> ness. Yet the *joy* should be the condition as would be thought on,
> rather than the separation at the time. This is going backward, even
> to be affected by the separation—when there is the joy as
> manifested in, "My Lord and my God."   295-8

Thereafter, Jesus appeared to various and ultimately all of
the disciples. On the road to Emmaus, where as Joshua he had
caused the sun to stand still, the resurrected Jesus visited with
two of his followers. In an upper room where the eleven
disciples were assembled, Jesus suddenly appeared and
showed them—especially the doubting Thomas—the scars in
his hands and side. Later he appeared again to them in Galilee
at the Sea of Tiberias and there caused them to catch a
multitude of fish. Jesus then ate with them and commanded
Peter to "feed my sheep." This command, though, was not
given to Peter alone.

> And so may ye in the present, even as was bidden to thy neighbor,
> thy brother in the Lord, "Feed my lambs . . . feed my sheep." This is
> the work of thy hands in the present; and these directed not by the
> eye-service of man but to the oneness of purpose of desire to bring
> into the hearts of men again and again *hope*, encouragement; and to
> *sow* again and again the seed that bear the fruits of the Spirit . . .
> patience, gentleness, kindness, brotherly love, long-suffering! For
> against such there is no law.   1529-1

Apparently the disciples and followers of Jesus felt it was
safe to return to Jerusalem from Galilee. The following Cayce
reading describes some of their activities after the resurrection.

> ... with the return from Galilee and the activities there upon the
> ascension (which was fifty days after the resurrection), Mary the
> mother of Christ became a dweller in the house or home of John—
> who joined with those in Bethany; for John, as may be well known,
> was the wealthiest of the disciples of the Christ. His estate would be
> counted in the present, in American money, as being near to a
> quarter of a million dollars; or to the estate where he was a power

with those in the Roman and Jewish power at the period. 295-8

Jesus later met with his disciples in Jerusalem and told them to "tarry" there until they had received the power of the Holy Spirit. He led them along the road to nearby Bethany, where he blessed them.

And it was here that Jesus ascended into heaven.

... [There were] five hundred who beheld Him as He entered into glory and saw the angels, heard their announcement of the event that must one day come to pass—and will only be to those who believe, who have faith, who look for and who expect to see Him as He is.   3615-1

The total mission of our Elder Brother—the Christ—had now been completed. Its fulfillment came in Jesus' surrender of self and in his death and resurrection. He showed the way of selflessness through his death; his resurrection signaled God's acknowledgment that death, the penalty of man's error, had been overcome.

The period of resurrection—here we find that in which ye *all* may glory. For without the fact of His overcoming death, the whole of the experience would have been as naught.   5749-10

For death hath no sting, it hath no power over those that know the resurrection ... how the resurrection brought to the consciousness of man that power that God hath given to man, that may reconstruct, resuscitate, even every atom of a physically sick body, that may resurrect even every atom of a sin-sick soul, may resurrect the soul that it lives on and on in the glory of a resurrected, a regenerated Christ in the souls and hearts of men!   1158-5

Another Cayce reading puts it in this manner:

But when the Prince of Peace came into the earth for the completing of His OWN development in the earth, *He* overcame the flesh *and* temptation. So He became the first of those that overcame death in the body, enabling Him to so illuminate, to so revivify that body as to take it up again, even when those fluids of the body had been drained away by the nail holes in His hands and by the spear piercing His side.   1152-1

God had now removed the punishment of death He had imposed upon the Master in Eden when, as Adam, he erred. The Master had now overcome the wages of sin.

All humanity could also now overcome the sting of death—

the penalty of disobeying the laws of God. But it could only be overcome by a total and complete surrender to the will of God. Jesus had provided the paradoxical key for obtaining the freedom of the soul: One must lose one's life in order to gain it; in discarding self—or selfishness—we find our true selves.

It was now finished. The long journey was over. For the first time in all His sojourns on earth, the Master could now rise to the victorious embrace of the Father and ascend to the glory which had awaited Him from the beginnings of time.

Amid the tumult of the angels and heavenly hosts, there were choruses of joy and praise for this Beloved One of the Father who had so loved His brothers and sisters that He had suffered and given His all for them. He asked only in return that they love one another.

By the visible example of the Master—the Christ—the trail was now blazed; the road was now marked and lighted for others to follow. And the haunting memory of the abode of the Father—the true home of the soul—had been rekindled in the hearts and minds of those who seek.

CHAPTER SEVENTEEN

Jesus: His Return

So Christ, having been offered once to bear the sins of many, will appear a second time, not to deal with sin but to save those who are eagerly waiting for him. *(Hebrews 9:28)*

The Essenes and others had expected a suffering, a priestly, and a kingly messiah. Such expectations were based upon prophecy in the Old Testament and elsewhere.[1]

Jesus obviously had fulfilled the suffering messiah concept, but the kingly and priestly aspects were not so obvious. The writers of the New Testament went to great lengths to supply these missing elements. The book of Hebrews discusses in copious detail the new priesthood Jesus established through his connection with Melchizedek. The gospels note the lineage of King David, and Jesus was mockingly anointed the "king of the Jews," but the usual incidents of royalty and kingship were notably missing from the life of Jesus.

Jesus' ultimate kingly ministry was first broached in the books of Enoch and is mentioned often in both the Old and New Testaments. His actual kingship, however, is expected to be supplied in his Second Coming, a subject which is an integral part of the New Testament.

Much of the 24th chapter of Matthew is an account by Jesus of his future return. He describes wars and other iniquities and refers to the abominations prophesied by Daniel as signals of the time of his coming. He warns against false prophets but promises to shorten the days of desolation for the sake of his elect. The sun and moon shall be darkened, and then the sign of the Son of man shall appear in the heavens. He shall be seen "coming on the clouds of heaven with power and great glory," and the angels "will gather his elect from the four winds, from one end of heaven to the other."

An earlier passage from Matthew adds:

> For the Son of man is to come with his angels in the glory of his Father, and then he will repay every man for what he has done. Truly, I say to you, there are some standing here who will not taste death before they see the Son of man coming in his kingdom.   (Matthew 16:27-28)

The return of Jesus was thus thought by his followers to be imminent. A Cayce reading explains the meaning of the above quote, indicating it was misunderstood by those who heard it. It actually meant:

Those individuals that were in hearing and in keeping of those things presented by the Master in that experience would be in the manifested form in the earth during the periods of fulfillments in the earth of the prophecies spoken of.   262-60

In other words, they would reincarnate at the time of his return.

The return of Jesus or his Second Coming probably should be viewed on more than one level. It first may relate to the reception of the Christ Consciousness in an individual. It may also pertain to the arrival of the Christ Consciousness on a national or international scale in our dealings with one another, or the promised "millennium." Finally, it may mean the actual physical return of Jesus in the skies in the manner in which he left. On this occasion, he will dispense the final judgment.

Jesus promised to be with those who call upon him in any age and time.

Is He abroad today in the earth? Yea, in those that cry unto Him from every corner . . . And He comes again in the hearts and souls

and minds of those that seek to know His ways.   5749-5

Another Cayce reading states that he is not in a body in the
earth, but that he "may come at will to him who *wills* to be one
with, and acts in love to make same possible." (5749-4) Also:

There is that access, then, that way, to the Throne of grace, of
mercy, of peace, of understanding, within thine own self. For He
hath promised to meet thee in thine own temple, in thine own body,
through thine own mind ... And then enter into the Holy of Holies,
within thine own consciousness; turn within; see what has
prompted thee. And He has promised to meet thee there. 922-1

The veil isolating the Temple Holy of Holies was rent and
torn symbolically at the death of Jesus. We are now free to meet
God—and the Master—within our own inner bodily temple.
Paul reminds us: "Know ye not that ye are the temple of God,
and that the Spirit of God dwelleth in you?" (I Corinthians 3:16)

Chapter 20 of the Book of Revelation describes the binding
of the devil or Satan for a thousand years during which his
influence on earth will not be felt. Jesus' elect will rule with him
on earth at this time; they are called those of the "first
resurrection." Thereafter Satan will be let loose again on earth
for a season. The "second resurrection" occurs sometime
afterward in the final judgment, when Satan is cast out forever.

Some Biblical passages seem to refer to this thousand-year
period, or millennium, in connection with the Second Coming
of Jesus. The following Cayce reading, apparently from John
the Beloved, also contemplates the millennium:

Q-7. *When Jesus the Christ comes the second time, will He set up
His kingdom on earth and will it be an everlasting kingdom?*

A-7. Read His promises in that ye have written of His words, even
as "I gave." He shall rule for a thousand years. Then shall Satan be
loosed again for a season.   5749-4

Another reading adds:

... for a thousand years He will walk and talk with men of every
clime. Then in groups, in masses, and then they shall reign of the
first resurrection for a thousand years; for this will be when the
changes materially come.   364-8

During this millennium period, there apparently will be a new
age of love and understanding among the nations and in the
dealings of individuals one with the other. The distracting and

misleading influence of the devil will be absent. This age seems
to be one characterized by a return of the Master—or at least of
his spirit. Throughout, he shall be the reigning monarch—the
kingly messiah at last.

There are other Biblical references to the Second Coming
which appear to pertain to his return at the final judgment at
the end of this world. His return will be in the clouds in the
manner in which he was seen to leave. And there are Cayce
readings which speak in this manner.

**For, He shall come as ye have seen Him go, in the *body* He
occupied in Galilee. The body that He formed, that was crucified on
the Cross, that rose from the tomb, that walked by the sea, that
appeared to Simon, that appeared to Philip, that appeared to "I,
even John."   5749-4**

When will his actual return be? Although a Cayce reading
indicates that the year 1998 may somehow relate to the return
of the Master, the readings and the Bible agree that only God—
not even the Master—knows when he will return.

**Q-10. He said He would come again. What about His Second
Coming?**
**A-10. The time no one knows. Even as He gave, not even the Son
himself. *Only* the Father. Not until His enemies—and the earth—
are wholly in subjection to His will, His powers.**
Q-11. Are we entering the period of preparation for His coming?
A-11. Entering the test period, rather.   5749-2

**. . . as has been promised through the prophets and the sages of
old, the time—and half time—has been and is being fulfilled in this
day and generation, and . . . soon there will again appear in the earth
that one through whom many will be called to meet those that are
preparing the way for His day in the earth. The Lord, then, will
come, "even as ye have seen him go."   262-49**

Just as the Essenes and others were necessary for the
preparation of the birth of the Master as Jesus, so too is
preparation required for his return. He will come again "when
those that are His have made the way clear, *passable.*" (262-49)
For he cannot come again until there is the seeking for him.
(1908-1)

The preparation for his return requires an expectancy and a
high standard of individual conduct.

Let thy daily life be free from criticism, from condemnation, from hate, from jealousy. And as ye give power to the Spirit of Peace, so may the *Prince of Peace*, the love of God, manifest.   3976-23

The chronicle of the Master therefore is not one that is contained and confined or which ended 2,000 years ago. Rather it is continuous and growing—stretching to eternity. He is available daily to those who wait upon him. He also seeks to be a part of the conduct of the nations of the world. And he will come again—in all his glory—to judge this world. His kingdom is forever, and it stretches throughout the heavens. It is a realm which he has earned and into which he beckons and invites each of us.

CHAPTER EIGHTEEN

The Message of Old

But the Counselor, the Holy Spirit, whom the Father will send in my name, he will teach you all things, and bring to your remembrance all that I have said to you. **(John 14:26)**

The writers of the New Testament were preoccupied with Jesus' Second Coming and were not concerned with matters of death and the hereafter. They were convinced that his return was imminent, and it took precedence over all else. What was the importance of subsequent lives if the final judgment is so close that physical death will not be experienced? Similarly, there was no need to write down the sayings and philosophy of Jesus, for they could be remembered until the end time. After all, Jesus had promised his disciples that they would see the Son of man returning in His glory.

It would only be as the disciples were growing old and some had already experienced death that the value of making a historical written record of Jesus and his teachings would become apparent. Even then, the accounts would not emphasize philosophy and metaphysical doctrines but would tell how to be saved. The writings would have a missionary zeal stressing salvation through faith. This message was the "good news," which is the literal meaning of the word "gospel." It would be centered upon spiritual experiences rather than doctrinal ideology.

For any who still may have difficulty with the concept of prior lives of the Master and insist that such knowledge must be spelled out clearly in the scriptures, the above should be kept in mind.

They should also recall the occasional statements in the New Testament that the full story of Jesus and the mysteries of God could not be shared with the general public. Paul and others insisted there was a message which was not written because the people were not yet able to receive it.

> The unspiritual man does not receive the gifts of the Spirit of God, for they are folly to him, and he is not able to understand them because they are spiritually discerned.   (I Corinthians 2:14)

> But I, brethren, could not address you as spiritual men, but as men of the flesh, as babes in Christ. I fed you with milk, not solid food; for you were not ready for it; and even yet you are not ready . . .   (I Corinthians 3:1-2)

Jesus, too, spoke of the need to withhold the full wisdom from those who were not spiritually advanced. After stating to his disciples, "he that hath ears to hear, let him hear," Jesus continued:

> To you has been given the secret of the kingdom of God, but for those outside everything is in parables.   (Mark 4:11)

And it is the parables of Jesus which are the fodder of the gospels.

The famous early Church theologian Origen noted that "divine matters are brought down to men somewhat secretly." He sagely observed that they "are all the more secret in proportion to one's disbelief or unworthiness."[1] He then added:

> This wisdom, therefore, is written more clearly and perfectly in our hearts, if it has been revealed to us according to the revelation of the mystery, which was kept secret for long ages, but is now disclosed through the prophetic writings and through the appearing of our Lord and Savior

Jesus Christ, to whom be glory for ever more.[2]

It is essential to look at prophetic and other writings of Jesus' time, which in many cases lie outside the Bible, to find the real and underlying philosophy of the earliest Christians as they had received it from Jesus. "It would be unwise to insist that only those things are true that may be found in the Bible and that one is not permitted to investigate further."[3]

There were secret versions of some of the gospels and other books which the early Christian authors claimed had hidden meaning understandable only to the spiritual initiate. Some of these documents are still available, but often their meaning is cryptic. We have examined many of these works as well as writings of ancient groups who claimed to know the secret and hidden meaning of God's revelations to man. Very often these documents are in harmony with the Cayce story of the Master's many lives. These sources have also included materials from recent archaeological finds which generally have not yet been assimilated into traditional Christian interpretations of the gospels.

It is imperative that Christianity re-examine its origins and early doctrines. It should do so in the light of these recently available documents and even other ancient sources which have in ages past been relegated to heresy—with or without good reason. As one scholar puts it:

> The Church of today, still laboring under the credal follies of its Councils from the fourth century onwards, has not got around to making the theological studies, and the ordinary Bible reader is denied the explanatory notes and comments which would introduce him to the Essene and Jewish interpretations.[4]

It is time Christianity rediscovered its message of old.

In the early Christian book, *Acts of Thomas,* King Misdaeus asks Judas Thomas the name of his Master and Judas answers, "Thou canst not hear his true name at this time; but the name that was given him is Jesus Christ."[5] As we have seen, the Bible records discussions between Jesus and his disciples as to who they and the general public thought he had been—or, in effect, what they thought his true name was. Just as the *Acts of*

Thomas indicates, the Bible records Peter answering only that Jesus was the Christ, the Son of God. The Ethiopian *Book of Enoch* also indicates that the Son of man was revealed by God only to the holy and elect ones. (1 Enoch 62:7) But Jesus did use certain terms and titles for himself in the Bible which, on close examination, seemingly give some of his true names, identify him, and connect him with earlier lives.

One of these titles is that of "Son of man." It has been mentioned in earlier chapters but deserves further comment in view of Jesus' strong identification with it.

The Hebraic meaning of "Son of man" implies a member of the human race, but it is a man as conceived of by God rather than a man as we find him in his present state. The title is used in the Bible in Daniel 7:13 in a messianic designation of "one like the Son of man" who will appear on the clouds before the Ancient of Days and receive his eternal kingdom over all peoples and nations. The title appears frequently in the Enochian books, which were held in high esteem by the Essenes and early Christians. The messianic term "Son of man" may actually have originated in the Enoch books, and they, like Daniel, used the title in referring to a coming messiah. Jesus used the "Son of man" title 82 times in the gospels in referring to himself. It was a messianic term in current usage at the time, and one that Jesus went to extreme lengths with which to identify. As we have earlier seen, it had been used historically in referring also to Adam and Enoch.

The "True Teacher" or "Teacher of Righteousness" of the Essenes, mentioned so frequently in their documents, epitomized the Son of man. It was believed by them that this soul comes among us from time to time "to call us back to our better selves, to the path of concern for others, to love and goodness of heart."[6] He is our home and the goal toward which we strive. "Through him, in spirit, we reach out to wonders infinite and glories incomparable."[7] In earlier chapters, we have seen this messianic Teacher of Righteousness identified in Essene documents as Asaph and possibly Joseph. He was expected to come back as the messiah.

The Son of man was also known by the Gnostics and other early Christian groups as the Heavenly Man or Sky Man who descends to earth from time to time as a mere mortal in order to impart spiritual direction to people. This "Heavenly Man" title was another title for the Teacher of Righteousness of the Essenes who would return in the end times as the messiah.[8]

> When we are given access to the legacy of the Essenes, we are able to appreciate what they were seeking to transmit. It was for the high purpose of redeeming the Elect and finally earth itself, and incorporating the faithful in the Messianic personality, that the Heavenly Man, in whose image Adam had been created, had incarnated in the True Teacher in the End Times.[9]

Some of Jesus' followers recognized Adam's appearance in Jesus, and we can observe these concepts in the Pauline writings. Paul wrote of the first Adam and the last Adam and linked him with Jesus, Paul's messiah and true teacher of the end times.

This Heavenly Man, Adam Kadmon, Sky Man, or Archetypal Man is associated with and called Wisdom in many of these ancient writings.[10] The characterization of Hermes as the personification of Wisdom, discussed in the Hermes chapter, should also be recalled.

The eighth chapter of Proverbs is considered to be a veneration of Wisdom. Its hidden meaning and identification with the Heavenly Man, the messiah, can now be conjectured however. And its authorship by Asaph, an incarnation of the Master, is a possibility in view of the similarity in language and style to Asaph's psalms and the fact that Asaph was a contemporary of Solomon, to whom the proverb compilation is normally attributed. Listen again to the language of Proverbs 8:22-31:

> The Lord created me at the beginning of his work,
> the first of his acts of old.
> Ages ago I was set up, at the first before the beginning of the earth.
> When there were no depths I was brought forth,
> when there were no springs abounding with water.
> Before the mountains had been shaped, before the hills, I was brought forth;
> before he had made the earth with its fields, or the

first of the dust of the world.
When he established the heavens, I was there,
when he drew a circle on the face of the deep,
when he made firm the skies above, when he
established the fountains of the deep,
when he assigned to the sea its limit, so that the
waters might not transgress his command, when
he marked out the foundations of the earth,
then I was beside him, like a master workman; and
I was daily his delight, rejoicing before him always,
rejoicing in his inhabited world and delighting in
the sons of men.

The above serves nicely as a beautiful and poetic version of the Edgar Cayce account of creation and the role of the Master in it.

Another Essene and early Christian doctrine was that of the Logos or the Word. The Gospel of John opens with this terminology. Philo, the first-century A.D. Jewish historian, wrote of the Egyptian Essenes, who were known as the Therapeuts. According to them, this Word, or Logos, exemplifies and lights the path for all mortals in traveling and finding their way back to God and becoming again Sons of God. The Therapeuts—and apparently Philo—believed that the Word or Logos was God's Firstborn, the Beginning (Adam), and was incarnate in Jesus. Hermes also was called the "Logos." Another word for the "Logos" is the "Nous" or Mind. In a couple of gnostic documents Hermes is also called the "Nous."[11]

A further legacy of the Essenes is a strong emphasis on a priestly messiah, who is identified as Christ Jesus in the Epistle to the Hebrews. The link here is made through a connection with Melchizedek, who, according to Cayce, was an incarnation of the Master.

Another title of significance is "the Elect One." It was a designation by God for Enoch as well as the messiah in the book, 1 Enoch. In Luke 9:35, God says at the Transfiguration: "This is my Son, my Chosen; listen to him." The better translation of the Greek text should probably read: "This is my Son, the Elect One; hear him." It is a possible identification of Jesus with Enoch from the highest source.

Jesus called himself the "good shepherd." This same designation was used in ancient documents for Hermes and for Zend.

The messiah was referred to in the Old Testament as the "branch" from the vine of Israel. (i.e., Jeremiah 23:5) The priest, Jeshua, was identified as this messianic branch. Jesus too used the terminology of the vine and the branch. Possibly because Israel would fail to recognize and claim him as the messiah, Jesus substituted himself for Israel as the "vine." His followers became the "branches." (John 15:5)

The first Christian martyr, Stephen, called Jesus "The Righteous One." (Acts 7:52) Such designation calls to mind the Essene messianic title of "Teacher of Righteousness" as well as the name Melchizedek, the actual meaning of which is "king (or Lord) of Righteousness."

All these titles and philosophies are important for us because they seem to identify Jesus with persons whom Edgar Cayce said were former incarnations of the Master. Such identifications, often by the Master himself, cannot be discounted simply as coincidence or accident. The manner and context in which they were given support the concept that the Master's complete mission encompassed multiple lives.

There were, as we have seen, numerous groups which believed that the messiah or Jesus had come to earth on more than one occasion for our spiritual advancement.

It is becoming increasingly apparent from the records available to us today that the Essenes prepared the way for the Christian Church and that they "helped to shape both the Church's soul and its body."[12] The first Christians—the followers of Jesus—were Essenes, or at least quasi-Essenes, as one scholar terms them.[13] The Essenes, we may recall, believed that the soul who would be the messiah had come to earth numerous times on behalf of humanity's salvation. He had, for example, been their Teacher of Righteousness.

Among the Gnostics, who encompassed a large number and variety of factions, are early Christians who also believed that this life of Jesus was not his first. The Gnostics have already been discussed, and we know them through the eyes of their critics as well as their own writings, including those found recently at Nag Hammadi, Egypt. Their demise occurred as a result of an organized effort by the Church to codify its theology into a single creed. From the gnostic writings, we now know that they had many traditions about Jesus which were secret and "hidden" from the masses who, in the second century, became the "catholic" church.[14] The gnostic "Testimony of Truth" condemns orthodox Christians who profess to speak for Christianity but who do not actually know who Christ is.[15]

But there are other early Christian groups, such as the Nazarenes, Ebionites, and Elkasites, who believed in the multiple lives of the messiah or Christ and whose backgrounds and identities are not so well known. Rediscovering them will be revelatory.

Shortly after the departure of Jesus, the apostles and others who had been close to him established the Church of Jerusalem. It became the Mother Church of Christianity and was headed by James, the brother of Jesus, until his martyrdom in 62 A.D. Those who founded and comprised this Church were Jewish and known as the Nazarenes. They held to many of the old Jewish customs and, as reflected in the New Testament, had difficulty adjusting to the outreach by Paul and others to the Gentiles of the Mediterranean area.

After the destruction of Jerusalem in 70 A.D., the Mother Church relocated across the Jordan River in the district of Pella. Its factions were known variously thereafter as the Nazarenes, Ebionites, and Elkasites. Their belief in the many lives of the Master is documented not only by them but also by their adversaries, who more and more included the Gentilean Christians. St. Jerome said disdainfully of the Ebionites in the fourth century A.D.:

> It is they who are called Nazarenes, who believe
> in Christ, Son of God, born from the Virgin Mary,
> but who, by wishing to be both Jews and
> Christians, are neither one nor the other.[16]

On the other hand, the Ebionites regarded themselves as the true mother church of Christianity and "guardian of the truth as it is in Jesus."[17] It has also been suggested that there are historical connections between these Jewish-Christian Ebionites and the Essenes of Qumran.[18]

The Gentilean Roman and Eastern Churches, however, grew

primarily out of the teachings of Paul. He focused totally on Jesus' crucifixion, resurrection, and ascension and was not interested in the details of Jesus' life or what he had said or taught. He may not even have been familiar with these details. Their promulgation was left to the Jerusalem Church and its immediate successors.

As the Roman and Eastern Churches became more organized, they began to simplify their theology so as to broaden its appeal and to accommodate the religious rites and beliefs of the Greek and Roman populations which they served. Numerous Councils were convened during the fourth and fifth centuries, and certain beliefs of the original Mother Church, those of the Judeo-Christians, were declared heretical. As we have seen earlier, the belief in the multiple lives of the Master was one such casualty. These Judeo-Christian churches declined and were virtually wiped out in the Muslim tide which subsequently swept the Middle East.

In looking at the writings of the early orthodox Church, we witness a new religion obsessed with renunciation of "heresy." Archaeological finds in this century permit us to examine objectively some of these heretical beliefs and to compare them with the well-known, standardized, clerical doctrines. When we discern the sources of the so-called "heresies," we find that many of them may be traceable to the apostles and followers who knew Jesus and probably to the Master himself. In its place was imposed a simple, mandatory, credal, hierarchical theology which was promulgated some two hundred or more years after the death of Jesus. It was an orthodoxy stressing ritual baptism, confession of the Church creed, participation in worship, and obedience to the clergy. It reflected a fear, not only of certain Christian factions but also of individual insight from God and of the inner guidance of the soul.

Thus, the Roman and Eastern Orthodox Churches, in haste to standardize Christian theology, lost some of the original teachings of Jesus. These teachings were maintained by the Nazarenes, Ebionites, Elkasites, and others until these groups passed into oblivion a few centuries later. They were not extreme, fanatical factions but remnants of the inner core of Jesus' faithful followers. They are the ones who should have had the teachings of Jesus—even the hidden mysteries—in their purest and most unadulterated form.

One of their important beliefs had been the conviction that the Master had come many times to help his erring brothers return to the fold of the Father.

CHAPTER NINETEEN
Our Heritage

The Spirit himself and our spirit bear united witness that we are children of God. And if we are children we are heirs as well: heirs of God and coheirs with Christ, sharing his sufferings so as to share his glory.

(Romans 8:16-17; Jerusalem Bible)

Scattered throughout the past and caressing the pages of time like a refreshing breeze has been the entrance at seemingly low periods in humanity's history of persons spiritually advanced far beyond their peers. These figures have arrived at significantly important times in a pattern or scheme suggestive of divine wisdom and orchestration. If it can be said that humanity has spiritually progressed during the recorded tenure on earth and if any such progress can be attributed to the religious endeavors of mortals, then these few spiritual pioneers have played a remarkable catalytic role in humanity's spiritual evolution. The Cayce readings indicate the Master soul was involved in each of these spiritual surges which taught that God is One.

The Master's story stretches from Eden to Egypt, to Persia, Babylon, Judea—even fabled Atlantis. And, of course, there is the city of Jerusalem, where he had such varied experiences— royalty, priesthood in the Temple, and eventually crucifixion on the cross. Possibly these Jerusalem experiences were in themselves fulfillment of the expectations for a kingly, priestly, and suffering messiah.

There are numerous other lives of the Master about whose locale we can only guess. Maybe he spent lifetimes in what we know as India, China, Japan, Europe, and the Americas, but the record is silent. Possibly Edgar Cayce would have clearly identified these other areas of the Master's lives if his audience had been of a different background than Judeo-Christian. But one can suspect that the Master's mark has been made upon all true religions and that his footprints have been left upon the sands of all lands.

Each life of the Master is made a living example for us to follow. Amilius the spirit. Adam the created. Enoch or Hermes the Great Initiate and sage. Melchizedek the mystical priest. Joseph the head of state and forgiver. Joshua the faithful warrior leader. Asaph the artisan. Jeshua the priest and scribe. Zend the spiritual leader. And Jesus who loved and suffered his way to Christhood. The pattern of each of these lives of the Master is charged and enlivened, however, by the power of his ultimate Christhood.

The term "Christ" comes from the Greek word *christos*, meaning anointed one. By this name, Christians historically have confessed their belief that Jesus was the messiah.[1]

Q-1. What is the meaning and significance of the words Jesus and Christ as should be understood and applied . . .?

A-1. . . . Jesus is the man—the activity, the mind, the relationships that He bore to others. Yea, He was mindful of friends, He was sociable, He was loving, He was kind, He was gentle. He grew faint, He grew weak—and yet gained that strength that He has promised in becoming the Christ, by fulfilling and overcoming the world! Ye are made strong—in body, in mind, in soul and purpose—by that power in Christ. The *power*, then, is in the Christ. The *pattern* is in Jesus.   2533-7

The Christ Consciousness is described in another reading as "the awareness within each soul, imprinted in pattern on the mind and waiting to be awakened by the will, of the soul's oneness with God." (5749-14)

There are a number of philosophical issues that historically have plagued Christianity but which seem to be answered by the lives of Jesus and the concepts from them as provided by Edgar Cayce. Our heritage is thus clarified and made more meaningful.

Much debate has centered on the role of grace in dissolving the effect of our sins and errors—our karma. The resolution as found in the Cayce readings is not that grace automatically erases sin. Rather, it recognizes the divine initiative and cleansing power of grace but conditions its operation on our use of grace or forgiveness in dealing with others.

For only as ye forgive those who have blamed thee without a cause, who have spoken vilely of thee without reason, can the giver of life and light forgive thee . . .   3660-1

A closely allied issue is that of faith versus works. Does salvation come through our faith or through the works we have done? One New Testament account says that we are saved through faith, "not of works, lest any man should boast." (Ephesians 2:8-9) Another, however, says "faith, if it have not works, is dead." (James 2:17) The Cayce answer seems to be a combination of both concepts. Faith is determined not by outward works, most assuredly, but by the inner motive of faith and love exemplified in our acts of kindness, patience, cooperation, forbearance, tolerance, and mercy toward each other. Thus, salvation comes through faith, but true faith is characterized by certain spiritual works.

Was Jesus a man who became God or was he God who became a man? This issue was one of the main subjects debated at the first Council of the Church at Nicea in 325 A.D. A Christian theologian from Alexandria named Arius claimed that Jesus was a man who became God through his total faith and acceptance of God's will. The Council was divided on the subject but eventually condemned this idea and sent Arius into exile. The Council of Constantinople in 553, in denouncing Origenism, also touched upon the subject of whether or not Jesus earned his Christhood through numerous bodies and names; however, it concluded somewhat ambiguously that such belief was heresy *unless* one also admitted that God humbled Himself and became a man. The Cayce readings say that the Master voluntarily left his original state with God and erred and suffered through many lives until returning to godhood. When

he came as Jesus, he had already completed the return to God
but chose to finish his earthly mission. As Jesus, he was thus
both God and man.

Are we ourselves gods in the making? Is such a belief
blasphemous? In defending himself against an accusation of
blasphemy, Jesus referred to and reiterated the statement of
the Psalm in the Old Testament that "ye are gods." He also
said, "What I do you can do"—apparently meaning that even
we can achieve Christhood or godhood. The spiritual
philosophy of the Edgar Cayce psychic readings is based upon
the conviction that humanity through the mercy of God and
through following the example of the Christ can attain and
return to a lost godhood—that state of original perfection and
oneness of our purpose and our will with God's.

The heritage the Master left us is also one of responsibility
and duty.

When Jesus said on the cross, "It is finished," he meant that
his earthly mission of showing the way to overcome sin had
been achieved. It had been done by meeting and overcoming his
prior errors. This concept is borne out in one possible
interpretation of his words, which is, "The debt is paid." The
philosophy of twentieth-century theologian, Rudolph Steiner,
similarly suggests:

> Indeed, an understanding of karma [and
> reincarnation] is essential to the understanding of
> what is meant by the traditional Christian doctrine
> that Christ in passing through the Mystery of
> Golgotha redeemed man from his sins.[2]

The purpose for which the Master had originally entered the
earth was finished; he had shown us the way back to the glory of
God. The earthly debt, which he had incurred along the way,
had also been paid. But his work was not finished; it was left in
the hands of us who are still bound to materiality and the earth
plane. Until the last sheep is back in the folds of the Father, the
Master's work is unfinished. It is our challenge to complete this
work of the Master soul who so ably completed his earthly part
in it and promised to be with us always.

**And as ye would be the channel to hasten that glorious day of the
coming of the Lord, then do with a might that thy hands find to do to**

make for the greater manifestations of the love of the Father in the earth. For, into thy keeping, and to His children and to His sons, has He committed the keeping of the saving of the world, of the souls of men . . .   262-58

The significance of the birth and mission of Jesus thus applies to each of us:

For as ye behold the face of thy friend, of thy neighbor, of thy foe, yea, thine enemy, ye behold the image of thy Savior.

For ye are all His, bought not only with the birth of the God-Child into flesh but with the death—that ye might know that He, thy Brother, thy Savior, thy Christ, has been and is the Way to the Father in this material plane.

For as He chose to enter, so ye have entered. As He chose to live, so may ye live. As He chose to give of Himself that there might be a greater understanding, a greater knowledge; yea, the showing forth of the wisdom of God that God is love, poured forth upon the children of men in this experience.   262-103

Finally, how does the idea and meaning of prior lives of Jesus affect conventional Christianity?

To a very large degree, no basic changes in Christian behavior are required. The essential ingredients of fundamental Christianity remain intact. Salvation is based upon repentance, belief, and a total commitment to God as exemplified in the life of Jesus. In any event, as the Cayce readings say for the subject of reincarnation generally, if the concept is spiritually helpful, use it; if not, then discard it.

On the other hand, many do find a very positive heritage in the many lives of the Master. They may, through an inner knowing, recognize a story almost lost from Christianity but one which in fact was a part of ancient messianic beliefs and an indispensable element of faith for many early Christians. For them, the lives of the Master provide a rich and powerful legacy.

They find that the narrative of Christ is not limited to the story of Jesus. Rather, it is clothed in a mission and tradition stretching from Adam—nay, even from the input of Amilius in spirit form—through legendary and important figures in the history of the world. The role of the Master thus becomes broader and grander in concept. Christianity is richer when depicted in such a magnificent mural and more beautifully woven tapestry.

For these people, our debt to Jesus Christ is far greater than ever conceived by conventional Christianity. The suffering, caring, and love of the Master are freely given, not in just one life, but in many. We can truly recognize in the religion which he founded a new human consciousness whose anthem is love.

The story of Jesus without the impact of his many appearances is like listening to an orchestral performance with only the percussion instruments present. The basic beat is there, but absent are the harmony, the overtones, and full beauty of all the parts and pieces playing together. With the knowledge of his lives, we begin to hear the complete concert in all its stirring and eloquent glory.

We can now also more easily identify with the life of Jesus and ascertain its applicability to us. We can begin to understand the credibility of Jesus' statement to his followers that they—and we—may do the things he did—and even greater. After all, the Master experienced all that we may encounter. He is not just God whose life experience as Jesus would inherently differ from ours. His story *is* ours, and it is our hope. It is a narrative retrieved from the past which not only affirms his deity but emphasizes his humanity. It portrays the way of return to the Father.

> . . . as the Son entered into the earth throughout the ages, as man counts time, there was the growth; the growth that made for that purposefulness that the world, the earth and the fullness thereof might be a *living* example of the *glory* of the Son. And as man counteth shortcomings *many* there were, yet tempted in all—even in that experience when "yet without sin" He presented His body before the Throne of grace and mercy . . .   262-82

As he progressed from error to perfection, so may we. Even his role as savior beckons as the capstone of our spiritual growth.

> . . . *each* and every soul *must become, must be* the *savior* of some soul! to even *comprehend* the purpose of the entrance of the Son *into* the earth—that man might have the closer walk with, yea the open door to, the very heart of the living God!   1472-3

And how do we become a "savior" to some soul?

> . . . smile upon those that are downhearted and sad; lift the load from those that find theirs too heavy to bear, in gentleness, in

kindness, in long-suffering, in patience, in mercy, in brotherly love. And as ye show forth these to thy fellow man, the ways and the gates of glory open before thee.   **272-8**

Perfection like that of Jesus seems overwhelming until we understand that like Jesus we do not have to achieve it in one lifetime. It may be accomplished, in the often-repeated advice of the Cayce readings, "here a little, there a little, line upon line, and precept upon precept." In the process, we learn patience, just as did the Master in his many appearances.

And yet, the urgency of the salvation theme is in no way lessened by multiple lives. Although the Father may allow us ample time to make the journey home, the pain and sorrow of meeting our errors over and over again, until they are learned or forgiven through grace, is so great that there should be no temptation to prolong the ordeal.

Thus, the lives of the Master—the rest of the Jesus story— has the potential to speak to each of us with a meaningful message of action and hope.

It is a message which should unite and bring all divisions of Christianity together in a singular effort. Jesus' creed and theology is simple. It is the love of God and all persons which was his hallmark from the beginning and throughout his many lives on our terrestrial plane.

We find . . . contentions arising in that called in the present denominationalism, and each one crying . . . "Lo, unless ye do this or that ye have no part in Him." "He that loves me will keep my commandments." What are the commandments? "Thou shalt have no other *God* before me," and "Love thy neighbor as thyself." In this is builded the whole *law* and gospel of every age that has said, "There is ONE God!"   **364-9**

The heritage of his lives should also make us realize that the Master is not limited uniquely to Christianity. His lives have touched and are a part of every religious thought which teaches that God is One. We are thus by this dynamic all brought together in love and ecumenism.

Finally, the lives of the Master is a chronicle that cries lovingly and patiently to each of us. It is given in the words and deeds of the Master and spoken by him in clarion and plaintive tones. It says:

"Come home.

"Come home, O pilgrim, come home.

"Come home to the glory prepared for you from the foundations of time.

"The Creator longs to welcome you home.

"You have been on a long and distant journey.

"Come home.

"Come home, prodigal, for I too have traveled that road—even to the cross.

"Come home; I have shown you the way.

"Come home.

"Come and follow me."

And for the faithful follower who answers his call, the Master has promised:

To him who overcomes I will grant to sit with me on my throne, even as I also overcame and have sat down with my Father on his throne.

He who overcomes I will make a pillar in the temple of my God, and he shall not go out again . . .

He who has ears, let him hear . . .

(Revelation 3:21, 12, and 22; Lamsa translation)

FOOTNOTES

CHAPTER ONE
Edgar Cayce

1. Richard H. Drummond, *Unto the Churches* (Virginia Beach: A.R.E. Press, 1978), pp. 17-18.

2. Lynn Elwell Sparrow, *Edgar Cayce and the Born Again Christian* (Virginia Beach: A.R.E. Press, 1985), pp. 45-67.

3. Hugh Schonfield, *The Essene Odyssey* (Longmead, England: Element Books, Ltd., 1984), p. 2.

4. Sylvia Cranston and Carey Williams, *Reincarnation: A New Horizon in Science, Religion, and Society* (New York: Julian Press, 1984), pp. 213-214.

5. Charles F. Pfeiffer, *The Dead Sea Scrolls and the Bible* (New York: Weathervane Books, 1969), pp. 136 and 145.

CHAPTER TWO
Edgar Cayce's Story of the Master

1. Hippolytus, "Refutatio," vol. 10, 2, as quoted in *The Other Bible*, ed. Willis Barnstone (San Francisco: Harper & Row, 1984), p. 636.

CHAPTER THREE
Past Lives?

1. Drummond, *Unto the Churches*, p. 21.

2. Flavius Josephus, *Antiquities of the Jews*, Book XVIII, 1, (3), trans. William Whiston (Grand Rapids: Kregel Publications, 1960), p. 376.

3. Flavius Josephus, *Wars of the Jews*, Book II, 8, (10-11), trans. William Whiston (Grand Rapids: Kregel Publications, 1960), pp. 477-478.

4. *Ibid.*, Book III, 8, (5), pp. 515-516.

5. James Bonwick, *Egyptian Belief and Modern Thought*, reprinted edition (Indian Hills: Falcon Wing's Press, 1956), pp. 82-83.

6. Drummond, *Unto the Churches*, pp. 20-24.

7. *Ibid.*, pp. 85-88.

8. F.L. Cross and E.A. Livingstone, eds., *The Oxford Dictionary of the Christian Church* (London: Oxford University Press, 1974), p. 957. And see R.

Bultmann, Z.N.T.W. xxiv (1925), pp. 100-146, cited in C.H. Dodd, *The Interpretation of the Fourth Gospel* (London: Cambridge University Press, 1970), p. 121.

9. Dodd, *The Interpretation of the Fourth Gospel*, pp. 121-124.

10. E.S. Drower, *The Secret Adam* (Oxford: Clarendon Press, 1960), p. xiv.

11. Cross and Livingstone, *The Oxford Dictionary of the Christian Church*, pp. 957.

12. Dodd, *The Interpretation of the Fourth Gospel*, p. 122.

13. Hippolytus, "The Refutation of All Heresies," in *The Ante-Nicene Fathers*, 10 vols., eds. Alexander Roberts and James Donaldson (Grand Rapids: Eerdman's Publishing Co., 1965), V:47-58.

14. Joseph Head and Sylvia Cranston, comps., *Reincarnation: An East West Anthology* (Wheaton: Theosophical Publishing House, 1981), pp. 321-324.

15. *Ibid.*, p. 42.

16. Dodd, *The Interpretation of the Fourth Gospel*, pp. 99-100.

CHAPTER FOUR
Amilius

1. *The Gospel According to Thomas*, trans. A. Guillanmont, Henri-Charles Peuch, Giles Quispel, Walter Till, and Yassah 'Abd el Misah (Leiden: E.J. Brill, 1959), p. 13.

2. *New Catholic Encyclopedia*, 17 vols., reprinted edition (Palatine, Illinois: Jack Heraty & Associates, 1981), XI:702.

3. Edgar Evans Cayce, *Edgar Cayce on Atlantis* (New York: Warner Books, 1968), pp. 59-60.

4. Drower, *The Secret Adam*, pp. 21-22.

5. *Ibid.*, note 1, p. 22.

6. Hugh Schonfield, ed., *The Authentic New Testament*, note 59, p. 309, quoted in Drower, *The Secret Adam*, note 2, p. 21.

CHAPTER FIVE
Adam

1. Manly P. Hall, *An Encyclopedic Outline of Masonic, Hermetic, Qabbalistic and Rosicrucian Symbolical Philosophy* (Los Angeles: Philosophical Research Society, Inc., 1957), p. CXXVI.

2. *Encyclopedia Judaica*, 16 vols. (Jerusalem: Keter Publishing House, 1972), II:234.

3. *Ibid.*, II:239.

4. James H. Charlesworth, ed., *The Old Testament Pseudepigrapha*, Vol. I (Garden City: Doubleday & Co., 1983), p. 152.

5. *Encyclopedia Judaica,* II:236.

6. *Ibid.,* II:237.

7. *Ibid.,* II:241.

8. George W.E. Nickelsburg, "Some Related Traditions in the Apocalypse of Adam, the Books of Adam and Eve, and 1 Enoch," in *The Rediscovery of Gnosticism,* vol. II, Proceedings of the Conference at Yale, March 1978, ed. Bentley Layton (Leiden: E.J. Brill, 1981), pp. 521-538.

9. Charlesworth, *The Old Testament Pseudepigrapha,* I:719.

10. James H. Charlesworth, ed., *The Old Testament Pseudepigrapha,* Vol. II (Garden City: Doubleday & Co., 1985), p. 292.

11. Josephus, *Antiquities of the Jews,* Book I, 2, (3), p. 27.

12. Birger A. Pearson, "Sethian Gnosticism," in *The Rediscovery of Gnosticism,* vol. II, ed. Bentley Layton (Leiden: E.J. Brill, 1981), p. 493.

13. *Ibid.,* p. 495.

14. *Eugnostos the Blessed* (NHC III, 3, 81) and *The Sophia of Jesus Christ* (NHC III, 4, 105) in *The Nag Hammadi Library,* gen. ed. James Robinson (San Francisco: Harper & Row, 1977, p. 217.

15. *The First Book of Adam and Eve* in *The Forgotten Books of Eden,* ed. Rutherford H. Platt, Jr. (New York: Bell Publishing Co., 1980), p. 28.

16. Hall, *An Encyclopedic Outline of . . .,* p. CXXVII.

17. Charlesworth, *The Old Testament Pseudepigrapha,* I:990.

18. *Ibid.,* I:994.

19. F. Legge, *Forerunners and Rivals of Christianity,* 2 vols. (New York: Peter Smith, 1950), I:lxi.

20. Drower, *The Secret Adam,* pp. 92-94.

22. Carl Jung, *Psychology and Alchemy, Collected Works of Carl Jung,* the Bollingen Series, 20 vols. (Princeton: Princeton University Press, 1958-1970), XII:368.

23. Drower, *The Secret Adam,* p. 102.

24. Schonfield, *The Essene Odyssey,* pp. 149-150.

25. *Encyclopedia Judaica,* II:240.

26. Charlesworth, *The Old Testament Pseudepigrapha,* II:252.

CHAPTER SIX

Enoch

1. Elizabeth Clare Prophet, *Forbidden Mysteries of Enoch* (Los Angeles: Summit University Press, 1983), p. 27.

2. *Ibid.,* pp. 27-30.

3. *Ibid.*, p. 32.

4. R.H. Charles, ed. and trans., *The Book of Enoch* (Oxford: Clarendon Press, 1893), pp. 148-150; as quoted in Prophet, *Forbidden Mysteries of Enoch,* p. 19.

5. Prophet, *Forbidden Mysteries of Enoch,* p. 34.

6. *Encyclopedia Judaica,* VI:794.

7. Charlesworth, *The Old Testament Pseudepigrapha,* Vol. I.

8. *Encyclopedia Judaica,* VI:795.

9. Charlesworth, *The Old Testament Pseudepigrapha,* I:9.

10. Nickelsburg, "Some Related Traditions in the Apocalypse of Adam, the Books of Adam and Eve, and 1 Enoch," in *The Rediscovery of Gnosticism,* vol. II, p. 537.

11. Birger A. Pearson, vol. ed., *Nag Hammadi Codices IX and X,* in *Nag Hammadi Studies,* gen. ed. James Robinson (Leiden: E.J. Brill, 1981), p. 29.

12. *Encyclopedia Judaica,* VI:795.

13. Charlesworth, *The Old Testament Pseudepigrapha,* I:94-96.

14. *Ibid.,* I:223.

15. *Ibid.,* I:229-231.

16. *Ibid.,* I:238.

17. *Ibid.,* I:229.

18. W.H. Church, "As Above, So Below: An Exploration of the Origins of Hermetic Philosophy," *The A.R.E. Journal,* vol. IX, no. 3 (May 1974), p. 91.

19. Carl Jung, *Alchemical Studies, Collected Works of Carl Jung,* the Bollingen Series, 20 vols. (Princeton: Princeton University Press, 1958-1970), XIII:137n.

20. *Encyclopedia Judaica,* VI:794.

21. *The Second Book of Adam and Eve* in *The Forgotten Books of Eden,* ed. Rutherford H. Platt, Jr. (New York: Bell Publishing Co., 1980), p. 81.

CHAPTER SEVEN
Hermes

1. *Books of Hermes* as quoted in Jessica Madigan, *The Past Lives of Jesus and Mary,* 2 vols. (Los Angeles: Mei Ling Publications, 1970), I:11.

2. W.H. Church, *Many Happy Returns* (San Francisco: Harper & Row, 1984), p. 78.

3. Hall, *An Encyclopedic Outline of . . .,* p. XXXVII.

4. Manly P. Hall, *Twelve World Teachers* (Los Angeles: Philosophers Press, 1937), pp. 30-31.

5. *Ibid.,* p. 33.

6. *The Encyclopedia of Philosophy*, 8 vols., ed. Paul Edwards (New York: Macmillan Publishing Co. and The Free Press, 1972), III:490.

7. C.H. Dodd, *Historical Tradition in the Fourth Gospel* (Cambridge: Cambridge University Press, 1965), p. 319.

8. Kurt Rudolph, *Gnosis* (New York: Harper & Row, 1983), pp. 131-132.

9. Dodd, *The Interpretation of the Fourth Gospel*, pp. 110-112.

10. *Ibid.*, p. 112 and note 2, p. 125.

11. Church, "As Above, So Below," p. 100.

12. Carl Jung, *Aion, Collected Works of Carl Jung,* the Bollingen Series, 20 vols. (Princeton: Princeton University Press, 1958-1970), IXii:201-202.

13. Pfeiffer, *The Dead Sea Scrolls and the Bible*, pp. 140 and 143.

14. Hall, *An Encyclopedic Outline of...*, p. XLIV and Peter Tompkins, *Secrets of the Great Pyramid* (New York: Harper & Row, 1971), p. 218.

15. *Encyclopedia Judaica*, VIII:372.

16. Charlesworth, *The Old Testament Pseudepigrapha*, I:228.

17. Jung, *Alchemical Studies, Collected Works of Carl Jung*, XIII:137n.

18. Jung, *Psychology and Alchemy, Collected Works of Carl Jung*, XII:370.

19. Hall, *Twelve World Teachers*, p. 33.

20. Hall, *An Encyclopedic Outline of . . .*, p. XXXVII.

21. *Ibid.*

22. *Ibid.*, p. XXXVIII.

23. Dodd, *The Interpretation of the Fourth Gospel*, pp. 30-31.

24. Hall, *An Encyclopedic Outline of . . .*, p. XXXIX.

25. *Ibid.*, p. XL.

26. *Ibid.*

27. Dodd, *The Interpretation of the Fourth Gospel*, pp. 33-34.

28. Robert W. Krajenke, *A Million Years to the Promised Land* (New York: Bantam Books, Inc., 1973), p. 71.

CHAPTER EIGHT

Melchizedek

1. Millar Burrows, *More Light on the Dead Sea Scrolls* (New York: Viking Press, 1968), p. 332.

2. *The Jerusalem Bible*, gen. ed. Alexander Jones (Garden City: Doubleday & Co., 1966), note g, p. 31.

3. M. Delcor, "Melchizedek from Genesis to the Qumran Texts and the

Epistle to the Hebrews," *Journal of Jewish Studies* (1971), p. 122.

4. Church, *Many Happy Returns,* p. 106.

5. *The Jewish Encyclopedia,* 12 vols. (London: Funk and Wagnells Co., 1904), VIII:450.

6. *Ibid.*

7. *Encyclopedia Judaica,* II:1289.

8. Legge, *Forerunners and Rivals of Christianity,* II:173.

9. Charlesworth, *The Old Testament Pseudepigrapha,* II:671 and 673.

10. *Ibid.,* II:693.

11. Delcor, "Melchizedek from Genesis . . .," p. 132.

12. Charlesworth, *The Old Testament Pseudepigrapha,* I:95.

13. W.D. Davies, "Commentary on Habakkuk 7:13," in *Christian Origins of Judaism* (Philadelphia: Westminster Press, 1962), p. 113.

14. Theodore Gaster, *The Dead Sea Scriptures in English Translation* (New York: Doubleday & Co., 1956), note 3, p. 29.

15. André Dupont-Sommer, *The Jewish Sect of Qumran and the Essenes* (Bath, England: Vallentine, Mitchell & Co., Ltd., 1956), p. 160.

16. Delcor, "Melchizedek from Genesis . . .," p. 124.

17. *Ibid.,* p. 250.

18. *Melchizedek* in *The Nag Hammadi Library,* gen. ed. James Robinson (San Francisco: Harper & Row, 1977), p. 403.

19. *Ibid.,* p. 399.

20. Pearson, ed., *Nag Hammadi Codices IX and X,* pp. 28-29.

21. Thomas Sugrue, *There Is a River* (Virginia Beach: A.R.E. Press, 1984), pp. 315-316.

22. *Encyclopedia Judaica,* XI:1290.

CHAPTER NINE
Joseph

1. Roland DeVaux, *The Early History of Israel* (Philadelphia: Westminster Press, 1978), pp. 303-320.

2. Werner Keller, *The Bible as History* (New York: Bantam Books, 1982), p. 89.

3. *Encyclopedia Britannica,* 30 vols., 15th edition (Chicago and London: Encyclopedia Britannica, Inc., 1977), I:401-403.

4. Robert Graves and Raphael Patai, *Hebrew Myths* (New York: Greenwich House, 1983), p. 27.

5. *Ibid.*, p. 263.

6. Josephus, *Antiquities of the Jews,* Book I, 3, (3), p. 28.

7. *The Testaments of the Twelve Patriarchs* in *The Forgotten Books of Eden,* ed. Rutherford H. Platt, Jr. (New York: Bell Publishing Co., 1980), pp. 259-260.

8. *Ibid.,* p. 265.

9. *Ibid.,* p. 267.

10. Charlesworth, *The Old Testament Pseudepigrapha,* II:187.

11. *Ibid.,* pp. 188 and 196.

12. *Ibid.,* p. 470.

13. *Ibid.,* p. 191.

14. *Ibid.,* p. 197.

15. *Ibid.,* p. 226.

16. Ray Stanford, *The Fatima Prophecy* (Austin: Association for the Understanding of Man, 1972), pp. 43-50.

17. Schonfield, *The Essene Odyssey,* p. 36.

18. *Ibid.,* pp. 37-38.

19. *The Jewish Encyclopedia,* VI:248.

20. *Ibid.,* pp. 248 and 252.

21. William Neil, *Harper's Bible Commentary* (New York: Harper & Row, 1975), p. 62.

22. *Ibid.,* pp. 54-65.

CHAPTER TEN
Joshua

1. David and Pat Alexander, eds., *Eerdman's Handbook to the Bible* (Herts, England: Lion Publishing, 1973), p. 210.

2. *Great People of the Bible and How They Lived* (Pleasantville: The Reader's Digest Association, Inc., 1974), p. 95.

3. John L. McKenzie, ed., *Dictionary of the Bible* (New York: Macmillan Publishing Co., 1965), p. 351.

4. Alexander, *Eerdman's Handbook to the Bible,* p. 210; *Great People of the Bible and How They Lived,* pp. 332-333.

5. Joan Comay and Ronald Brownrigg, *Who's Who in the Bible,* 2 vols. (New York: Bonanza Books, 1980), II:172.

6. Charlesworth, *The Old Testament Pseudepigrapha,* II:260-261.

7. Comay and Brownrigg, *Who's Who in the Bible,* II:172.

8. Isaac Asimov, *Asimov's Guide to the Bible, The Old Testament* (New York: Avon Books, 1971), p. 208.

9. *Encyclopedia Judaica*, X:271.

10. *Ibid.*, X:267.

11. *Ibid.*

12. *Ibid.*

CHAPTER ELEVEN
Asaph

1. Keller, *The Bible as History*, p. 96.

2. DeVaux, *The Early History of Israel*, p. 296.

3. Charlesworth, *The Old Testament Pseudepigrapha*, II:165.

4. Schonfield, *The Essene Odyssey*, p. 51.

5. Charlesworth, *The Old Testament Pseudepigrapha*, II:366.

6. Schonfield, *The Essene Odyssey*, pp. 8-9, 44, and 57.

7. *Ibid.*, p. 46.

8. *Ibid.*, pp. 9 and 44-45.

9. *Ibid.*, pp. 50-51.

10. *Ibid.*, p. 97.

CHAPTER TWELVE
Jeshua

1. *Great People of the Bible . . .*, pp. 196-249.

2. Joan Comay, *Who's Who in the Old Testament* (New York: Bonanza Books, 1971), p. 207.

3. *Encyclopedia Judaica*, X:1.

4. *Ibid.*, X:2.

5. *Great People of the Bible . . .*, p. 274.

6. *Ibid.*, p. 276.

7. Editorial comments preceding the Book of Zechariah in the New Scofield Reference edition of the *Holy Bible* (New York: Oxford University Press, 1967), p. 964.

8. *Encyclopedia Judaica*, X:2.

9. McKenzie, *Dictionary of the Bible*, p. 459.

10. Alexander, *Eerdman's Handbook to the Bible*, p. 204.

11. *Ibid.*, pp. 205-208.

CHAPTER THIRTEEN
Zend

1. Ruhi M. Afnan, *The Great Prophets* (New York: Philosophical Library, 1960), p. 113.

2. *Ibid.*, p. 114.

3. Hall, *Twelve World Teachers*, p. 69.

4. Afnan, *The Great Prophets*, p. 122.

5. Hall, *Twelve World Teachers*, p. 72.

6. John A. Hardon, *Religions of the World* (Garden City: Doubleday & Co., 1968), p. 206.

7. Robert O. Ballou, ed., *The Portable World Bible* (New York: Penguin Books, 1985), pp. 179-180.

8. Afnan, *The Great Prophets*, pp. 109-110.

9. Hardon, *Religions of the World*, p. 206.

10. Hall, *Twelve World Teachers*, p. 70.

11. *Ibid.*, p. 72.

12. *Ibid.*, p. 74.

13. *Ibid.*, p. 75.

14. Hardon, *Religions of the World*, p. 207.

15. Hall, *Twelve World Teachers*, pp. 76-77.

16. Legge, *Forerunners and Rivals of Christianity*, I:lxii.

17. Hardon, *Religions of the World*, p. 205.

18. *Ibid.*, p. 204.

19. Afnan, *The Great Prophets*, p. 119.

20. *Ibid.*

21. *Ibid.*, p. 122.

22. Hardon, *Religions of the World*, p. 208.

23. Ballou, *The Portable World Bible*, pp. 189-190.

24. Hardon, *Religions of the World*, p. 208.

25. *Ibid.*, p. 207.

26. Afnan, *The Great Prophets*, p. 138.

27. *Ibid.*, p. 125.

28. *Ibid.*, p. 131.

29. Jeffrey Furst, *Edgar Cayce's Story of Jesus* (New York: Coward-McCann, Inc., 1969), p. 98.

30. Afnan, *The Great Prophets*, pp. 125-126.

31. Joseph Gaer, *What the Great Religions Believe* (New York: Dodd, Mead, and Co., 1963), pp. 217 and 227.

32. As quoted in Afnan, *The Great Prophets*, p. 110.

33. *Ibid.*, p. 142.

34. *Holy Bible*, New Scofield Reference edition, p. 993.

35. Drower, *The Secret Adam*, p. 92.

36. Pfeiffer, *The Dead Sea Scrolls and the Bible*, p. 142.

37. John H. Sieber introduction to *Zostrianos* in *The Nag Hammadi Library*, ed. James Robinson (San Francisco: Harper & Row, 1977), p. 368.

38. Pearson, "Sethian Gnosticism," in *The Rediscovery of Gnosticism*, vol. II, p. 497.

39. Hall, *Twelve World Teachers*, p. 77.

40. *Ibid.*

CHAPTER FOURTEEN
Jesus: His Early Life

1. Anne Read, *Edgar Cayce on Jesus and His Church* (New York: Paperback Library, 1970), p. 11.

2. McKenzie, *Dictionary of the Bible*, pp. 758-759.

3. *Ibid.*, p. 668.

4. Schonfield, *The Essene Odyssey*, p. 75.

5. *Ibid.*

6. Legge, *Forerunners and Rivals of Christianity*, p. 155.

7. *Ibid.*, p. 156.

8. *Ibid.*, p. 712.

9. Janet Bock, *The Jesus Mystery* (Los Angeles: Aura Books, 1980), p. 2.

10. *Ibid.*

11. *Ibid.*, pp. 3 and 6.

12. *Ibid.*

13. *Ibid.*, pp. 23, 29, 47-49.

14. *Ibid.*, pp. 207-227.

15. *Ibid.*, p. 207.

16. *Ibid.*, p. 49.

17. *Ibid.*, p. 50.

18. *Ibid.*, p. 74.

CHAPTER FIFTEEN

Jesus: His Ministry

1. Furst, *Edgar Cayce's Story of Jesus,* p. 212.

CHAPTER SIXTEEN

Jesus: His Death and Resurrection

1. George M. Lamsa, trans., *Holy Bible: From Ancient Eastern Manuscripts* (Philadelphia: A.J. Holman Co., 1957), p. 986.

2. John Dominic Crossan, *Four Other Gospels* (Minneapolis: Winston Press, 1985), p. 153.

CHAPTER SEVENTEEN

Jesus: His Return

1. Pfeiffer, *The Dead Sea Scrolls and the Bible,* pp. 126-134.

CHAPTER EIGHTEEN

The Message of Old

1. Origen, "The Scriptures Are Divinely Inspired," as quoted in *The Living Testament (The Essential Writings of Christianity Since the Bible),* eds. M. Basil Pennington, Alan Jones, and Mark Booth (San Francisco: Harper & Row, 1985), p. 41.

2. *Ibid.*

3. Cranston and Williams, *Reincarnation—A New Horizon in Science, Religion, and Society,* p. 213.

4. Schonfield, *The Essene Odyssey,* p. 147.

5. Rappaport, *Myth and Legend of Ancient Israel,* Vol. III, pp. 97, 200, and 204, as cited in Schonfield, *The Essene Odyssey,* p. 126.

6. Schonfield, *The Essene Odyssey,* pp. 136-137.

7. *Ibid.*

8. *Ibid.*, pp. 136-139.

9. *Ibid.*, p. 141.

10. *Ibid.*, p. 164.

11. Treatises No. 25, Codex VI and No. 23, Codex VI. See Jean Doresse, *The Secret Books of the Egyptian Gnostics* (New York: Viking Press, 1960), p. 243.

12. Dupont-Sommer, *The Jewish Sect of Qumran and the Essenes,* p. 164.

13. *Ibid.*, pp. 148-153.

14. Elaine Pagels, *The Gnostic Gospels* (New York: Random House, 1979), p. xix.

15. *Ibid.*, p. 103.

16. Dupont-Sommer, *The Jewish Sect of Qumran and the Essenes*, p. 158.

17. F.F.Bruce, *Peter, Stephen, James and John—Studies in Non-Pauline Christianity* (Grand Rapids: Eerdman's Publishing Co., 1979), p. 118.

18. Pfeiffer, *The Dead Sea Scrolls and the Bible*, p. 144.

CHAPTER NINETEEN
Our Heritage

1. McKenzie, *Dictionary of the Bible*, p. 432.

2. Stewart Easton, *Man and World in the Light of Anthroposophy* (Spring Valley: The Anthroposophic Press, 1982), p. 178.

BIBLIOGRAPHY

Afnan, Ruhi M. *The Great Prophets*. New York: Philosophical Library, 1960.

Asimov, Isaac. *Asimov's Guide to the Bible, The Old Testament*. New York: Avon Books, 1971.

Ballou, Robert O., ed. *The Portable World Bible*. New York: Penguin Books, 1985.

Bock, Janet. *The Jesus Mystery*. Los Angeles: Aura Books, 1980.

Bonwick, James. *Egyptian Belief and Modern Thought*, reprinted edition. Indian Hills: Falcon Wing's Press, 1956.

Bruce, F.F. *Peter, Stephen, James and John—Studies in Non-Pauline Christianity*. Grand Rapids: Eerdman's Publishing Co., 1979.

Burrows, Millar. *More Light on the Dead Sea Scrolls*. New York: Viking Press, 1968.

Cayce, Edgar Evans. *Edgar Cayce on Atlantis*. New York: Warner Books, 1968.

Charlesworth, James H., ed. *The Old Testament Pseudepigrapha*, Vol. I. Garden City: Doubleday & Co., 1983.

_____ *The Old Testament Pseudepigrapha*, Vol. II. Garden City: Doubleday & Co., 1985.

Church, W.H. "As Above, So Below: An Exploration of the Origins of Hermetic Philosophy." *The A.R.E. Journal*, Vol. IX, No. 3:91-103.

_____ *Many Happy Returns*. San Francisco: Harper & Row, 1984.

Comay, Joan. *Who's Who in the Bible*. New York: Bonanza Books, 1971.

Comay, Joan, and Brownrigg, Ronald. *Who's Who in the Bible*, Vol. 2. New York: Bonanza Books, 1980.

Cranston, Sylvia, and Williams, Carey. *Reincarnation: A New Horizon in Science, Religion, and Society*. New York: Julian Press, 1984.

Crossan, John Dominic. *Four Other Gospels*. Minneapolis: Winston Press, 1985.

Davies, W.D. "Commentary on Habakkuk 7:13." In *Christian Origins of Judaism*. Philadelphia: Westminster Press, 1962.

Delcor, M. "Melchizedek from Genesis to the Qumran Texts and the Epistle to the Hebrews." *Journal of Jewish Studies* (1971).

DeVaux, Roland. *The Early History of Israel*. Philadelphia: Westminster Press, 1978.

222

Dictionary of the Bible. Edited by John L. McKenzie. New York: Macmillan Publishing Co., 1965.

Dodd, C.H. *Historical Tradition in the Fourth Gospel.* Cambridge: Cambridge University Press, 1972.

———. *The Interpretation of the Fourth Gospel.* Cambridge: Cambridge University Press, 1970.

Doresse, Jean. *The Secret Books of the Egyptian Gnostics.* New York: Viking Press, 1960.

Drower, E.S. *The Secret Adam.* Oxford: Clarendon Press, 1960.

Drummond, Richard H. *Unto the Churches.* Virginia Beach: A.R.E. Press, 1978.

Dupont-Sommer, André. *The Jewish Sect of Qumran and the Essenes.* Bath, England: Vallentine, Mitchell & Co., 1956.

Easton, Stewart C. *Man and World in the Light of Anthroposophy.* Spring Valley: The Anthroposophic Press, 1982.

Eerdman's Handbook to the Bible. Edited by David and Pat Alexander. Hertfordshire, England: Lion Publishing, 1973.

Encyclopedia Britannica, 15th ed., vol 1. Chicago and London: Encyclopedia Britannica, Inc., 1977.

Encyclopedia Judaica, vols. II, VI, VII, X and XI. Jerusalem: Keter Publishing House, 1972.

The Encyclopedia of Philosophy, Vol. 3. Edited by Paul Edwards. New York: Macmillan Publishing Co. and The Free Press, 1972.

Eugnostos the Blessed. In *The Nag Hammadi Library,* edited by James Robinson. San Francisco: Harper & Row, 1977.

The First Book of Adam and Eve. In *The Forgotten Books of Eden,* edited by Rutherford H. Platt, Jr. New York: Bell Publishing Co., 1980.

Furst, Jeffrey. *Edgar Cayce's Story of Jesus.* New York: Coward-McCann, Inc., 1969.

Gaer, Joseph. *What the Great Religions Believe.* New York: Dodd, Mead and Co., 1963.

Gaster, Theodore. *The Dead Sea Scriptures in English Translation.* Garden City: Doubleday & Co., 1956.

The Gospel According to Thomas. Translated by A. Guillanmont, Henri-Charles Peuch, Giles Quispel, Walter Till and Yassah 'Abd al Masih. Leiden: E.J. Brill, 1959.

Graves, Robert, and Patai, Raphael. *Hebrew Myths.* New York: Greenwich House, 1983.

Great People of the Bible and How They Lived. Pleasantville, New York: The Reader's Digest Association, Inc., 1974.

Hall, Manly P. *An Encyclopedic Outline of Masonic, Hermetic, Qabbalistic and*

Rosicrucian Symbolical Philosophy, 11th ed. Los Angeles: Philosophical Research Society, Inc., 1957.

_____ *Twelve World Teachers.* Los Angeles: Philosophers Press, 1937.

Hardon, John A. *Religions of the World.* Garden City: Doubleday & Co., 1968.

Hippolytus. "Refutatio." In *The Other Bible.* Edited by William Barnstone. San Francisco: Harper & Row, 1984.

_____ "The Refutation of All Heresies." In *Ante-Nicene Fathers,* Vol. V. Edited by Alexander Roberts and James Donaldson. Grand Rapids: Eerdman's Publishing Co., 1965.

Holy Bible: From Ancient Eastern Manuscripts. Translated by George M. Lamsa. Philadelphia: A.J. Holman Co., 1957.

Holy Bible, New Scofield Reference Edition. Edited by C.I. Scofield. New York: Oxford University Press, 1967.

Holy Bible, Revised Standard Version, New Oxford Annotated Bible. Edited by Herbert G. May and Bruce M. Metzger. New York: Oxford University Press, 1977.

The Jerusalem Bible. General editor Alexander Jones. Garden City: Doubleday & Co., 1966.

The Jewish Encyclopedia, vols. VI and VIII. London: Funk and Wagnalls Co., 1904.

Josephus, Flavius. *Antiquities of the Jews.* Translated by William Whiston. Grand Rapids: Kregel Publications, 1960.

_____ *Wars of the Jews.* Translated by William Whiston. Grand Rapids: Kregel Publications, 1960.

Jung, Carl. *Aion.* In *Collected Works of Carl Jung,* Bollingen Series, vol. 9ii. Princeton: Princeton University Press, 1958-1970.

_____ *Alchemical Studies.* In *Collected Works of Carl Jung,* Bollingen Series, vol. 13. Princeton: Princeton University Press, 1958-1970.

_____ *Psychology and Alchemy.* In *Collected Works of Carl Jung,* Bolligen Series, vol. 12. Princeton: Princeton University Press, 1958-1970.

Keller, Werner. *The Bible as History.* New York: Bantam Books, 1982.

Krajenke, Robert W. *A Million Years to the Promised Land.* New York: Bantam Books, Inc., 1973.

The Last Jubilee: A Sermon; "Melchizedek Texts." In *The Dead Sea Scriptures.* Introduction by Theodore H. Gaster. Garden City: Anchor Press/Doubleday & Co., 1976.

Legge, F. *Forerunners and Rivals of Christianity,* vols. I & II. New York: Peter Smith, 1950.

Madigan, Jessica. *The Past Lives of Jesus and Mary,* vol. I. Los Angeles: Mei Ling Publications, 1970.

Melchizedek. In *The Nag Hammadi Library,* edited by James Robinson. San Francisco: Harper & Row, 1977.

Neil, William. *Harper's Bible Commentary.* New York: Harper & Row, 1975.

New Catholic Encyclopedia, vol. XI. Reprinted edition. Palatine, Illinois: Jack Heraty & Associates, 1981.

Nickelsburg, George W.E. "Some Related Traditions in the Apocalypse of Adam, the Books of Adam and Eve, and 1 Enoch." In *The Rediscovery of Gnosticism,* vol. II. Edited by Bentley Layton. Leiden: E.J. Brill, 1981.

Origen. "The Scriptures Are Divinely Inspired." In *The Living Testament (The Essential Writings of Christianity Since the Bible)* edited by M. Basil Pennington, Alan Jones, and Mark Booth. San Francisco: Harper & Row, 1985.

The Oxford Dictionary of the Christian Church. Edited by F.L. Cross and E.A. Livingstone. London: Oxford University Press, 1974.

Pagels, Elaine. *The Gnostic Gospels.* New York: Random House, 1979.

Pearson, Birger A. *Nag Hammadi Codices, IX and X.* In *Nag Hammadi Studies,* edited by James Robinson. Leiden: E.J. Brill, 1981.

"Sethian Gnosticism." In *The Rediscovery of Gnosticism,* vol. II, edited by Bentley Layton. Leiden: E.J. Brill, 1981.

Pfeiffer, Charles F. *The Dead Sea Scrolls and the Bible.* New York: Weathervane Books, 1969.

Prophet, Elizabeth Clare. *Forbidden Mysteries of Enoch.* Los Angeles: Summit University Press, 1983.

Read, Anne. *Edgar Cayce on Jesus and His Church.* New York: Paperback Library, 1970.

Reincarnation, An East-West Anthology. Compiled by Joseph Head and Sylvia Cranston. Wheaton: Theosophical Publishing House, 1981.

Rudolph, Kurt. *Gnosis.* New York: Harper & Row, 1983.

Schonfield, Hugh. *The Essene Odyssey.* Longmead, United Kingdom: Element Books, Ltd., 1984.

The Second Book of Adam and Eve. In *The Forgotten Books of Eden,* edited by Rutherford H. Platt, Jr. New York: Bell Publishing Co., 1980.

Sieber, John H. Introduction to *Zostrianos* in *The Nag Hammadi Library,* edited by James Robinson. San Francisco: Harper & Row, 1977.

The Sophia of Jesus Christ. In *The Nag Hammadi Library,* edited by James Robinson, San Francisco: Harper & Row, 1977.

Sparrow, Lynn Elwell. *Edgar Cayce and the Born Again Christian.* Virginia Beach: A.R.E. Press, 1985.

Stanford, Ray. *The Fatima Prophecy.* Austin: Association for the Understanding of Man, 1972.

Stearn, Jess. *The Sleeping Prophet.* New York: Doubleday & Co., Inc., 1967.

Sugrue, Thomas. *There Is a River.* Virginia Beach: A.R.E. Press, 1970.

The Testaments of the Twelve Patriarchs. In *The Forgotten Books of Eden,* edited by Rutherford H. Platt, Jr. New York: Bell Publishing Co., 1980.

Tompkins, Peter. *Secrets of the Great Pyramid.* New York: Harper & Row, 1971.

Glenn Sanderfur is an attorney and former President of the Federal Intermediate Credit Bank of Louisville. He currently serves as Director of Development for the Association for Research and Enlightenment, Inc., where he is a frequent lecturer on reincarnation and the lives of Jesus.

THE WORK OF EDGAR CAYCE TODAY

The Association for Research and Enlightenment, Inc. (A.R.E.®), is a membership organization founded by Edgar Cayce in 1931.

• 14,145 Cayce readings, the largest body of documented psychic information anywhere in the world, are housed in the A.R.E. Library/Conference Center in Virginia Beach, Virginia. These readings have been indexed under 10,000 different topics and are open to the public.

• An attractive package of membership benefits is available for modest yearly dues. Benefits include: a bi-monthly magazine; lessons for home study; a lending library through the mail, which offers collections of the actual readings as well as one of the world's best parapsychological book collections, names of doctors or health care professionals in your area.

• As an organization on the leading edge in exciting new fields, A.R.E. presents a selection of publications and seminars by prominent authorities in the fields covered, exploring such areas as parapsychology, dreams, meditation, world religions, holistic health, reincarnation and life after death, and personal growth.

• The unique path to personal growth outlined in the Cayce readings is developed through a worldwide program of study groups. These informal groups meet weekly in private homes.

• A.R.E. maintains a visitors' center where a bookstore, exhibits, classes, a movie, and audiovisual presentations introduce inquirers to concepts from the Cayce readings.

• A.R.E. conducts research into the helpfulness of both the medical and nonmedical readings, often giving members the opportunity to participate in the studies.

For more information and a color brochure, write or phone:

A.R.E., P.O. Box 595
Virginia Beach, VA 23451, (804) 428-3588